# Words *of* Love

## Quotations from the first blush to the final sigh

Selected and edited by
Jordan L. Linfield & Joseph Krevisky

RANDOM HOUSE
REFERENCE

*Words of Love: Quotations from the First Blush to the Final Sigh*

Copyright © 2002 by Innovation Press

This book is available for special purchases in bulk by organizations and institutions, not for resale, at special discounts. Please direct your inquiries to the Random House Special Sales Department, toll-free 888-591-1200 or fax 212-572-4961.

Please address inquiries about electronic licensing of reference products, for use on a network or in software or on CD-ROM, to the Subsidiary Rights Department, Random House Reference, fax 212-940-7352.

Earlier editions of this work were published in 1995 as *Quotations for Lovers* and in 1997 as *Words of Love: Quotations from Plato to Madonna*.

**Library of Congress Cataloging-in-publication data is available.**

Typeset and printed in the United States of America.
Page design: Nancy Etheredge, REM Studio
Page Composition: G&H SOHO, Inc. Hoboken, NJ

0 9 8 7 6 5 4 3 2 1
January 2002
ISBN 0-375-71982-2

New York   Toronto   London   Sydney   Auckland

# Contents

# Introduction

Love is more than hearts and flowers.
Love is more than moon and June.
Love is more than forever after.
Love is deception and treason.
Love is rapture and laughter.
Love is foreplay and afterplay.
Love is reaching the stars and feeling
    post-coital tristesse.

In *Words of Love: Romantic Quotations from Plato to Madonna* we share the most perceptive, witty, astute and caring quotations culled and treasured over years. Many of the entries are amusingly candid and forthright. Some entries are poignantly evocative. But all are truthful. For here is love as women and men truly recall and experience it.

# Absence

This is the sad bed
of chosen chastity
because you are miles
& mountains away.
—ERICA JONG, "The Sad Bed"


Morning without you is dwindled dawn.
—EMILY DICKINSON
*Selected Poems and Letters of Emily Dickinson*


When you are away, I'm restless, lonely,
Wretched, bored, dejected; only
Here's the rub my darling dear
I feel the same when you are near.
—SAMUEL HOFFENSTEIN, "When You're Away"
*Poems in Praise of Practically Nothing*


Your absence has not taught me how to be alone, it merely
has shown that when together we cast a single shadow on
this wall.
—DOUG FETHERLING, "Your Absence Has Not Taught Me"

Men are merriest when they are from home.
—WILLIAM SHAKESPEARE
*Henry V*


Wives in their husbands' absences grow subtler
And daughters sometimes run off with the butler.
—GEORGE GORDON, Lord Byron
*Don Juan*


Our hours in love have wings; in absence, crutches.
—COLLEY CIBBER
*Xerxes*


Where you used to be, there's a hole in the world, which I
find myself constantly walking around in the daytime, and
falling into at night. I miss you like hell.
—EDNA ST. VINCENT MILLAY
*Letters of Edna St. Vincent Millay*


All along, one of my complaints was his absence from
home, and even worse, his absence when he *was* home.
—SONIA JOHNSON
*From Housewife to Heretic*


The heart may think it knows better: the senses know that
absence blots people out.
—ELIZABETH BOWEN
*The Death of the Heart*

# Abstinence

I married the world—the world is my husband. That is why I am so young. No sex. Sex is the most tiring thing in the world.
—ELSA MAXWELL (attributed)


Who will in time present from pleasure refrain, shall, in time to come, the more pleasure obtain
—JOHN HEYWOOD
*A Dialogue Containing the Number in Effect of All the Proverbs in the English Tongue*


"May worry you for a while," the trustee advised. "You may have trouble at first. Specially if you're used to gettin' yours wet every night. You'll get over it, though," he said confidently. "It won't kill you. You'll just think it will."
—JAMES JONES
*From Here to Eternity*


I will have nought to do whether with lover or husband . . . albeit he come to me with an erection. . . . I will live at home unbulled.
—ARISTOPHANES
*Lysistrata* (oath taken by women in sex strike against war)


Abstainer: a weak person who yields to the temptation of denying himself a pleasure.
—AMBROSE BIERCE
*The Devil's Dictionary*

And he, whom in itching no scratchyng will forbear,
He must bear the smarting that shall follow there.
—JOHN HEYWOOD
*A Dialogue Containing the Number in Effect of All the Proverbs in the English Tongue*


No sex is better than bad sex.
—GERMAINE GREER (attributed)


Ain't misbehavin'
Savin' all my love for you.
—ANDY RAZAF, "Ain't Misbehavin'"


Abstinence sows sand all over
The ruddy limbs and flaming hair,
But desire gratified
Plants fruits of life and beauty there.
—WILLIAM BLAKE
*Complete Writings*


# Adolescence

Wanton kittens make sober cats.
*English Proverb*


Fourteen-year-old, why do you giggle and dote,
Fourteen-year-old, why are you such a goat?
I am fourteen years old and that's the reason,
I giggle and dote in season.
—STEVIE SMITH, "The Conversationalist"

Everything you are and do from fifteen to eighteen is what you are and will do the rest of your life.
—F. SCOTT FITZGERALD, letter to daughter, September 19, 1938

So much alarmed that she is alarming.
All Giggle, Blush, half Pertness, and half Pout.
—GEORGE GORDON, Lord Byron
*Beppo*

Don't count your boobies until they are hatched.
—JAMES THURBER
*Fables of Our Times*

My salad days;
When I was green in judgment; cold in blood.
—WILLIAM SHAKESPEARE
*Antony and Cleopatra*

She would eat the cheeseburgers and Dairy Queen sundaes they bought for her while they fished in her panties for whatever it is that men fish for in that primitive space.
—TOM ROBBINS
*Even Cowgirls Get the Blues*

The sexual memory of which I was drenched during that season in Brooklyn, whenever I forlornly unloosed the flood gates, was of uneasy darkness, sweat, reproving murmurs, bands and sinews of obdurate elastic, lacerating little hooks and snaps, whispered prohibitions, straining erections, stuck zippers and a warm miasmal odor of secretions from inflamed and obstructed glands.
—WILLIAM STYRON
*Sophie's Choice*

Too chaste an adolescence makes for a dissolute old age.
—ANDRÉ GIDE

*Journals*, 1939–1950


God, how I envied girls. . . . Whatever it was on them, it
didn't dangle between their legs like an elephant trunk.
No wonder boys talked about nothing but sex. That thing
was always there. Every time I went to the john, there it
was, twitching around like a little worm on a fishing hook.
When we took baths, it floated around in the water like a
lazy fish and God forbid we should touch it. It sprang to
life like lightning leaping from a cloud.
—JULIUS LESTER, "Being a Boy"

*Ms.*, 1973


Nothing to do but wait.
In the stale heat
of the attic, in the rippled
full-length mirror, she posed
in velvet, in chiffon, in
her mother's useless clothes,
waiting for her breasts
to blossom and fill
the loose bodice of
her grief.
  —JULIE KANE, "Thirteen"


*See also:* YOUTH.

# Adultery

Cease hunting married game: trouble and grief more often come to you than real enjoyment.
—HORACE


I went into my marriage knowing I would commit adultery at the earliest chance I had. (It was a goal: committing adultery, in fact it was one of the reasons for getting married.)
—JOSEPH HELLER
*Something Happened*


No adultery is bloodless.
—NATALIE GUINZBERG
*The City and the House*


Lady Capricorn, he understood, was still keeping open bed.
—ALDOUS HUXLEY
*Antic Hay*


She could commit adultery at one end and weep for her sins at the other, and enjoy both operations at the same time.
—JOYCE CARY
*The Horse's Mouth*


Her exotic daydreams do not prevent her from being small-town bourgeois at heart, clinging to conventional ideas or committing this or that conventional violation of the conventional, adultery being the most conventional way to rise above the conventional.
—VLADIMIR NABOKOV, "Madame Bovary"
*Lectures on Literature*

As I grow older and older,
And totter toward the tomb,
I find that I care less and less
Who goes to bed with whom.
—DOROTHY L. SAYERS
*Such a Strange Lady* by Janet Hitchman


Adultery is extravagance.
—MAXINE HONG KINGSTON
*The Woman Warrior*


When your man comes home late, tells you,
      you're gettin' old
When your man comes home late, tells you,
      you're gettin' old
That's a true sign he's got someone else bakin' his jelly roll.
*Blues Song*


Adultery may or may not be sinful, but it is never cheap.
—RAYMOND POSTGATE
*Somebody at the Door*


The first breath of adultery is the freest: after it, constraints aping marriage develop.
—JOHN UPDIKE
*Couples*


From outrage (matrimony) to outrage (adultery) there arose nought but outrage (copulation) yet the matrimonial violator of the matrimonially violated had not been outraged by the adulterous violator of the adulterously violated.
—JAMES JOYCE
*Ulysses*

{ 8 }

Musical beds is the faculty sport around here.
—EDWARD ALBEE
*Who's Afraid of Virginia Woolf?*


Do not adultery commit
Advantage rarely comes of it.
—ARTHUR HUGH CLOUGH, "The Last Decalogue"


The bonds of wedlock are so heavy it takes two to carry
them—sometimes three.
—HONORÉ DE BALZAC
*The Physiology of Marriage*


Now at least I know where he is.
—QUEEN ALEXANDRA, after the death of King Edward VII, whose
infidelities she had accepted with tolerance and understanding


One man's mate is another man's passion.
—EUGENE HEALY
*Mr. Sandman Loses His Life*


She was too fond of her most filthy bargain.
—WILLIAM SHAKESPEARE
*Othello*


     It is natural
For a woman to be wild with her husband when he
Goes in for secret love.
—EURIPIDES
*Medea* (translated by Rex Warner)

Such is the way of an adulterous woman; she eateth, and wipeth her mouth, and saith, I have done no wickedness.
*Proverbs*

Little drops of water, little grains of sand
Every sensible woman got a back-door man.
—SARA MARTIN, "Strange Loving Blues"

*See also:* INFIDELITY.

# Affairs

The happiest moment of any affair takes place after the loved one has learned to accommodate the lover and before the maddening personality of either party has emerged like a jagged rock from the receding tides of lust and curiosity.
—QUENTIN CRISP

I can understand companionship. I can understand bought sex in the afternoon. I cannot understand the love affair.
—GORE VIDAL
*The Sunday Times*, 1973

But an affair wants to spill, to share its glory with the world. No act is so private it does not seek applause.
—JOHN UPDIKE
*Couples*

Let's face it, I have been momentary,
A luxury
. . .
I give you back your heart
I give you permission.
—ANNE SEXTON, "For My Lover, Returning to His Wife"


The maternal instinct leads a woman to prefer a tenth share of a first-rate man to the exclusive possession of a third-rate one.
—GEORGE BERNARD SHAW
*Man and Superman*


The number of affairs a man has after his marriage is probably equal to the number he didn't have before it.
—RICHARD J. NEEDHAM
*A Friend in Needham*


There are few people who are not ashamed of their love affairs when the infatuation is lover.
—FRANÇOIS, Duc de La Rochefoucauld
*Réflexions ou sentences et maximes morales*


# Age and Aging

I grow old . . . I grow old
I shall wear the bottoms of my trousers rolled
. . .
I have heard the mermaids singing each to each;
I do not think they will sing to me.
—T.S. ELIOT, "Love Song of J. Alfred Prufrock"

Old meat makes good soup.

*Italian Proverb*


Already I am no longer looked at with lechery and love.
My daughters and sons have put me away with marbles
   and dolls,
Are gone from the house
My husband and lovers are pleasant and somewhat
   polite
And night is night.
—GWENDOLYN BROOKS, "A Sunset of the City"


So much has been said and sung of beautiful young girls,
why doesn't somebody wake up to the beauty of old
women.
—HARRIET BEECHER STOWE
*Uncle Tom's Cabin*


Poor ghost, old love, speak
with your old voice
of flaming insight
that kept us awake all night
In one bed and apart.
—ROBERT LOWELL, "The Old Flame"


And while she murmurs love, he counts her years.
—JUVENAL
*Satire VI* (translated by William Gifford)


Why, Thais, do you constantly call me old? No one,
Thais, is too old for some things.
—MARTIAL
*Epigrams* (translated by Walter C.A. Ker)

How many loved the moments of glad grace,
And loved your beauty with love false or true,
But one man loved the pilgrim soul in you,
And loved the sorrows of your changing face.
And bending down beside the glowing bars
Murmur, a little sad, "From us fled Love.
He paced upon the mountains far above,
And hid his face amid a crowd of stars."
—WILLIAM BUTLER YEATS, "When You Are Old"
*The Countess Kathleen*


In your amours you should prefer old women to young
ones. They are so grateful.
—BENJAMIN FRANKLIN, letter, June 25, 1745


Quite a few women told me, one way or another, that they
thought it was sex, not youth, that's wasted on the young . . .
—JANET HARRIS
*In Praise of Ms. America*


Dawn love is silver
Wait for the west:
Old love is gold love
Old love is best.
—KATHERINE LEE BATES, "For a Golden Wedding"


But you, may bitter age and time attack you,
bringing the stealthy wrinkles to your face!
And as the mirror mocks your haggard beauty,
may white hairs as you pull them, multiply.
—SEXTUS AURELIUS PROPERTIUS

Young I was, but now am old,
But I am not yet grown cold;
I can play and I can twine
'Bout a virgin like a vine:
In her lap I can lie
Melting, and in fancy die
And return to life, if she
Clasps my cheek, or kisseth me;
Thus, and thus it appears
That our love outlasts our years.
—ROBERT HERRICK
  *Hesprides*


Love at the close of our days
is apprehensive and tender.
Slow brighter, brighter farewell rays
of one last love in its evening splendor
. . .
The blood runs thinner, yet the heart
remains as ever deep and tender.
—FYODOR TYATCHEV, "Last Love"


I wept for my youth, sweet passionate
            young thought,
And cozy women dead that at my side
Once lay: I wept with bitter longing,
            not
Remembering how in my youth I cried.
—STANLEY KUNITZ, "I Dreamed That I Was Old"


There is something sadder than growing old—remaining a
child.
—CESARE PAVESE
  *The Burning Brand Diaries*

Old age has disgraces of its own: do not add to them the
shame of vice.
—CATO, The Elder
*Apothegms*


I have everything now I had twenty years ago—except it's
all lower.
—GYPSY ROSE LEE
*Newsweek,* September 16, 1968


Grow old along with me!
The best is yet to be
The last of life, for which the first was made.
—ROBERT BROWNING, "Rabbi Ben Ezra"


. . . she thinks me young,
Although she knows my days are past the best.
—WILLIAM SHAKESPEARE, "Sonnet 138"


If the young only knew; if the old only could.
*French Proverb*


The young feel tired at the end of an action;
The old at the beginning.
—T.S. ELIOT


Sex with older men? I say grab it. But if your man has
had a heart attack don't try to jump start his pacemaker
whisper "This could be your last one, let's make it good."
—PHYLLIS DILLER
*The Joys of Aging and How to Avoid Them*

I dread no more the first white in my hair,
Or even age itself, the easy shoe,
The cane, the wrinkled hands, the special chair:
Time, doing this to me, may alter too
My sorrow, into something I can bear.
—EDNA ST. VINCENT MILLAY, "Sonnet"


Don't look back. Something may be gaining on you.
—SATCHEL PAIGE, last words in his notebook.


. . . I saw my wrinkles in their wrinkles. You know, one looks at herself in the mirror every morning, and she doesn't see the difference, she doesn't realize she is aging. But then she finds a friend who was young with her, and the friend isn't young anymore, and all of a sudden, like a slap on her eyes, she remembers that she, too, isn't young anymore.
—INGRID BERGMAN
    *The Egotists* by Oriana Fallaci


# Alimony

Divorce comes from the old Latin word "divorcerum" meaning "having your genitals torn out through your wallet." And the judge said, "All the money and we'll shorten it to alimony."
—ROBIN WILLIAMS


Marriage is but for a little while. It is alimony that is forever . . .
—QUENTIN CRISP
    *The Naked Civil Servant*

You never realize how short a month is until you pay alimony.
—JOHN BARRYMORE (attributed)


. . . women should not be cowed into believing that to ask for alimony is to be unliberated, or that their husbands provide alimony out of the largesse of their noble hearts.
—SUSAN C. ROSS
*The Rights of Women*


The wages of sin is alimony.
—CAROLYN WELLS (attributed)


In these days of Women's Lib, there is no reason why a wife, whose marriage has not lasted and who has no child, should have a bread ticket for life.
—SIR GEORGE BAKER
*The Observer*, April 3, 1973


Judges, as a class, display, in the matter of arranging alimony, that reckless generosity that is found only in men who are giving away somebody else's cash.
—P.G. WODEHOUSE
*Louder and Funnier*


He doesn't make much money
Just five thousand per
A judge who thinks he's funny
Says "You'll pay six to her."
—GUS KAHN, "Makin' Whoopee"

No one is going to take women's liberation seriously until women recognize that they will never be thought of as equals . . . until they eschew alimony.
—NORMAN MAILER
*Love Talk*

# Anger

If you seek Nirvana in the crotch . . . and that's all there is and it disappoints you, you become angry and hostile. . . . We are angered because we have asked of sex what it cannot give.
—JUDIANNE DENSEN-GERBER
*Walk in My Shoes*

The angry lover tells himself many a lie.
—PUBLILIUS SYRUS
*Sententiae*

When late I attempted your pity to move,
Why seemed you so deaf to my prayers?
Perhaps it was right to dissemble your love.
But—why should you kick me downstairs?
—ISAAC BICKERSTAFFE
*An Expostulation*

The anger of lovers renews their love.
—TERENCE
*The Woman of Andros*

# Anxiety

There is no such thing as pure pleasure; some anxiety always goes with it.
—OVID

*Metamorphoses*

Habitually they walk about with tightened buttocks and rigid pelvic musculature. Just as people grind their teeth, tighten their jaws, hunch their shoulders, or curl their toes in an unconscious response to anxiety, these women clamp their vaginas . . . Their vaginal "clench" is a habitual response to tension.
—AVODAH OFFIT

*The Sexual Self*

Anxiety is the first time you can't do it a second time; panic is the time you can't do it the first time.
—WILLIAM A. NOLEN, "Impotence"

*Esquire*, November 1981

# Aphrodisiacs

Love charms are temporary things if your mojo ain't total.
—TONI CADE BAMBARA

*Gorilla My Love*

Like iron or some kind of crowbar standing all the time he must have eaten oysters.
—JAMES JOYCE

*Ulysses*

There is no aphrodisiac like innocence.
—JEAN BAUDRILLARD
*Cool Memories*


Power is the ultimate aphrodisiac.
—HENRY KISSINGER
*The Guardian*, November 28, 1976


The moon is nothing
But a circumambulating aphrodisiac
Divinely subsidized to provoke the world
Into a rising birthrate.
—CHRISTOPHER FRY
*The Lady's Not for Burning*


Fame is a powerful aphrodisiac.
—GRAHAM GREENE
*Radio Times*, September 10, 1964


Variety is the one simply and absolutely foolproof aphrodisiac.
—AUTHOR UNKNOWN


Bring you magics, spells, and charms
To enflesh my thighs and arms.
Is there no way to beget
In my limbs their former heat?
. . .
Find that medicine, if you can,
For your dry, decrepit man;
Who would fain his strength renew
Were it but to pleasure you.
—ROBERT HERRICK, "To His Mistress"

Love is its own aphrodisiac and is the main ingredient for
lasting sex.
—MORT KATZ
*Marriage Survival Kit*

# Arousal

Arousal is a miracle. . . . Don't try to hide it. [It is] an
unsolicted endorsement, a standing ovation, a sponta-
neous demonstration.
—*Playboy*, December1981

> . . . for the vilest things
> Become themselves in her, that the holy priests
> Bless her when she is riggish.
> —WILLIAM SHAKESPEARE
> *Antony and Cleopatra*

There are a number of mechanical devices which increase
sexual arousal, particularly in women. Chief among these
is the Mercedes-Benz 380SL convertible.
—P.J. O'ROURKE
*Modern Manners*

# Asking

The lame tongue gets nothing.
—WILLIAM CAMDEN
*Remains Concerning Britain*

Whether they give or refuse, it delights women to have been asked.
—OVID
*Ars Amatoria*


By all the soft Pleasures a Virgin can share,
By the critical Minute no Virgin can bear
By the question I burn to ask, but don't dare
I pr'y thee now hear me dear Molly.
—ANONYMOUS, "The Gallant Schemer's Petition to the Honorable
Mrs. F_____s "
*Merry Muses* by J.S. Farmer


He that is too proud to ask is too good to receive.
—THOMAS FULLER
*Gnomologia: Adagies and Proverbs*


# Attraction

What attracts us to a woman rarely binds us to her.
—CHURTON COLLINS
*Aphorisms*


Be mysterious.
—JOHN BOUVIER, advice to his daughter Jacqueline [Kennedy Onassis]


To each his own love, mine for me.
—ATILIUS
*Fragment*

Husbands would never go whoring
They would stay with the ones they adore
If wives were but half alluring
After the act as before.

*The Greek Anthology*


Love stories have so overworked the power of love's gaze,
that finally people agreed to discount it. We hardly dare,
nowadays, to admit that two human beings loved one
another because they looked at one another. Yet—love
dawns thus, and only thus. The rest—comes afterwards.
Nothing is more true, more real, than the primeval mag-
netic disturbances that two souls may communicate to one
another, through the tiny sparks of a moment's glance.
—VICTOR HUGO

*Ideal Marriage* by Van de Velde


Venus is spoilt by serving her in darkness;
Surely you know, sight is the path of love.
—SEXTUS AURELIUS PROPERTIUS


I have a big flaw in that I am attracted to thin, tall, good-
looking men who have one common denominator. They
must be lurking bastards.
—EDNA O'BRIEN


# Aversion

'Tis safest in matrimony to begin with a little aversion.
—RICHARD SHERIDAN

*The Rivals*

Man can start with aversion and end with love, but if he begins with love and comes around to aversion he will never get back to love.
—HONORÉ DE BALZAC
*The Physiology of Marriage*

# Awakening

Awake, my Fanny, leave all meaner things;
This morn shall prove what rapture swiving brings.
—JOHN WILKES
*An Essay on Women*

# Awe

For he [Henry Miller] captured something in the sexuality of men as it had never been seen before, precisely that it was man's sense of awe before women, his dread of her position one step closer to eternity (for in that step were her powers) which made men detest women, revile them, humiliate them, defecate symbolically upon them, do everything to reduce them so that one might dare to enter them and take pleasure of them
—Norman Mailer
*The Prisoner of Sex*

# Bachelors

We bachelors grin, but you married men laugh—till your hearts ache.
—JOHN RAY
*English Proverbs*


What is it, then, to have, or have no wife
But single thralidom, or double strife?
—FRANCIS BACON
*The World*


No lack to lack a wife.
—JOHN HEYWOOD
*A Dialogue Containing the Number in Effect of All the Proverbs in the English Tongue*


Nowadays all married men live like bachelors, all bachelors live like married men.
—OSCAR WILDE
*The Picture of Dorian Gray*


A bachelor never quite gets over the idea that he is a thing of beauty and a boy forever.
—HELEN ROWLAND

I'd be equally as willing
For a dentist to be drilling
Than ever let a woman in my life.
—ALAN JAY LERNER
*My Fair Lady*


Said a fussy old bachelor named Harridge:
"Connubial life I disparage.
Every time I get hot
And poke some girl's spot,
She thinks it is an offer of marriage."
—ANONYMOUS
*The New Limerick* by Gershon Legman


A bachelor is a cagey guy
And he has loads of fun.
He sizes all the cuties up
And never Mrs. one.
—ANONYMOUS
*A Treasury of Atrocious Puns* by Bennett Cerf


Down to Gehenna or up to the Throne
He travels the fastest who travels alone.
—RUDYARD KIPLING, "The Winners"


I belong to Bridegooms Anonymous. Whenever I feel like
getting married they send over a lady in a housecoat and
hair curlers to burn my toast for me.
—DICK MARTIN
*Playboy*, 1969


Lord of yourself, uncumber'd with a wife.
—JOHN DRYDEN
*Epistles*

Benedick: "I will live a bachelor."
Don Pedro: "I shall see thee, ere I die, look pale with love."
Benedick: "With anger, with sickness, or with hunger, my lord, not with love."
—WILLIAM SHAKESPEARE
   *Much Ado About Nothing*


# Bashfulness

Love requires Boldness, and scorns Bashfulness.
—THOMAS FULLER
   *Gnomologia: Adagies and Proverbs*


Modesty is a Virtue, Bashfulness is a Vice.
—BENJAMIN FRANKLIN
   *Poor Richard's Almanac*


The bashful always lose.
   *French Proverb*


# Battle of the Sexes

When Eve ate this particular apple, she became aware of her womanhood, mentally. And mentally she began to experiment with it. She has been experimenting ever since. So has man. To the rage and horror of both of them.
—D.H. LAWRENCE
   *Fantasia of the Unconscious*

In the sex war, thoughtlessness is the weapon of the male, vindictiveness of the female.
—CYRIL CONNOLLY
*Unquiet Grave*


# Beauty

Love is a great beautifier.
—LOUISA MAY ALCOTT
*Little Women*


Beauty—a deceitful bait with a deadly hook.
—JOHN LYLY
*Euphues and His England*


To me, fair friend, you never can be old
For as you were when first your eye I eyed
Such seems your beauty still.
—WILLIAM SHAKESPEARE, "Sonnet 104"


"To be born a woman is to know—
Although they do not talk of it in school—
That we must labour to be beautiful."
—WILLIAM BUTLER YEATS, "Adam's Curse"


Beauty is very well at first sight; but who ever looks at it when it has been in the house three days?
—GEORGE BERNARD SHAW
*Man and Superman*

There is a garden in her face
Where roses and white lilies blow.
—THOMAS CAMPION, "There Is a Garden in Her Face"


Love built on beauty, soon as beauty, dies.
—JOHN DONNE
*Elegies*: "The Anagram"


Beauty is but a flower
Which wrinkles will devour.
—THOMAS NASHE, "Summer's Last Will and Testament"


Remember that the most beautiful things in the world are
the most useless; peacocks and lilies for instance.
—JOHN RUSKIN
*Three Stones of Venice*


What a strange illusion it is to suppose that beauty is
goodness.
—LEO TOLSTOY
*The Kreutzer Sonata*


Oh no, it wasn't the aeroplanes. It was beauty that killed
the beast.
—JAMES CREELAND AND RUTH ROSE
*King Kong*


If they be adorned with beauty they be strait laced and
made so high in the instep, that they disdain them most
that desire them.
—JOHN LYLY
*Euphues and His England*

A beautiful woman should break her mirror early.
—BALTASAR GRACIÁN


If you get simple beauty and naught else,
You get about the best thing God invents.
—ROBERT BROWNING, "Fra Lippo Lippa"


Beauty is a short-lived reign.
—SOCRATES (cited by Diogenes Laertius)


There is no excellent beauty that hath not some strange-
ness in the proportion.
—FRANCIS BACON
*Essays: On Beauty*


What is lovely never dies,
But passes into other loveliness.
—THOMAS BAILEY ALDRICH, "A Shadow of the Night"


Beauty unchaste is beauty in disgrace.
—HOMER
*The Odyssey* (translated by Alexander Pope)


What I fancy, I approve,
No dislike there is in love:
Be my mistress short or tall
And distorted there withal:
Be her forehead, and her eyes
Full of incongruities:
Has she thin hair, hath she none
She's to me a paragon.
—ROBERT HERRICK
*Hesperides*

All heiresses are beautiful.
—JOHN DRYDEN
*King Arthur*


Bait: A preparation which renders the hook more palatable. The best kind is beauty.
—AMBROSE BIERCE
*The Devil's Dictionary*


Beauty for some provides escape,
Who gain a happiness in eyeing
The gorgeous buttocks of the ape
Or autumn sunsets exquisitely dying.
—ALDOUS LEONARD HUXLEY, "The Ninth Philosophical Song"


Well I know
What is this beauty men are babbling of:
I wonder only why they prize it so.
—EDNA ST. VINCENT MILLAY, "Love is Not Blind, I See With a
Single Eye"


Beauty draws more than oxen.
—GEORGE HERBERT
*Jacula Prudentum*


Beauty soons grows familiar to the lover,
Fades in his eye, and palls upon the sense.
—JOSEPH ADDISON
*Cato*


Beauty will not buy beef.
—THOMAS FULLER
*Gnomologia: Adagies and Proverbs*

Beauty is never satisfied
with beauty. Helen
gazing in her glass,
framed by lecherous curtains,
the enchanted bed,
knew herself beautiful. Yet she felt life pass
about her.
—KATHLEEN SPIVACK, "Mythmaking"


Beauty stands
In the admiration only of weak minds
Led captive.
—JOHN MILTON
*Paradise Regained*


But beauty vanishes; beauty passes;
However rare—rare it be;
And when I crumble who will remember
This lady of the West Country?
—WALTER DE LA MARE, "Here Lies a Most Beautiful Lady"


I am tired of all this nonsense of beauty being only skin
deep. That's deep enough. What do you want—an adorable
pancreas?
—JEAN KERR


He who follows Beauty
Breaks his foolish heart.
—BERTYE YOUNG WILLIAMS, "Song Against Beauty"


Beauty, like male ballet dancers, makes some men afraid.
—MORDECAI RICHLER, "Song of a Smaller Hero"

Man soon tires of mere beauty. In fact, the inconstant
creature as soon tires of mere anything.
—ARNOLD HAULTAIN
*Hints for Lovers*


Beauty is a simple passion
but, oh my friends, in the end
you will dance the fire dance in iron shoes.
—ANNE SEXTON, "Snow White and the Seven Dwarfs"


Her hairs are wires of gold,
her cheeks are made of lilies and roses,
her brows are arches,
her eyes sapphires,
her looks lightning,
her mouth coral,
her teeth pearls,
her paps alabaster,
her body straight,
her belly soft,
and from thence downward to her knees is
all sugar candy.
—BARNABE RICH


No woman can be a beauty without a fortune.
—GEORGE FARQUHAR
*The Beaux' Stratagem*


'Tis not a lip, or eye, we beauty call,
But the joint force and full result of all.
—ALEXANDER POPE
*Essay on Criticism*

Beauty's the thing that counts
In women: red lips
And black eyes are better than brains.
—MARY J. ELMENDORF, "Beauty Is the Thing"


Beauty like hers is genius.
—DANTE GABRIEL ROSSETTI, "Genius in Beauty"


Beauty isn't everything! But then what is?
—SANFORD WILSON
*The Madness of Lady Bright*


So you can have your beauty
It's skin deep and it only lies.
—BOB DYLAN, "Long Time Gone"


# Bed

No, no, I'll never farm your bed
Nor your smock-tenant be.
—APHRA BEHN, "A Song"


. . . a bed fortified with the crazy molecules of a thousand
fornications . . .
—NORMAN MAILER
*Prisoner of Sex*


Groan, went the bed.
—THOMAS PYNCHON
*V*

Many a fair nymph has in a cave been spread,
And much good love without a feather bed.
—JUVENAL
Satire VI (translated by John Dryden)


Bored of the foolish things that girls must dream
Because their beds are empty of delight.
—ROY CAMPBELL, "The Sisters"


Bed is the poor man's opera.
Italian Proverb


. . . this love's hallow'd temple, this soft bed.
—JOHN DONNE, "To His Mistress Going to Bed"


The bed is for lascivious toyings meet,
There use all tricks, and shed shame underneath.
—OVID
Elegia XIV (translated by Christopher Marlowe)


There goes a saying, and 'twas shrewdly said,
Old fish at table, young flesh in bed
—ALEXANDER POPE, "January and May"


It isn't the ecstatic leap across that I deplore, it's the weary
trudge home.
—ANONYMOUS, a comment on single beds


The grave of lost illusions.
—ANONYMOUS

Name it I would: but being blushing red,
The rest I'll speak, when we meet both in bed.
—ROBERT HERRICK, "What Shame Forbids to Speak"


The place where marriages are decided.
—ANONYMOUS


For I've been born and I've been wed—
All of man's peril comes of bed.
—C.H. WEBB, "Dum Vivimus Vigilamus"


We are not sure yet if flesh
Has merely sprung a trap,
But, between not-knowing and the knowing
Beds will span the gap.
—JOAN FINNIGAN, "Honeymoon"


. . . on love
wet sheets, we play again
the ancient comedy,
Your orifice, my oracle
—HARRY HOWITH, "Joanne"


. . . there is no sanctuary in one bed from the memory of
another.
—CYRIL CONNOLLY


At night, alone, I marry the bed.
—ANNE SEXTON, "The Ballad of the Lonely Masturbator"

# Betrayal

My love, I have betrayed you seventy times
In this brief period since our stars met:
. . .
Forgot you, worshipped others, flung a flower
To meaner beauty, proved an infidel.
—CONRAD AIKEN, "Sonnet IV"


I loved you despite your betrayals, how would I have felt
had you been faithful?
—JEAN RACINE
*Andromache*


As a rule the person found out in a betrayal of love holds,
all the same, the superior position of the two. It is the
betrayed one who is humiliated.
—ADA LEVERSON
*Love's Shadow*


In me you've found the man you care for.
And, for a while, you'll richly pay me
With kindness, kisses and endearments—
And then, as usual, you'll betray me.
—HEINRICH HEINE, "Ich Liebe Solche Weissen Glieder" (translated by
Louis Untermeyer)


She's fickle and false and there we agree;
For I am as false and fickle as she:
We neither believe what either can say;
And neither believing we neither betray.
—JOHN DRYDEN, "Hourly I Die"
*Amphitryon*

# Bigamy

Two cats and one mouse,
Two wives in one house,
Two dogs and one bone
Never agree in one.
—JOHN RAY
*English Proverbs*


Bigamy is having one wife too many. Monogamy is the same.
—OSCAR WILDE


When two rites make a wrong.
—ANONYMOUS


One wife at a time is enough for most people.
—MR. JUSTICE SMITH
*The Observer*, May 13, 1979


One wife is too much for one husband to hear,
But two at a time there's no mortal can bear.
This way, and that way, and which way I will,
What would comfort the one, t'other wife would take ill.
—JOHN GAY
*The Beggar's Opera*


# Blindness of Love

Though love is blind, yet 'tis not for want of eyes.
—THOMAS FULLER
*English Proverbs*

But love is blind, and lovers cannot see
The petty follies that themselves commit
—WILLIAM SHAKESPEARE
*The Merchant of Venice*


The swarthy girl is tawny, the scrawny is a gazelle, the dumb is modest, that she is half-dead with consumption is slender, and that she is bloated with enormous dugs, is Ceres herself.
—LUCRETIUS
*De Rerum Natura*


# Blondes

It was a blonde. A blonde to make a bishop kick a hole in a stained-glass window.
—RAYMOND CHANDLER
*Farewell My Lovely*


Hazel Morse was a large, fair woman of the type that incites some men when they use the word "blonde" to click their tongues and wag their heads roguishly.
—DOROTHY PARKER
*Big Blonde*


She was a blonde—with a brunette past.
—GWYN THOMAS
BBC TV, October 20, 1969


A chaste woman ought not to dye her hair yellow.
—MENANDER
*Fragments*

That gentlemen prefer blondes is due to the fact that, apparently, pale hair, delicate skin and an infantile expression represent the very apex of frailty which every man longs to violate.

—ALEXANDER KING


It is possible that blondes also prefer gentlemen.

—MAMIE VAN DOREN (attributed)


Being blonde is definitely a different state of mind . . . the artifice of being blonde has some incredible sort of sexual connotation.

—MADONNA

*Rolling Stone*, March 23, 1989


Gentlemen prefer blondes, but take what they can get.

—DON HEROLD (attributed)


# Blushes

There's a blush for won't and a blush for shan't
And a blush for having done it;
There's a blush for thought and a blush for naught
And a blush for just begun it.

—JOHN KEATS, "Sharing Eve's Apple"


In a blush, love finds a barrier.

—VIRGIL

*Ciris*

Blushing is virtue's color.
—JOHN RAY
*English Proverbs*


Faults done by night will blush by day.
—ROBERT HERRICK, "The Vision"


Whoever blushes is already guilty, true innocence is
ashamed of nothing.
—JEAN-JACQUES ROUSSEAU
*Émile*


Girls blush, sometimes, because they are alive,
Half wishing they were dead to save the shame.
The sudden blush devours them, neck and brow;
They have drawn too near the fire of life, like gnats,
And flare up bodily, wings and all. What then?
Who's sorry for a gnat . . . or girl?
— ELIZABETH BARRETT BROWNING
*Aurora Leigh*


# The Body

The basic Female Body comes with the following acces-
sories: garter belt, panti-girdle, crinoline, camisole, bustle,
brassiere, stomacher, chemise, virgin zone, spike heels,
nose ring, veil, kid gloves, fishnet stockings, fichu, ban-
deau, Merry Widow, weepers, chokers, barrettes, bangles,
beads, lorgnette, feather boa, basic black, compact, Lycra
stretch one-piece with modesty panel, designer peignoir,
flannel nightie, lace teddy, bed, head.
—MARGARET ATWOOD
*Michigan Quarterly Review*

A woman watches her body uneasily, as though it were an unreliable ally in the battle for love.
— LEONARD COHEN
*The Favorite Game*


For women . . . bras, panties, bathing suits, and other stereotypical gear are visual reminders of a commercial, idealized feminine image that our real and diverse female bodies can't possibly fit. Without these visual references, each individual woman's body demands to be accepted on its own terms. We stop being comparatives. We begin to be unique.
— GLORIA STEINEM, "In Praise of Women's Bodies"
*Ms.*, April 1981


i like my body when it is with your
body. . . .
— E.E. CUMMINGS


This is a waist the spirit breaks its arm on.
— RANDALL JARRELL
*A Girl in a Library*


The sexual organs are the most sensitive organs of the human being. The eye or the ear seldom sabotage you. An eye will not stop seeing if it doesn't like what it sees, but the penis will stop functioning if he doesn't like what he sees. I would say that the sexual organs express the human soul more than any other limb of the body. They are not diplomats. They tell the truth ruthlessly. It is nice to deal with them and their caprices, but they are even more meshuga than the brain.
— ISAAC BASHEVIS SINGER
*The New York Times Magazine*, November 26, 1978

What ever happens with us, your body
will haunt mine —
—ADRIENNE RICH
*Twenty One Love Poems*


The fate of man
Turns on the body of woman.
—WILLIAM EVERSON, "The Man-Fate"


The most effective lure that a woman can hold out to a
man is the lure that he fatuously conceives to be her
beauty. This so-called beauty, of course, is almost always
an illusion. The female body, even at its best, is very defec-
tive in form; it has harsh curves and very clumsily distrib-
uted masses; compared to it the average milk jug or even
cuspidor, is a thing of intelligent and gratifying design.
—H.L. MENCKEN
*A Mencken Chrestomathy*


# Boredom

. . . entering our lives' third quarter she'd been bored stiff
with me and I bored limp with her. . . .
—JOHN BARTH
*Letters*


Bore: a man in love with another woman.
—MARY PETTINGBONE POOLE (attributed)


It is impossible to become bored in the presence of a
mistress.
—STENDHAL

When you are bored with yourself,
Marry and be bored with someone else.
—DAVID PRYCE-JONES
*Owls and Satyrs*


In love there are no vacations no such thing. Love has to
be lived fully with its boredom and all that.
—MARGUERITE DURAS


She, while her lover pants upon her breast,
Can mark the figures on an Indian chest.
—ALEXANDER POPE
*Epistle to a Lady*


What shall we do with ourselves this afternoon? And the
day after that, and the next thirty years?
—F. SCOTT FITZGERALD
*The Great Gatsby*


# Brain

My brain? It's my second favorite organ.
—WOODY ALLEN AND MARSHALL BRICKMAN
*Sleeper*


Sex on the brain is the wrong place to have it.
—MALCOLM MUGGERIDGE (attributed)


I have a brain and a uterus and I use them both.
—PATRICIA SCHROEDER (attributed)

For while we have sex on the mind, we truly have none in the body.
—D.H. LAWRENCE, "Leave Sex Alone"
*Pansies*


But if God wanted us to think just with our wombs, why did He give us a brain?
—CLARE BOOTH LUCE
*Life*, October 18, 1970


And not a girl goes walking
Along the Cotswold lanes
But knows men's eyes in April
Are quicker than their brains.
—JOHN DRINKWATER, "Cotswold Love"


We're equal partners, that is plain;
Our life cannot grow dull or shoddy.
While I have such a lovely brain
And you have such a lovely body.
—LOUIS UNTERMEYER, "Equals"


I think I have a dick in my brain. I don't need one between my legs.
—MADONNA
*Madonnarama* by bell hooks


We have too much sex on the brain and too little of it elsewhere
—NORMAN DOUGLAS
*An Almanac*

*See also:* THE MIND.

# Breakfast

Never make love to a woman before breakfast for two reasons. One it is tiring. Two, you may meet some one else during the day that you like better.

—ENRICO CARUSO (attributed)


The sexual organs are simply the means of exchanging sexual sensations. The real business is transacted at the emotional level. Thus, the foundation of sexual happiness—or misery—is laid not in the bedroom but at the breakfast table.

—DAVID R. REUBEN

*Reader's Digest*, January 1973


My wife and I tried two or three times in the last forty years to have breakfast together, but it was so disagreeable that we had to stop.

—WINSTON CHURCHILL

*The New York Times*, December 4, 1950


The glances over cocktails
That seemed so sweet;
Don't seem quite so amorous
Over shredded wheat.

—BENNY FIELDS

*Reader's Digest*, December 1947


Breathes there a man with soul so dead
Who never to his wife hath said:
Breakfast be damned, come to bed.

—SAMUEL HOFFENSTEIN

The problem with marriage is that it ends every night after making love, and it must be rebuilt every morning before breakfast.

—GABRIEL GARCIA MARQUEZ

*Love in the Time of Cholera*

# Breakup

Since there is no help, come let us kiss and part—
Nay, I have done you get no more of me;
And I am glad, yea glad with all my heart,
That thus so cleanly I myself can free.
Shake hands for ever, cancel all our vows
And when we meet at anytime again,
Be it not seen in either of our brows
That we one jot of former love retain.

—MICHAEL DRAYTON, "Since There Is no Help, Come Let Us Kiss and Part"

You must live through the time when everything hurts.

—STEPHEN SPENDER, "The Double Shame"

She always believed in the old adage: "Leave them while you're looking good."

—ANITA LOOS

*Gentlemen Prefer Blondes*

I leave before being left. I decide.

—BRIGITTE BARDOT

*Newsweek,* March 5, 1973

Cast not out the foul water till you bring in the clean. Part not with that way of living you had, till you are sure of a better.

—JAMES KELLY

*A Complete Collection of Scottish Proverbs*

*See also:* PARTING; THE END OF LOVE.

# Breasts

. . . her friendly bust
gives promise of pneumatic bliss.

—T.S. ELIOT, "Whispers of Immortality"

How do you like them? Like a pear, a lemon, à la Montgolfier, half an apple, or a cantaloupe? Go and choose, don't be embarrassed.

—COLETTE

*Journey for Myself*

A full bosom is actually a millstone around a woman's neck . . . [Breasts] are not parts of a person but lures slung around her neck, to be kneaded and twisted like magic putty, or mumbled and mouthed like lolly ices.

—GERMAINE GREER

*The Female Eunuch*

Breasts and bosoms I have known
Of varied shapes and sizes
From poignant disappointments
To jubilant surprises.
—WALDO PIERCE

*An Almanac of Words at Play* by W.R. Espy


If you are a girl worry that your breasts are too round.
Worry that your breasts are too pointed . . . If you are a
boy, worry that you will get breasts.
—DELIA EPHRON

*Teenage Romance*


When I hold you in the night
Kiss your breast upon the right
Then you say: "My love, beware!
That one is my husband's share.

Take the left one, lover bold;
That is yours, to have and hold.
Yours is much the better part
For it lies above my heart."
—DEEMS TAYLOR, "Turn to the Left"


Anyone who gives a surgeon six thousand dollars for
breast augmentation should give some thought to invest-
ing a little more in brain augmentation.
—MIKE ROYKO

# Brides

It has been said that a bride's attitude towards her betrothed can be summed up in three words: Aisle, Altar, Hymn.
—FRANK MUIR AND DENIS NORDEN, "A Jug of Wine"
*Upon My Word*

Bride: A woman with a fine prospect of happiness behind her.
—AMBROSE BIERCE
*The Devil's Dictionary*

"Who gives this woman?" Then
Whoever does is silly.
She's given herself to countless men.
So why not now to Willy?
—GEOFFREY R. RIDDLEHOUGH, "Give Away"

Bride loved old words, and found her pleasure marred
On the first night, her expectations jarred,
And thirty inches short of being a yard.
—JAMES VINCENT CUNNINGHAM, "Five Epigrams"

*See also:* WIVES.

# Brothel

No one was ever made wretched in a brothel.
—CYRIL CONNOLLY (attributed)

Prisons are built with stones of law, brothels with bricks
of religion.
—WILLIAM BLAKE
*Proverbs of Hell*


# Buttocks

Many women loathe their backside, that blind and public
mass which belongs to everyone before belonging to
them.
—JEAN-PAUL SARTRE
*Erotic Art and the West* by Robert Melville


. . . the shadow and substance of that warm divide that
tends to drive all mankind to mutest adoration.
—GILBERT SORRENTINO
*Mulligan's Stew*


My wife with buttocks of spring.
—ANDRÉ BRETON, "Freedom of Love"


Think you can run around with a behind like that and get
away with it in court? This is a case of intentional assault
with a dangerous weapon.
—BERTOLT BRECHT
*The Caucasian Chalk Circle*


. . . a thumb-pinch of tush peeking out over each thigh.
—RICHARD PRICE
*Ladies Man*

. . . the most beautiful part of her was the long-sloping fall of the haunches from the socket of the back, and the slumberous round stillness of the buttocks. Like hillocks of sand the Arabs say, soft and downward-slipping with a long slope
—D.H. LAWRENCE

*Lady Chatterley's Lover*

He kissed the plump mellow smellow melons of her rump, on each plump melonous hemisphere, in their mellow yellow furrow, with obscure prolonged provocative melonsmelonous osculation.
—JAMES JOYCE

*Ulysses*

# Buxomness

When a woman that's buxom a dotard does wed
'Tis madness to think she'd be ty'd to his bed.
—AUTHOR UNKNOWN, "When a Woman's That's Buxom" (1682)

So buxom, blithe and debonair.
—JOHN MILTON

*Comus*

# Celibacy

. . . my celibacy . . . more a passive habit than an active policy . . .
—JOHN BARTH
*Letters*

Marriage has many pains, but celibacy has no pleasures.
—SAMUEL JOHNSON
*Rasselas*

I tend to agree that celibacy for a time is worth considering, for sex is dirty if all it means is winning a man, conquering a woman, beating someone out of something, abusing each other's dignity in order to prove that I am a man, I am a woman.
—TONI CADE BAMBERA

As to marriage or celibacy, let man take which course he will, he will be sure to repent.
—SOCRATES

The worst form of self-abuse.
—PETER DE VRIES
*The New York Times*, June 12, 1983

Marriage may often be a stormy lake, but celibacy is almost always a muddy horsepond.
—THOMAS LOVE PEACOCK
*Melincourt*


I can live without it all—
love with its blood pump,
sex with its messy hungers,
men with their peacock strutting
their silly sexual baggage,
their wet tongues in my ear.
—ERICA JONG
*About Women* by S. Berg and S.J. Marks


[Celibacy] happens to be the most common human sexual adventure.
—KURT VONNEGUT, JR.
*Palm Sunday*


[Celibacy] an alternative preferable to the degradation of most male-female relationships.
—DANA DENSMORE
*Sexing the Millenium* by Linda Grant


# Chance

Which to defend is harder than to get:
And ought not be prophaned on either part,
For though 'tis got by chance, 'tis kept by art.
—JOHN DONNE
*The Expostulation*

# Change

I loved thee once, I'll love no more,
Thine be the grief and is the blame;
Thou are not what thou wast before —
What reason should I be the same?
—ROBERT AYTOUN
*To an Inconstant Mistress*


Love is like linen often changed, the sweeter.
—PHINEAS FLETCHER
*Sicelides*


"Yes," I answered you last night;
"No," this morning, sir, I say:
Colors seen by candlelight
Will not look the same by day.
—ELIZABETH BARRETT BROWNING, "The Lady's 'Yes'"


A new love drives out the old.
*French Proverb*


"You gave me the key of your heart, my love;
Then why did you make me knock?"
"Oh that was yesterday, saints above!
And last night—I changed the lock!"
—JOHN BOYLE O'REILLY, "Constancy"


'Tis good to be off wi' the old love
Before you are on wi' the new.
—RICHARD EDWARDS, "Damon and Pythias"

And I shall find some girl perhaps
And a better one than you
With eyes as wise, but kinder
And lips so soft, but true
And I dare say she will do.
—RUPERT BROOKE, "The Chilterns"


In youth, it was a way I had,
To do my best to please.
And change, with every passing lad
To suit his theories.

But now I know the things I know.
And do the things I do,
And if you do not like me so,
To hell, my love, with you.
—DOROTHY PARKER, "Indian Summer"


# Charm

You know what charm is: a way of getting the answer yes
without having asked a clear question.
—ALBERT CAMUS
*The Fall*


It's a sort of bloom on a woman. If you have it, you don't
need to have anything else; and if you don't have it, it
doesn't much matter what else you have.
—JAMES M. BARRIE
*What Every Woman Knows*

# Chastity

Beauty and chastity have always a mortal quarrel between them.
*Spanish Proverb*

Be thou chaste as ice, pure as snow, thou shall not escape calumny.
—WILLIAM SHAKESPEARE
*Hamlet*

Chastity: The most unnatural of sexual perversions.
—AMBROSE BIERCE
*The Devil's Dictionary*

Bolts and bars will not keep our wives and daughters chaste.
—MOLIÈRE
*L'École des maris*

Banish all objects of lust, shut up all youth into the severest discipline that can be exercised in any hermitage, ye can not make them chaste, that came not hither so.
—JOHN MILTON
*Areopagetica*

If she seems not chaste to me,
What care I how chaste she be?
—SIR WALTER RALEIGH, "Shall I Like Hermit Dwell"

God's rarest blessing.
—GEORGE MEREDITH

The cement of civilization and progress.
—MARY BAKER EDDY

To love pure and chaste from afar.
—JOE DARION, "The Impossible Dream"


I had prayed to you for chastity and said, "Give me chastity and continence but not yet." For I was afraid that you would answer my prayer at once and cure me too soon of the disease of lust, which I want satisfied, but not quelled.
—ST. AUGUSTINE
*Confessions*


Chaste as the icicle
That's curdled by the frost from purest snow
And hangs on Dian's temple.
—WILLIAM SHAKESPEARE
*Coriolanus*


Chastity is curable, if detected early.
—GRAFFITO


If not chastity, then cautiously.
*Latin Proverb*


We may come to realize that chastity is no more a virtue than malnutrition.
—ALEX COMFORT
*The New York Times*, February 18, 1968

# Choice of Lover

Are you the new person drawn to me?
To begin with, take warning, I am surely
Far different from what you suppose.
. . .
Do you suppose you will find in me your ideal
Do you think it is so easy to have me become your lover?
—WALT WHITMAN, "Are You the New Person Drawn to Me?"


He'd have given me rolling lands.
House of marble and billowing farms
. . .
You—you'd only a lilting song
Only a melody, happy and high
. . .
He'd have given me laces rare,
Dresses that glimmered with frosty sheen
. . .
You—you'd only to whistle low,
Gaily I followed wherever you led.
I took you and let him go—
Someone ought to examine my head.
—DOROTHY PARKER, "The Choice"


Your true jilt uses men like chess-men, she never dwells
so long on any single man as to overlook another who
may prove more advantageous; nor gives one another's
place, until she has seen that it is in her interest; but if one
is more useful to her than others, brings him in over the
heads of all others.
—ALEXANDER POPE
*Thoughts on Various Subjects*

I can love both fair and brown;
Her whom abundance melts, and her whom want betrays;
Her who loves loneness best, and her who masks and
     plays;
Her whom the country formed and whom the town;
Her who believes and her who tries.
Her who still weeps with spongy eyes;
And her who is dry cork, and never cries.
I can love her, and her, and you and you,
I can love any, so she be not true.
—JOHN DONNE, "The Indifferent"


Every man needs two women, a quiet homemaker, and a
thrilling nymph.
—IRIS MURDOCH


Everybody winds up kissing the wrong person goodnight.
—ANDY WARHOL
*From A to B and Back Again*


When I am dead, you'll find it hard, says he
To ever find another like me.
What makes you think, as I suppose you do,
I'll ever want another man like you?
—EUGENE T. WARE, "He and She"


Finding a man is like finding a job; it's easier to find one
when you already have one.
—PAIGE MITCHELL (attributed)


You need somebody to love while you're looking for
someone to love.
—SHELAGH DELANEY
*A Taste of Honey*

# Class Distinctions

When Adam delved and Eve span,
Who was then the gentleman?
—JOHN BALL
*Speech*, 1381


He is a fool who kisseth the maid when he may kiss the
mistress.
—JAMES HOWELL
*Proverbs*


The sex is turn'd all whore; they love the game:
And mistresses and maids are all the same.
—JUVENAL
*Satire VI* (translated by John Dryden)


Night makes no difference between the priest and the
        clark;
Joan as my lady is as good i' the dark.
—ROBERT HERRICK
*Hesperides*


Love in a hut, with water and a crust,
Is—Love forgive us!—cinders, ashes, dust;
Love in a palace is perhaps at last
More grievous torment than a hermit's fast.
—JOHN KEATS, "Lamia"


# The Closet

Tell your secret to your servant, and you make him your master.
—NATHANIEL BAILEY
*An Universal Etymological English Dictionary*

To whom thy secret thou dost tell,
To him thy freedom thou dost sell.
—BENJAMIN FRANKLIN
*Poor Richard's Almanac*


# Clothes

What a man enjoys about a woman's clothes are his fantasies of how she would look without them.
—BRENDAN FRANCIS (attributed)


A sweet disorder in dress
Kindles in clothes a wantonness.
—ROBERT HERRICK
*Hesperides*


I bet she snaps a mean garter.
—RAYMOND CHANDLER
*Farewell My Lovely*


. . . the heartthrob of garterbelt boils down to nothing but elastic.
—SEYMOUR KRIM
*Views of a Nearsighted Cannoneer*


That girdle will not gird me.
—THOMAS FULLER
*Gnomologia: Adagies and Proverbs*


Your dresses should be tight enough to show you're a woman and loose enough to show you're a lady.
—EDITH HEAD (attributed)

Ah, when at night my lady sweet
Loosens the honeyed linen from her thigh,
Girdle and smock and all warm things lie
Fall'n in a snowdrift round her feet;
. . .
Yea, as I feast upon my lady's clothes,
I dream I was a bee, and they a rose.
—RICHARD LE GALLIENNE
*English Poems*


A dress has no meaning unless it makes a man want to take it off.
—FRANÇOISE SAGAN
*The Observer*, 1969


In olden days a glimpse of stocking
Was looked on as something shocking
Now, heaven knows,
Anything goes.
—COLE PORTER, "Anything Goes"


She wore far too much rouge last night and not quite enough clothes. That is always a sign of despair in a woman.
—OSCAR WILDE
*An Ideal Husband*


Away with silks, away with lawn,
I'll have no scenes or curtains drawn;
Give me my mistress as she is,
Dress'd in her nak'd simplicities:
For as my heart e'en so my eye
Is won by flesh, not drapery.
—ROBERT HERRICK, "Clothes Do But Cheat and Cozen Us"

Oh, what a tangled web we weave
When bras we put on to deceive.
—LEONARD LEWIS LEVINSON
*Bartlett's Unfamiliar Quotations*

Seamed stockings aren't subtle but they certain do the job. You shouldn't wear them when out with someone you're not prepared to sleep with. . . . If you really want your escort paralytic with lust, stop frequently to adjust the seams.
—CYNTHIA HEIMEL
*Sex Tips for Girls*

*See also:* DRESS; FETISHES; LINGERIE.

# Commitment

Never give all the heart, for love
Will hardly seem worth thinking of
To passionate women if it seems
certain. . . .
—WILLIAM BUTLER YEATS, "Never Give All the Heart"

Women would be more charming if one could fall into their arms without falling in her arms.
—AMBROSE BIERCE
*Epigrams*

It's gonna be a long drag, but we'll make it.
—JANIS JOPLIN (attributed)

# Communication

Mute: marriages
the ten-ton block of ice
obstructing the throat, the heart
the red filler of the liver
the clogged life
. . .
Speak the dream
Follow the red thread
of images
Defrost the glacier
with the live heat
of your breath,
propelled by the heart's explosion.
—ERICA JONG, "Mute Marriages"


Love makes mute of those who habitually speak most fluently.
—MADELEINE DE SCUDÉRY
*Choix de pensées: "De l'amour"*


A sound marriage is not based on complete frankness; it is based on sensible reticence.
—MORRIS L. ERNST


Often the diffference between a sucessful marriage and a mediocre one consists of leaving about three or four things a day unsaid.
—HARLAN MILLER


There is nothing like desire from preventing the thing one says from bearing any resemblance to what one has in one's mind.
—MARCEL PROUST
*Remembrance of Things Past: The Guermantes Way*

{ 65 }

Talking in bed ought to be the easiest
Lying together there goes back so far
An emblem of two people being honest
Yet more and more time passes silently
. . .
It becomes still more difficult to find
Words once true and kind,
Or not untrue and not unkind.
—PHILIP LARKIN, "Talking in Bed"


Ultimately, the bond of all companionship, whether in marriage or friendship, is conversation.
—OSCAR WILDE
*De Profundis*


Sex is making a fool of yourself, exposing yourself as an asshole. That is why sex is so intimate. Making mistakes is one of the most revealing and intimate moments of sexual communication.
—JERRY RUBIN AND MIMI LEONARD
*The Battle Between the Sheets*


Women like silent men. They think they're listening.
—MARCEL ARCHANIL


In love there are two things: bodies and words.
—JOYCE CAROL OATES


Some nights he said he was tired, and some nights she said she wanted to read, and other nights no one said anything.
—JOAN DIDION
*Play It as It Lays*

O gentle Romeo
If thou dost love, pronounce it faithfully.
—WILLIAM SHAKESPEARE
*Romeo and Juliet*


They love indeed who quake to say they love.
—SIR PHILIP SIDNEY, "Sonnet LIV"


. . . walking at noon in the ghost town
surrounded by a silence

that sounds like the silence of the place
except that it came with us
and is familiar
and everything we are saying until now
was an effort to blot it out—
Coming out here we are up against it

Out here I feel more helpless
with you than without you . . .
—ADRIENNE RICH, "Trying to Talk to a Man"


Loneliness is never more cruel than when it is felt in close
propinquity with someone who has ceased to communicate.
—GERMAINE GREER
*The Female Eunuch*


We love in another's soul
whatever of ourselves
we can deposit in it:
the greater the deposit
the greater the love.
—IRVING LAYTON, "The Whole Bloody Bird"


*See also:* TALK.

# Compatibility

Though few would still subscribe
To the monogamic axiom
That strife below the hipbones
Need not estrange the heart.

—ROBERT GRAVES, "Call It a Good Marriage"


Considering the two of you
are just alike,
the worst wife and
the worst husband,
I find it quite remarkable
You aren't compatible.

—MARTIAL

*Select Epigrams of Martial* (translated and adapted by Donald C. Goertz)


you fit into me
like a hook in an eye
a fish hook
an open eye

—MARGARET ATWOOD

*Power Politics*


Getting along with men isn't what is important. The vital
knowledge is how to get along with a man, one man.

—PHYLLIS McGINLEY


I love her too, but our neuroses don't match.

—ARTHUR MILLER

*The Ride Down Mount Morgan*

It's true love because
If he said quit drinking martinis, but I kept on
drinking them
and next morning I couldn't get out of bed,
He wouldn't tell me he told me.
—JUDITH VIORST, "True Love"


Love and sex can go together and sex and unlove can go
together and love and unsex can go together. But personal
love and personal sex is bad.
—ANDY WARHOL
    *From A to B and Back Again*


Life has taught us that love does not consist in gazing at
each other but in looking outward together in the same
direction.
—ANTOINE DE SAINT-EXUPÉRY
    *Wind, Sand, and Stars*


# Compromise

Dear wife, give in or get out
. . .
So listen my love, here's a compromise:
If your aim is purity, be a pure bore by day;
When I come home at night, I want a rampant whore.
—MARTIAL
    *Select Epigrams of Martial* (translated and adapted by Donald C. Goertz)


If you cannot catch a bird of paradise, better take a wet hen.
—NIKITA KHRUSHCHEV
    *Time*, January 6, 1958

# Conception

Behold I was brought forth in iniquity,
And in sin did my mother conceive me.
*Psalms*

I shall demand perfect men and women out of my love-
spendings.
—WALT WHITMAN, "A Woman Waits for Me"

. . . but what he did know was if sex had meaning, con-
ception could not be empty of it. . . .
. . .
Sex can lead to conception and be as rewarding as cold
piss. . . .
—NORMAN MAILER
*The Prisoner of Love*

*See also:* PREGNANCY.

# Confession

The things she said to me,
as a man, I won't repeat.
The light of understanding
has made me discreet.
—FEDERICO GARCIA LORCA, "The Faithless Wife"

Never seek to tell thy love
Love that never told can be.
. . .
I told my love, I told my love
I told her all my heart
Trembling, cold, in ghastly fears
Ah! she doth depart.
—WILLIAM BLAKE, "Never Seek to Tell Thy Love"


Strange fits of passion have I known
And I will dare to tell,
But in the lover's ear alone,
What once to me befell.
—WILLIAM WORDSWORTH, "Strange Fits of Passion Have I Known"


You find it no great effort to disclose
Your crimes of murder, bigamy and arson
But can you tell them that you pick your nose?
—NORMAN CAMERON, "Punishment Enough"


Confession may be good for the soul but it doesn't get one
much reputation for sense.
—AUTHOR UNKNOWN


# Conquest

Still stoop to conquer: when she thwarts thee, yield;
Do all her bidding, thou shalt win the field;
Thus, when she argues, argue on her side;
What she approves, approve; deny what she denied;
Say and unsay; and as her face appears
Smile on her smiles, and weep on her tears.
—OVID

*Ars Amatoria*

The way to get on with a girl
Is to drift like a man in a mist,
Happy enough to be caught
Happy to be dismissed.

Glad to be out
of her way,
Glad to rejoin her in bed
Equally grieved or gay
To learn that she's living or dead.
—AUTHOR UNKNOWN, "Advice to Lovers"
*Some Irish Loving* by Edna O'Brien


# Conscience

A standing prick has no conscience.
*"English Proverb"*
*A Dictionary of Catchphrases* by Eric Partridge


Penis erectus non conscient ius.
—GERSHON LEGMAN
*The Limerick*


# Constancy

Let us not undervalue lips or arms
As reassurances of constancy
Or speech as necesssary communication
When troubled hearts go groping
through the dusk.
—ROBERT GRAVES, "The Starred Coverlet"

Dear were her charms to me,
Dearer her laughter free,
Dearest her constancy—
—GERALD GRIFFEN, "Eileen Aroon"


Doubt thou the stars are fire;
Doubt that the sun doth move
Doubt truth to be a liar
But never doubt I love.
—WILLIAM SHAKESPEARE
*Hamlet*


As you are woman, so be lovely;
As you are lovely so be various,
Merciful as constant, constant as various,
So be mine, as I yours forever.
—ROBERT GRAVES, "Pygmalion to Galatea"


Sigh no more ladies, sigh no more,
Men were deceivers ever,
One foot in the sea and one foot on shore
To one thing constant never.
—WILLIAM SHAKESPEARE
*Much Ado About Nothing*


I know not, I ask not, if guilt is in that heart,
But I know that I love thee, whatever thou art.
—THOMAS MOORE, "Come, Rest in This Bosom"
*Juvenile Poems*


Doth not a man's appetite change? A man loves the meat
in his youth that he cannot endure in his age.
—WILLIAM SHAKESPEARE
*Much Ado About Nothing*

There is nothing in this world constant, but inconstancy.
—JONATHAN SWIFT
*A Critical Essay on the Faculties of the Mind*

# Continence

Mr. Mercaptan went on to preach a brilliant sermon on that melancholy perversion known as continence.
—ALDOUS HUXLEY
*Antic Hay*

Continence is an angelic exercise.
—ST. AUGUSTINE
*On the Good of Marriage*

Continence, under some circumstances is a duty, but is never a virtue, it being without any moral quality whatever.
—R.G. WHITE
*Words and Their Uses*

# Contraception

The best contraceptive is a glass of water: not before, or after, but instead.
—AUTHOR UNKNOWN

Use contraceptives: No deposit—No return.
—GRAFITTO

Contraceptives should be used on all conceivable occasions.
—SPIKE MULLIGAN
*The Last Goon Show of All,* BBC TV


A pretty young maiden of France
Decided she'd "take a chance."
She let herself go
For an hour or so
And now all her sisters are aunts.
—ANONYMOUS LIMERICK
*More Playboy's Party Jokes*


Accidents will occur in the best-regulated families.
—CHARLES DICKENS
*David Copperfield*


Where are the children I might have had? . . . Drowned
to the accompaniment of the rattling of a thousand douche
bags.
—MALCOLM LOWRY
*Under the Volcano*


I remember when the women in my college dormitory
gritted their teeth and had a plastic article that looked that
it had been made by Mattel placed inside their bodies.
And I remember an absolutely uproarious all-female
brunch where a friend described her first experience with
a contraceptive device, which shot out of a bathroom window into the college quadrangle. She never retrieved it. I
wouldn't have either.
—ANNA QUINDLEN
*The New York Times,* June 17, 1987

Mary mother, we believe
That without sin you did conceive,
Teach us we pray thee, us believing
How to sin without conceiving.
—ANONYMOUS, "Maiden's Prayer"

# Cooking

There is no spectacle on earth more appealing than that of
a beautiful woman in the act of cooking dinner for someone she loves.
—THOMAS WOLFE
*The Web and the Rock*

Better a dinner of herbs where love is, than a stalled ox
and hatred therewith.
*Proverbs*

# Cosmetics

Where the countenance is fair, there need no colors.
—JOHN LYLY
*Euphues and His England*

Men say y'are fair; and fair ye are 'tis true;
But (Hark!) we praise the Painter now, not you.
—ROBERT HERRICK, "Upon a Painted Gentlewoman"

Give me a look, give me a face
That makes simplicity a grace;
Robes loosely flowing, hair as free:
Such sweet neglect more taketh me
Than all the adulteries of art;
They strike my eyes, but not my heart.
—BEN JONSON
*Epicoene or The Simple Woman*


Stupidity always preserves beauty. It keeps away the wrinkles, it is the divine cosmetic.
—CHARLES BAUDELAIRE
*Intimate Journals*


A girl whose cheeks are covered with paint
Has advantage with me over one whose ain't.
—OGDEN NASH, "Biological Reflection"


Your lover must not find the dressing table covered with lotions. Art conceals its art.
—OVID
*Ars Amatoria*


One sprinkles the most sugar where the tart is burnt.
*Dutch Proverb*


In the factory we make cosmetics; in the store we sell hope.
—CHARLES REVSON
*Fire and Ice* by A. Tobias

Wearing a face that she keeps in a jar by the door.
—JOHN LENNON AND PAUL McCARTNEY, "Eleanor Rigby"


There is no cosmetic for beauty like happiness.
—ANONYMOUS


All the cosmetic names seem obscenely obvious to me in their promise of sexual bliss. They are all firming or uplifting or invigorating. They make you tingle. Or glow. Or feel young. They were prepared with hormones or placentas or royal jelly. All the juice and joy in the lives of these women were to be supplied by the contents of the jars and bottles. No wonder they would spend twenty dollars for an ounce of face makeup or thirty for a half-ounce of hormone cream. What price bliss? What price sexual ecstasy?
—ERICA JONG
*How to Save Your Own Life*


# Courtesy

Politeness is a pleasant way for a man to get nowhere with a girl.
—AUTHOR UNKNOWN


When a man opens the car door for his wife, it's either a new car or a new wife.
—PRINCE PHILIP, Duke of Edinburgh
*Today*, March 2, 1988

Formal courtesy between husband and wife is even more important than it is between strangers.
—R.A. HEINLIN
*The Notebooks of Lazurus Long*

# Courtship

Better to be courted and jilted
Than never be courted at all.
—THOMAS CAMPBELL, "The Jilted Nymph"

. . . women that delight in courting are willing to yield.
—JOHN LYLY
*Euphues and His England*

Courtship to marriage, as a very witty prologue to a very dull play.
—WILLIAM CONGREVE
*The Old Bachelor*

She's a woman, therefore may be woo'd
She's a woman, therefore may be won.
—WILLIAM SHAKESPEARE
*Titus Andronicus*

Then, Julia, let me woo thee
. . .
My soul I'll pour into thee.
—ROBERT HERRICK, "The Night Piece: To Julia"

Why, having won her, do I woo?
. . .
. . . because in short
She's not and never can be mine.
—COVENTRY PATMORE, "The Married Lover"


*See also:* WOOING.


# Crying

With the persuasive language of a tear.
—CHARLES CHURCHILL, "The Times"


He said "I'm leaving mama; and your crying won't
make me stay.
The more you cry: the further I'm going away."
—IDA COX, "Misery Blues"


I woke up this morning with the blues
        all 'round my bed.
I woke up this morning with the blues
        all 'round my bed.
I felt just like somebody in my family was dead.
I began to moan and I began to cry,
I began to moan and I began to cry,
My sweet man went away didn't know the reason why.
—LIL JOHNSON, "You'll Never Miss Your Jelly"

Cry me a river
Cry me a river
For I cried a river over you.
—ARTHUR HAMILTON, "Cry Me a River"


# Cuckolds

You can't pluck roses without fear of thorns.
Nor enjoy a fair wife without fear of horns.
—BENJAMIN FRANKLIN


I pray thee, good Lord, that I may not be married. But if I
am to be married, that I may not be a cuckold. But if I am
to be a cuckold, that I may not know. But if I am to know,
that I may not mind.
—ISAK DINESEN, "The Poet"
*Seven Gothic Tales*


The cuckold is last that knows of it.
—WILLIAM CAMDEN
*Remains Concerning Britain*


The character of cuckoldry is perpetual; on whom it once
fasteneth, it holdeth forever.
—MICHEL DE MONTAIGNE
*Essays III*


He that thinks himself a cuckold carries live coals in his
heart.
—THOMAS FULLER
*Gnomologia: Adagies and Proverbs*

# Dalliance

Good for thee to have dalliance in a woman's arms.
—HOMER
*Iliad*

Sweet dalliance keepeth wrinkles long away;
Repentance follows them that refuse.
—HENRY CONSTABLE, "Sonnets to Diane"

# Dancing

Through dancing many maidens have been unmaidened . . .
—JOHN NORTHBROOKE
*Against Dicing*

Refrain from dancing which was the means that lost John
Baptist's head.
—JOHN LYLY
*Euphues and His England*

Dancing is a perpendicular expression of a horizontal
desire.
—ANONYMOUS

Dancing is wonderful training for girls, it's the first way you learn to guess what a man is going to do before he does it.
—CHRISTOPHER MORLEY
*Kitty Foyle*


# Darkness

In darkness there is no choice.
—J.C. AND A.W. HARE
*Guesses at Truth*


When the candles are out, all women are fair.
—PLUTARCH
*Conjugal Precepts*


Regarding what is below the girdle, it is impossible of two women to know an old one from a young one. In the dark all cats are grey.
—BENJAMIN FRANKLIN, letter, June 25, 1745


The dark night makes every woman beautiful . . . In the dark all blemishes are hid, every fault overlooked, that hour makes any woman fair . . . Do not let too strong a light come into your bedroom. There are in a beauty a great many things which are enhanced by being seen only in a half-light.
—OVID
*Ars Amatoria*

Night hath better sweets to prove
Venus now wakens and wakens love,
Come, let us our rites begin;
'Tis only daylight that makes sin.
—JOHN MILTON
*L'Allegro*


# Dating

Don't go with girls you'd be ashamed to marry.
—JOHN UPDIKE
*Couples*


Stop looking at the opposite sex as the enemy . . . Don't
tell your life story at a first meeting. Especially avoid talking about your personal problems. Don't describe your
long-term marital ambitions on the first date.
—ABBY HIRSCH


The traditional male-female dynamic is enjoyable. We like
doors opened for us and meals paid for on the first date.
Otherwise we think he's cheap.
—CHRISTINA HOFF SOMMERS
*Esquire*, February 1994


It's just time to marry, that's all . . . I'm so tired of dating!
I'm so tired of keeping up a good front!
—ANNE TYLER
*Breathing Lessons*

. . . men generally pay all the expenses on a date . . .
Either sex may bring a little gift, its value to be deter-
mined by the bizarreness of the sexual request to be made
later in the evening.
—P.J. O'ROURKE
*Modern Manners*


I feel that the moment a date happens that it is a social
encounter. And the question of sex needs to be negotiated
from the first moment on.
—CAMILLE PAGLIA
*Sex, Art, and American Culture*


# Death

In Heaven
If I cry to you then, will you hear or know?
—A.C. SWINBURNE, "The Triumph of Time"


Men have died from time to time and worms have eaten
them, but not for love.
—WILLIAM SHAKESPEARE
*As You Like It*


The difference between sex and death is, with death you
can do it alone and nobody's going to make fun of you.
—WOODY ALLEN
*The New York Times*, December 1, 1975


He loves too much who dies for love.
—RANDLE COTGRAVE
*Dictionary*

May I grow languid in the work of Venus, when I die, may I perish in the act; and, may a friend, weeping over my body, say this of me: He died as he lived.
—OVID
*Ars Amatoria*


Death is orgasm is rebirth is death is orgasm.
—WILLIAM BURROUGHS
*The Ticket that Exploded*


Death is the only pure, beautiful conclusion of a great passion.
—D.H. LAWRENCE
*Fantasia of the Unconscious*


When I am dead and over me bright April
Shakes out her rain-drenched hair
Though you should lean above me broken-hearted
I shall not care.
—SARA TEASDALE, "I Shall Not Care"


When I am dead my dearest
Sing no sad songs for me;
Plant thou no roses at my head,
Nor shady cypress tree:
Be the green grass above me
With showers and dewdrops wet;
And if thou wilt, remember,
And if thou wilt, forget.
—CHRISTINA ROSSETTI, "When I Am Dead"

True love makes the thought of death frequent, easy, without terrors; it merely becomes the standard of comparison, the price one would pay for many things.
—STENDHAL
*De l'Amour*


When Death to either shall come—
I pray it be first to me.
—ROBERT BRIDGES
*When Death to Either Shall Come*


# Debauchery

Debauchery and love can not live together.
—JEAN-JACQUES ROUSSEAU
*La Nouvelle Héloïse*


Not joy but joylessness is the mother of debauchery.
—FRIEDRICH W. NIETZSCHE
*Human All-Too-Human*


After a debauch, one feels oneself to be more solitary, more abandoned.
—CHARLES BAUDELAIRE
*Intimate Journals*


True debauchery is liberating because it creates no obligations. In it you possess only yourself; hence it remains the favorite pastime of great lovers of their own person.
—ALBERT CAMUS
*The Fall*

Debauchee: One who so earnestly pursued pleasure that
he has the misfortune to overtake it.
—AMBROSE BIERCE

*The Devil's Dictionary*

# Deceit

Venus lends deaf ears to love's deceits.
—OVID

*Amores*

When cheated, wife or husband feels the same.
—EURIPIDES

*Andromache*

Men in matters of love have as many ways to deceive as
they have words to utter.
—JOHN LYLY

*Euphues and His England*

Who can deceive a lover?
—VIRGIL

*Aeneid*

Deceit is the game of small minds and is therefore the
proper pursuit of women.
—PIERRE CORNEILLE

*Nicomède*

It is a double pleasure to deceive the deceiver.
—JEAN DE LA FONTAINE
*Caractères*

A man does not look behind the door unless he has stood there himself.
—HENRI DUBOIS

O what a tangled web we weave
When first we practice to deceive!
But when we've practiced quite a while
How vastly we improve our style!
—J.R. HOPE, "A Word of Encouragement"

If she be false, O then heaven mocks itself.
I'll not believe it.
—WILLIAM SHAKESPEARE
*Othello*

It is not difficult to deceive the first time, for the deceived possesses no antibodies, unvaccinated by suspicion, she overlooks latenesses, accepts absurd excuses, permits the flimsiest patching to repair great rents in the quotidian.
—JOHN UPDIKE
*Couples*

Love is only half the illusion; the lover but not his love, is deceived.
—GEORGE SANTAYANA
*The Life of Reason*

# Declarations of Love

I get no kick from champagne
Mere alcohol doesn't thrill me at all
So tell me why should it be true
That I get a kick out of you?
—COLE PORTER, "I Get a Kick Out of You"
*Anything Goes*


. . . when I look on you a moment, then can I speak no
more, but my tongue falls silent, and at once a delicate
flame courses beneath my skin, and with my eyes I see
nothing, and my ears hum, and a wet sweat bathes me,
and a trembling seizes me all over . . .
—SAPPHO


Night and day, you are the one.
—COLE PORTER, "Night and Day"
*Gay Divorcée*


Come to me
Not as a river willingly downward falls
To be lost in a wide ocean.
But come to me
As flood-time comes to shoreline
Filling empty bays
With a white stillness
Mating earth and sea.
—ANNE WILKINSON, "In June and Gentle Oven"


I want to do with you
What spring does
With the cherry trees.
—PABLO NERUDA

. . . .I gave you the whole sun and stars to play with. I gave you eternity in a single moment, strength of the mountains in one clasp of your arms, and the volume of the seas in one impulse of your soul . . . I have given you the greatest of all things; and you ask me to give you little things. I gave you your own soul: you ask for my body as a plaything. Was it not enough? Was it not enough?

—GEORGE BERNARD SHAW

*Getting Married*

You have opened up the prison gates of my womanhood. And all the passion that was unsatisfied in me for so many years, leaped into a wild reckless storm boundless as the sea.

—EMMA GOLDMAN, letter to Ben Reitman

if you do not love me I shall not be loved
if I do not love you I shall not love

—SAMUEL BECKETT, "Cascando"

Entreat me not to leave thee, and to return from not following after thee; for wither thou goest, I will go; and wither thou lodgest, I will lodge; thy people shall be my people, and thy God my God; where thou diest, will I die, and there will I be buried; the Lord do so to me, and more also, if aught but death part thee and me.

*The Book of Ruth*

# Defects in a Lover

Never look a worm in the apple of your eye.

—LANGSTON HUGHES

*Reader's Digest*, May 1973

I'm a one-hour mama, so no one-minute papa
Ain't the kind of man for me.
— PORTER GRANGER, "One-Hour Mama"


She wanted to be the reason for everything and so was
the cause of nothing.
— DJUNA BARNES
*Nightwood*


You're so mean and evil, you do things you ought
    not do.
But you've got my brand of honey, so I guess I'll have
to put up with you.
— JIMMY RUSHING AND COUNT BASIE, "Going to Chicago Blues"


In faith I do not love thee with mine eyes,
For they in thee a thousand errors note,
But 'tis my heart that loves what they despise.
— WILLIAM SHAKESPEARE, "Sonnet 141"


She has the bear's ethereal grace,
The bland hyena's laugh,
The footstep of the elephant,
The neck of the giraffe,
I love her still, believe me,
Though my heart its passion hides;
'She's all my fancy painted her,'
But oh, how much besides.
— LEWIS CARROLL, "My Fancy"
*College Rhymes*


The man I love got lowdown ways for true,
Well, I'm hinkty and lowdown too.
— W.C. HANDY, "The Basement Blues"

# Definitions of Love

Love is an act of endless forgiveness, a tender look which becomes a habit.
—PETER USTINOV
*Christian Science Monitor*, September 12, 1958


Love is the wisdom of the fool and the folly of the wise.
—SAMUEL JOHNSON
*Johnsonian Miscellanies*


Love is man unfinished.
—PAUL ÉLUARD, "Out of Sight in the Direction of My Body" (translated by Samuel Beckett)


Love is not the dying moan of a distant violin; it's the triumphant twang of a bedspring.
—S.J. PERELMAN (attributed)


Love is the best, most insidious, most effective instrument of social repression.
—RAINER WERNER FASSBINDER (attributed)


Love is an attempt to change a piece of the dream-world into reality.
—THEODOR REIK
*The Psychology of Sex Relations*


Love is a hole in the heart.
—BEN HECHT
*Winkleberg*

Love is the tact of every good,
The only warmth, the only peace.
—DELMORE SCHWARTZ, "For the One Who Would Take Man's Life
in His Hands"


Love is form, and cannot be without
important substance.
—CHARLES OLSEN, "The Maximus Poems"


It was gotten by despair
Upon impossibility.
—ANDREW MARVELL, "Definition of Love"


. . . love is always self-sacrifice, the sacrifice of identity,
will and body integrity, in order to fulfil and redeem the
masculinity of her lover.
—ANDREA DWORKIN, in a speech, 1975


Love is much nicer to be in than an automobile accident, a
tight girdle, a higher tax bracket or a holding pattern over
Philadelphia.
—JUDITH VIORST
*Redbook*, February 1975


Love is like quicksilver in the hand.
Leave the fingers open and it stays.
Clutch it and it darts away.
—DOROTHY PARKER


Love is the realization that one woman differs from another.
—MERVYN LEVY
*The Moons of Paradise*

Love is the delusion that one woman differs from another.
—H.L. MENCKEN
*A Mencken Chrestomanthy*


Love is not love until love's vulnerable.
—THEODORE ROETHKE
*The Dream*


Love is a mystery which, when solved, evaporates.
—NED ROREN
*Music From the Inside Out*


Love is sweet, but tastes better with bread.
*Yiddish Proverb*


Love is a sickness full of woes
All remedies refusing.
—SAMUEL DANIEL, "Love Is a Sickness"


If love is the answer, could you rephrase the question?
—LILY TOMLIN (attributed)


Love is the answer, but while you're waiting for the answer
sex raises some pretty good questions.
—WOODY ALLEN


Love doesn't make the world go 'round.
Love is what makes the ride worthwhile.
—FRANKLIN P. JONES (attributed)

Love is a game in which both players cheat.

—E.W. HOWE

*County Town Sayings*


Love is something far more than desire for sexual intercourse; it is the principal means of escape from loneliness which afflicts most men and women throughout the greater parts of their lives.

—BERTRAND RUSSELL


Love is an irresistible desire to be irresistibly desired.

—ROBERT FROST

*Comment*


Love is when two people who care for each other get confused.

—BOB SCHNEIDER (attributed)


Love is like a faucet, you can turn it off an' on,
But when you think you've got it, it's done turned off .
and gone.

*Blues Song*


Love is, above all, gift of oneself.

—JEAN ANOUILH

*Ardèle*


Love is just a four-letter word.

—BOB DYLAN (Title of song)

Love is a migraine
A bright stain on the vision
Blotting out reason.
—ROBERT GRAVES
*Symptoms of Love*


Love is so simple.
—JACQUES PRÉVERT (attributed)


Love is two minutes fifty-two seconds of squishing noises.
It shows your mind is not clicking.
—JOHNNY ROTTEN (attributed)


Love is a sour delight, a sugur'd grief, a living death, an
ever-dying life.
—THOMAS WATSON


Love is a fiend, a fire, a hell,
Where pleasure, pain, and repentence dwell.
—RICHARD BARNFIELD


Love, what is it? A cork and a bottle.
—ANDRÉ MALRAUX
*Man's Fate*


Love is my religion—I could die for it.
—JOHN KEATS


Love in young men, for the most part, is not love at all but
simply sexual desire and its accomplishment is its end.
—MIGUEL DE CERVANTES
*Don Quixote*

# Definitions of Marriage

Marriage is a lottery.

*English Proverb*

Marriage is a covenant which hath nothing free but the entrance.

—MICHEL DE MONTAIGNE

*Essays*

Marriage: The state or condition of a community consisting of a master, a mistress and two slaves, making in all, two.

—AMBROSE BIERCE

*The Devil's Dictionary*

Marriage is difficult enough; just plain monogamy. Polygamy is more difficult. And group marriage is just too difficult for anybody.

—MARGARET MEAD

# Definitions of Sex

Sex is the last refuge of the miserable.

—QUENTIN CRISP

*The Naked Civil Servant*

Sex is a shortcut to everything.

—ANNA CUMMINGS

*The Love Quest*

Sex is like money; only too much is enough.
—JOHN UPDIKE
*Couples*


Sex is a conversation carried out by other means.
—PETER USTINOV
*Speaking Frankly* by W. Lewis


# Delay

Delay is a great procuress.
—OVID
*Ars Amatoria*


Desires are nourished by delays.
—JOHN RAY
*English Proverbs*


Sweet reluctant amorous delay.
—JOHN MILTON
*Paradise Lost*


# Denial of Love

Roused by your naked grief and beauty,
For lust he will burn:
"Turn to me sweetheart! Why do you not turn?"
—ROBERT GRAVES, "A Lost Jewel"

You say it is only a trifle
You are asking;
it is true it is only a trifle
you are asking,
then it is only a trifle
I am refusing.
—MARTIAL
*Selected Epigrams of Martial* (translated and adapted by Donald C. Goertz)


I'd rather have my cake burn than you should turn it.
. . . Better to be deny'd than deceived . . .
A civil denial is better than a rude grant.
—THOMAS FULLER
*Gnomologia: Adagies and Proverbs*


[Perhaps] a great love is never returned.
—DAG HAMMARSKJÖLD
*Markings*


He that asketh faintly beggeth a denial.
*English Proverb*


# Desertion

[Men] are all but stomachs, and we all but food
They eat us hungrily, and when they are full
They belch us.
—WILLIAM SHAKESPEARE
*Othello*


I woke up this morning: with an awful aching head
My new man had left me; just a room and an empty bed.
—BESSIE SMITH, "Empty Bed Blues"

Did you ever wake up, just at the break of day
With your arms around the pillow, where your daddy
used to lay.

—MA GERTRUDE RAINEY, "Bad Luck Blues"

When you're going to pull out on someone, tell them first.

—JOHN IRVING

*The World According to Garp*

# Desire

To blurt it out in a word—we want laying.

—ARISTOPHANES

*Lysistrata*

The warm beast of desire that lies curled up in our loins
and stretches itself with a fierce gentleness.

—ALBERT CAMUS

*Notebooks*

The desire accomplished is sweet to the soul.

*Proverbs*

I know the nature of women, when you want to, they
don't want to; and when you don't want to, they desire
exceedingly.

—TERENCE

*Eunuchus*

A virgin's longing is a consuming fire,
A hundred times worse is a man's desire.
—JEAN-BAPTISTE LOUIS GRESSET
*Vert-Vert*


A true saying it is, desire hath no rest.
—ROBERT BURTON
*The Anatomy of Melancholy*


If you wish to drown, do not torture yourself with shallow
water.
*Bulgarian Proverb*


To drink is a small matter,
To be thirsty is everything.
—GEORGES DUHAMEL
*The Heart's Domain*


Want a thing long enough, and you don't.
*Chinese Proverb*


Hungry dogs will eat dirty puddings.
—ROBERT BURTON
*The Anatomy of Melancholy*


A man's desire is for the woman; but the woman's desire is
rarely other than for the desire of the man.
—SAMUEL TAYLOR COLERIDGE
*Table Talk,* July 23, 1837

There are two tragedies in life: One is not to get your
heart's desire. The other is to get it.
—GEORGE BERNARD SHAW
*Man and Superman*


Desire is the very essence of man.
—BARUCH SPINOZA
*Ethics*


He who desires, but acts not, breeds pestilence.
—WILLIAM BLAKE
*The Marriage of Heaven and Hell*


For love, and love alone of all our joys
By full possession does but fan the fire;
The more we still enjoy, the more we still desire.
—LUCRETIUS
*Concerning the Nature of Love* (translated by John Dryden)


Women wise increase desiring
By combining kind delays.
—WILLIAM CONGREVE, "The Reconciliation"


I came upon no wine
So wonderful as thirst.
—EDNA ST. VINCENT MILLAY, "Feast"


If you drive nature out with a pitchfork, she will soon find
a way back.
—HORACE
*Epistles*

It's ill-becoming for an old broad to sing about how bad
she wants it. But occasionally we do.
—LENA HORNE
*Time*, October 17, 1988


The desire of the man is for the woman, but the desire of
the woman is for the desire of the man.
—MADAME DE STAËL (attributed)


The shame of aging is not that desire should fail (who
mourns for something he no longer needs?): it is that
someone else must be told.
—W.H. AUDEN


'Tis not the meat, but 'tis the appetite
Makes eating a delight.
—JOHN SUCKLING, "Of Thee, Kind Boy"


O lyric Love, half angel and half bird
And all a wonder and a wild desire.
—ROBERT BROWNING
*The Ring and the Book*


The desire for possession is insatiable, to such a point that
it can survive even love itself. To love, therefore, is to ster-
ilize the person one loves.
—ALBERT CAMUS
*The Rebel*

# Destiny

Anatomy is not destiny.
—SIMONE DE BEAUVOIR (attributed)


Hanging and marriage, you know, go by destiny.
—GEORGE FARQUHAR
*The Recruiting Officer*


# Divorce

All women are stimulated by the news that any wife has left any husband.
—ANTHONY POWELL
*The Acceptance World*


So many persons think that divorce is the panacea for every ill, who find out, when they try it, that the remedy is worse than the disease.
—DOROTHY DIX
*Dorothy Dix, Her Book*


What God hath joined together no man shall ever put asunder: God will take care of that.
—GEORGE BERNARD SHAW
*Getting Married*


Only a marriage with partners strong enough to risk divorce is strong enough to avoid it . . .
—CAROLYN HEILBRUN, "Marriage Is the Message"
*Ms.*, August 1974

Tomorrow to fresh woods and pastures new.
—JOHN MILTON
*Lycidas*


The finest shoe often hurts the foot.
—JOHN CLARKE
*Paroemiologia Anglo-Latina*


The three "gets": get a lawyer, get a job, get laid.
—JUDITH CRIST, advice to women contemplating divorce
*New York*, May 8, 1972


The difference between divorce and legal separation is that legal separation gives a husband time to hide his money.
—JOHNNY CARSON (attributed)


In our family we don't divorce our men—we bury them.
—RUTH GORDON (attributed)


You don't know a woman until you have met her in court.
—NORMAN MAILER (attributed)


The happiest time of anyone's life is just after the first divorce.
—JOHN KENNETH GALBRAITH (attributed)


Cast not out the foul water till you bring in the clean.
—DAVID FERGUSSON
*Scottish Proverbs*

Divorces are made in heaven.
—OSCAR WILDE
*The Importance of Being Earnest*


When a marriage goes on the rocks, the rocks are there, right there.
—TENNESSEE WILLIAMS
*Cat on a Hot Tin Roof*
[stage directions: Big Mama points to the bed.]


Being divorced is like being hit by a Mack truck—if you survive you start looking very carefully to the right and left.
—JEAN KERR
*Mary, Mary*


A divorce is like an amputation, you survive, but there is less of you.
—MARGARET ATWOOD
*Time*, 1973


We lov'd, and we lov'd, as long as we could
Til our love was lov'd out in us both;
But our marriage is dead, when the pleasure has fled:
Twas pleasure that made it an oath.
—JOHN DRYDEN, "Marriage à la Mode"


I see no marriages fail sooner, or more troubled, than such as are concluded for beauty's sake, and huddled up for amourous desires.
—MICHEL DE MONTAIGNE
*Essays*

You can make divorce as easy as a dog license, but you can't burn away the sense of shame and waste.

—A. ALVAREZ

*Life After Marriage*


You don't dare entertain
questions like—can I start again?
seek divorce?

—DANNIE ABSE

*Portrait of a Marriage*


I don't want the cheese; I just want out of the trap.

*Spanish Saying*


*See also:* RECONCILIATION.


# Domination

When a man curls his lip, when he uses ridicule, when he grows angry, you have touched a raw nerve in domination.

—SHEILA ROWBOTHAM

*Woman's Consciousness, Man's World*


Who knows not Circe,
The Daughter of the Sun, whose charmed cup
Whoever tasted, lost his upright shape,
And downward fell into a groveling swine.

—JOHN MILTON

*Comus*

Disguise our bondage as we will,
'Tis woman, woman, rules us still.
—THOMAS MOORE, "Sov'reign Woman"


I always run into strong women who are looking for weak
men to dominate them.
—ANDY WARHOL


Do you come to me to bend me to your will
As conqueror to the vanquished
To make me a bond slave
To bear your children, wearing out my life
In drudgery and silence
No servant will I be.
If that be what you ask, O lover
I refuse you.
—CHRISTINA WALSH, "A Woman to Her Lover ('Proudly')"


*See also:* POWER.


# Don Juans

Unyielding pride, a desire to subjugate others, the provocative lord of battle, the need for ascendancy, these are his
predominant features. Sensuality is but a secondary importance compared to these.
—HIPPOLYTE TAINE
*Sexuality and Homosexuality* by Arno Karlen

If the Don Juans and Don Juanesses only obeyed their desires, they'd have very few affairs. They have to tickle themselves up imaginatively before they can start being casually promiscuous.

—ALDOUS HUXLEY

*Point Counter Point*


Any man that can't find what he is looking for in a thousand women is really looking for a boy.

—GERSHON LEGMAN

*Rationale of the Dirty Joke*


*See also:* PROMISCUITY.


# Double Standard

The pot calls the pan burnt-arse.

—JOHN CLARKE

*Paroemiologia Anglo-Latina*


When the goose drinks as deep as the gander, pots are soon empty and the cupboard bare.

—C.H. SPURGEON

*John Ploughman's Pictures*


As well as for the cow calf as for the bull.

—JOHN HEYWOOD

*A Dialogue Containing the Number in Effect of All the Proverbs in the English Tongue*

Thou rangest like a town bull, why art thou so incensed if
she tread awry?
—ROBERT BURTON
*Anatomy of Melancholy*


Women want monogamy
Man delights in novelty.
Love is woman's moon and sun
Man has other forms of fun.
Woman lives but in her lord
Count to ten and man is bored.
What this the gist and sum of it,
What earthly good can come of it.
—DOROTHY PARKER, "General Review of the Sex Situation"


We still have these double standards where the emphasis
is all on the male's sexual appetites—that it's OK for him
to collect as many scalps as he can before he settles down
and "pays the price." If a woman displays the same attitude, all the epithets that exist in the English language are
laid at her door, and with extraordinary bitterness.
—GLENDA JACKSON


# Dreams

A man doesn't dream about a woman because he thinks
her "mysterious"; he decides that she is "mysterious" to
justify his dreaming about her.
—HENRI DE MONTHERLANT, "The Goddess Cypris"

Dreaming is the poor retreat of the lazy, hopeless and imperfect lover.

—WILLIAM CONGREVE

*Love for Love*


I do not understand the capricious lewdness of the sleeping mind.

—JOHN CHEEVER

*John Cheever: The Journals*


Come to me in my dreams, and then
By day I shall be well again.
For then the night will be more than
The hopeless longing of day.

—MATTHEW ARNOLD, "Longing"


Forgo your dream, poor fool of love.

—CATULUS

*Carmina* (translated by Sir W. Marris)


Like a dog, he hunts in dreams.

—ALFRED, Lord Tennyson, "Locksley Hall"


(dreaming,
et
        cetera, of
Your smile
eyes, knees and of your Etcetera)

—E.E. CUMMINGS, "my sweet old etcetera"


*See also:* FANTASY.

# Dress

You must have women dressed, if it is only for the pleasure of imagining them as Venuses.
—GEORGE MOORE


Byron said, her costume began too late and ended too soon.
—WILLIAM C. HAZLITT
*Four Generations of a Literary Family*


. . . when Dwayne and Trout and I were boys, girls concealed their underpants at all costs and boys tried to see their underpants at all costs.
—KURT VONNEGUT, JR.
*Breakfast of Champions*


You don't have to signal a social conscience by looking like a frump. Lace knickers won't hasten the holocaust, you can ban the bomb in a feather boa just as well as without, and a mild interest in hemlines doesn't necessarily disqualify you from reading *Das Kapital* and agreeing with every word.
—JILL TWEEDIE


*See also:* CLOTHES; FETISHES; LINGERIE.


# Drinking

One more drink and I'd have been under the host.
—DOROTHY PARKER
*Wit's End*

Many a miss would not be a missus
If liquor did not add a spark to her kisses.
—E.L.C., "Listen"
*Life*, March 1933


Who loves not wine, women or song
Remains a fool his whole life long.
—MARTIN LUTHER (attributed)


Without Bacchus and Ceres, Venus grows cold.
*Roman Proverb*


Wine makes old wives wenches.
—JOHN CLARKE
*Paroemiologia Anglo-Latina*


Sex and a cocktail: they both lasted about as long, had the
same effect, and amounted to about the same thing.
—D.H. LAWRENCE
*Lady Chatterley's Lover*


A drunken woman is an open door.
*German Proverb*


Candy
is dandy
But liquor
is quicker.
—OGDEN NASH, "Reflections on Ice-Breaking"

Alcohol is like love. The first kiss is magic, the second is intimate, the third is routine. After that you take the girl's clothes off.
—RAYMOND CHANDLER
*The Long Goodbye*


It provokes the desire but takes away the performance. Therefore much drink may be said to be an equivocator: it makes him and it mars him, it sets him on and it takes him off.
—WILLIAM SHAKESPEARE
*Macbeth*


Absinthe makes the tart grow fonder.
—HUGH DRUMMOND
*Vintage Year* by S. Hicks


# Duration of Love

How long shall I love him, I can no more tell,
Then had I a Fever, when I should be well.
—SIR GEORGE ETHEREGE, "Song"
*She Would If She Could*


In time the Rockies may crumble
Gibraltar may tumble
(They're only made of clay)
But our love is here to stay.
—IRA GERSHWIN, "Our Love is Here to Stay"
*Goldwyn Follies*

# Ears

Love enters a man through his eyes; a woman through her ears.

*Polish Proverb*


There is nothing so virtuous as the ear of an abandoned woman.

—ALFRED De MUSSET

*Lorenzacchio*


The ears are chaste,
E'en though the eyes are bold.

—JEAN DE LA FONTAINE, "Le tableau"

*Contes et Nouvelles*


It is better to play with the ears than the tongue.

—JOHN DAVIES

*The Scourge of Folly*


Keep a guard over your eyes and ears as the inlets of your heart...

—ANNE BRONTË

*The tenant of Wildfell Hall*

# Embracing

Imparudis'd in one another's arms.
—JOHN MILTON
*Paradise Lost*


Let him rebuke who ne'er has known the pure platonic
    grapple,
Or hugged two girls at once behind a chapel.
—EZRA POUND
*L'Homme moyen sensuel*


Embrace me
My sweet embraceable you.
Embrace me
You irreplaceable you.
—IRA GERSHWIN, "Embraceable You"
*Girl Crazy*


Let us embrace, and from this very moment
Vow an eternal misery together.
—THOMAS OTWAY
*The Orphan*


There is no more disturbing experience in the rich gamut
of life than when a man discovers, in the midst of an
embrace, that he is taking the episode quite calmly . . . His
doubts and fears start from this point and there is no end
to them. He doesn't know, now, whether it's love or passion. In fact, in the confusion of the moment, he's not
quite sure if it isn't something else altogether, like forgery.
—E.B. WHITE
*New York Journal-American*, February 12, 1961

# The End of Love

You like potato and I like po-tah-to,
You like tomato and I like to-mah-to,
Potato, poh-tah-to, tomato, tomah-to
Let's call the whole thing off!
—IRA GERSHWIN, "Let's Call the Whole Thing Off"


I loved thee, Attis, once, in days long past.
—SAPPHO
*Greek Poetry for Everyone* by Lucas


There lives within the very flame of love
A kind of wick or snuff that will abate it.
—WILLIAM SHAKESPEARE
*Hamlet*


I no longer love her, that's certain, but how I loved her
My voice tried to find the wind to touch her hearing.
—PABLO NERUDA


At the beginning of love and at its end lovers are embarrassed to be left alone.
—JEAN DE LA BRUYÈRE


At the end, every flower loses its perfume.
*Italian Saying* (translated by Sir W. Marris)


'Tis hard to drop at once old-standing love.
—CATULLUS
*Carmina*

"I don't love you anymore" is the classic exit line in every relationship.
—JOHN GAGNON
*Human Sexualities*


After all, my estwhile dear,
My no longer cherished,
Need we say it was not love,
Just because it perished?
—EDNA ST. VINCENT MILLAY, "Passer Mortus Est"


No argument, no anger, no remorse,
No dividing of blame
There was poison in the cup—why should we ask
From whose hand it came?
No grief for our dead love . . .
—ROBERT GRAVES, "Hedges Streaked With Snow"


Yet each man kills the thing he loves,
By each let this be heard.
Some do it with a bitter look,
Some with flattering word.
The coward does it with a kiss,
The brave man with a sword!
—OSCAR WILDE, "The Ballad of Reading Gaol"


The flowers of our two hearts were bleeding to death
And perhaps we wept without either seeing the tears . . .
—JUAN RÁMON JIMÉNEZ, "Nudes"


The song is ended
But the melody lingers on.
—IRVING BERLIN, "The Song Is Ended"
*The Ziegfeld Follies*

Far away is close at hand
Close joined is far away,
Love shall come at your command
Yet will not stay.
—ROBERT GRAVES, "Song of Contrariety"
*Whipperginny*


The real genius for love lies not in getting into, but getting
out of love.
—GEORGE MOORE (attributed)


What shall I do
Now my love is gone?
Toss on an empty
Bed alone?
—PADRAIG O'BROIN, "Circle"


Love comes into your being like a tidal wave . . . Sometimes it withdraws like a wave, till there isn't such a thing
as a pool left, and every bit of your heart is as dry as sea-
weed beyond the wave's reach.
—PHYLLIS BOTTOME


Music I heard with you was more than music
And bread I broke with you was more than bread
Now that I am not with you, all is desolate
All that once was so beautiful is dead.
—CONRAD AIKEN, "Bread and Music"


When love grows diseas'd, the best thing to do is to put it
to a violent death; I can not endure the torture of a lingering and consumptive passion.
—SIR GEORGE ETHEREGE
*The Man of Mode*

So there are no more words and all is ended
The timbrel is stilled, the clarion laid away
And Love with streaming hair goes unattended
Back to the loneliness of yesterday.
—JOSEPH AUSLANDER, "So There Are No More Words"


When love turns away, now, I don't follow it. I sit and suf-
fer, unprotesting, until I feel the tread of another step.
—SYLVIA ASHTON-WARNER
*Teacher*


No, no, not love, not love. Call it by name.
Now that it's over, now that it is gone and can not hear us.
It was an honest thing, not noble. Yet no shame.
—EDNA ST. VINCENT MILLAY, "What Savage Blossom"
*Huntsman, What Quarry?*


Ah, when to the heart of man
Was it ever less than treason
To go with the drift of things
To yield with a grace to reason
And bow and accept at the end
Of a love or a season.
—ROBERT FROST
*Vogue*, March 14, 1963


The mind has a thousand eyes
The heart but one
Yet the life of a whole life dies
When love is done.
—FRANCIS WILLIAM BOURDILLON


Wise after the event, by love withered.
—ROBERT GRAVES, "Never Such Love"

I had lost the power to love.
—HENRY MILLER
*Nexus*


I thought when love for you died, I should die.
It's dead. Alone, strangely, I live on.
—RUPERT BROOKE


*See also:* BREAKUP; PARTING.


# The Enemy

Women are natural guerrillas. Scheming, we nestle in the
enemy's bed, avoiding open warfare, watching the
options, playing the odds.
—SALLY KEMPTON
*Esquire*, July 1970


"How can you lead us while you still copulate, relate to,
traffic with, and are penetrated by the enemy, 'the male?'"
—JUDIANNE DENSEN-GERBER
*Walk in My Shoes*


If man is my aggressor, my put-down, my oppressor,
would somebody tell me why I am sleeping in the enemy
camp.
—BONNIE CHARLES BLUH
*Woman to Woman: European Feminists*

# Engagement

We sat in the car park until twenty to one
And now I'm engaged to Miss Joan Hunter Dunn.
—SIR JOHN BETJEMAN, "Subaltern's Love-song"
*New Bats in Old Belfries*

No sooner met but they looked; no sooner looked but they loved; no sooner loved but they sighed; no sooner sighed but they asked one another the reason; no sooner knew the reason but they sought the remedy; and in these degrees have they made a pair of stairs to marriage, which they will climb incontinent, or else be incontinent before marriage.
—WILLIAM SHAKESPEARE
*As You Like It*

A positive engagement to marry a certain person at a certain time, at all haps and hazards, I have always considered the most ridiculous thing on earth.
—JANE WELSH CARLYLE

# Equality

. . . we have passed out and beyond the era when the wife was considered sexually as a passive implement, receptacle and incubator and have recognized and accepted her as an active, adult and equivalent sexual being.
—TH. VAN DE VELDE
*Ideal Marriage*

Man is willing to accept woman as an equal, as a man in skirts, as an angel, as a devil, a baby-face, a machine, an instrument, a bosom, a womb, a pair of legs, an encyclopedia, an ideal, or an obscenity: the only thing he won't accept her as is a human being, a real human being of the female sex.
—D.H. LAWRENCE

# Erogenous Zones

He moved his lips about her ears and neck as though in thirsting search for an erogenous zone. A waste of time, he knew from experience. Erogenous zones are either everywhere or nowhere.
—JOSEPH HELLER
*Good as Gold*

. . . strictly speaking, the whole body is an erotogenic zone.
—SIGMUND FREUD
*An Outline of Psychoanalysis*

There was a young student named Jones
Who'd reduce any maiden to moans.
    By his wonderful knowledge
    Acquired in college
Of the nineteen erogenous zones.
*Anonymous Limerick*

The erogenous zone is always shifting and it is the business of fashion to pursue it, without ever catching it up.
—JAMES LAVER (attributed)

# Erotica and Eroticism

. . . women are the only true erotica.
—JOHN CIARDI
*The Browser's Dictionary*

In this loveless everyday life eroticism is a substitute for love.
—HENRI LEFEBVRE
*Everyday Life in the Modern World*

Eroticism is like a dance: one always leads the other.
—MILAN KUNDERA
*Immortality*

Eroticism has its own moral justification because it says that pleasure is enough for me; it is a statement of the individual's sovereignty.
—MARIO VARGAS-LLOSA
*International Herald Tribune*, October 23, 1990

Eroticism is a realm stalked by ghosts. It is the place beyond the pale, both cursed and enchanted.
—CAMILLE PAGLIA
*Sexual Personae*

# Estrangement

My mother and father and I now lived in the intimacy of estrangement that exists between married couples who have nothing left in common but their incompatability.
—NADINE GORDIMER
*The Lying Days*

Sleep on, I sit and watch your tent of Silence
White as a sail upon this sandy sea
And I know the Desert's self is not more boundless
Than is the distance 'twixt yourself and me.
—LAURENCE HOPE, "Stars of the Desert"

When once estrangement has arisen between those who
truly love each other, everything seems to widen the
breach.
—MARY ELIZABETH BRADDON
*Run to Earth*

But that intimacy of mutual embarrassment, in which
each feels that the other is feeling something, having once
existed, its effect is not to be done away with.
—GEORGE ELIOT
*Middlemarch*

# Eternal Love

I shall love you until death do us part and then we shall be
together for ever and ever.
—DYLAN THOMAS, "Under Milkwood"

You are woman, so be lovely:
As you are lovely, so be various,
Merciful as constant, constant as various,
So be mine, as I yours for ever.
—ROBERT GRAVES, "Pygmalion to Galetea"
*Poems*

Bind the sea to slumber still,
Bind its odor to the lily,
Bind the aspen ne'er to quiver,
Then bind love to last for ever.
—THOMAS CAMPBELL, "How Delicious Is the Winning"


And I will love thee still, my dear
Till the seas gang dry.
—ROBERT BURNS, "A Red, Red Rose"


I love thee, I love but thee,
With a love that shall not die.
Till the sun grows old,
And the stars are cold,
And the leaves of the Judgment Book unfold.
—BAYARD TAYLOR, "Bedouin Song"


No, the heart that truly loved never forgets,
But as truly loves on to the close.
—THOMAS MOORE, "Believe Me, If All Those Endearing Young
   Charms"


It used to be "Love Me Forever" and now it's "Help Me
Make It Through the Night."
—ANNE TYLER
*Breathing Lessons*


To say that you can love one person all your life is like
saying that one candle will continue to burn as long as
you live.
—LEO TOLSTOY
*Kreutzer Sonata*

In a love affair, forever is at least over the weekend.
—ANONYMOUS


I'll see you again
Whenever springtime breaks through again.
—NÖEL COWARD
*Bittersweet*


But to see her was to love her,
Love but her, and love for ever.
—ROBERT BURNS, "Ae Fond Kiss"


Two such as you with such a master speed
Cannot be parted nor swept away
From one another once you are agreed
That life is only life forevermore
Together wing to wing and oar to oar.
—ROBERT FROST, "The Master Speed"


*See also:* LASTING LOVE.


# Excess

But love would not be love if it did not slip over into the
excessive.
—EDNA O'BRIEN
*Some Irish Loving*


Even nectar is poison if taken to excess.
*Hindu Proverb*

Moderation is a fatal thing: nothing succeeds as excess.
—OSCAR WILDE
*A Woman of No Importance*


# Excitement

We boil at different degrees.
—RALPH WALDO EMERSON
*Society and Solitude: Eloquence*


He who is not impatient is not in love.
*Italian Proverb*


Man lives by habit indeed, but what he lives for is thrills and excitement.
—WILLIAM JAMES


# Experience

To love women and never enjoy them, is as much to love wine and never taste it.
—JOHN LYLY
*Euphues and His England*


The best proof that experience is useless is that the end of one love does not disgust us from beginning another.
—PAUL BOURGET

Find a mate you can groove with. You'll then have an additional brain and sensory organs. The quantity of your experience will be at least doubled and the quality will differ because no two people perceive in exactly the same manner. With a warm, perceptive mate you'll be able to freely give and receive love.
—EUGENE SCHOENFELD


Drawn wells have the sweetest water.
—JOHN CLARKE
*Paroemiologia Anglo-Latina*


# Experimentation

Once, a philosopher; twice, a pervert.
—VOLTAIRE


Once doesn't count.
—LIN FIELD
*Mrs. Murphy's Laws*


When Eve ate the particular apple, she became aware of her womanhood, mentally. And mentally she began to experiment with it. She has been experimenting ever since. So has man. To the rage and horror of both of them.
—D.H. LAWRENCE
*Fantasia of the Unconscious*

# Eyes

When she raises her eyelids it's as if she were taking off all
her clothes.
—COLETTE
*Claudine and Annie*

Blue eyes say: Love me or I die; black eyes say: love me or
I kill thee.
*Spanish Proverb*

And in those eyes the love-light lies
And lies—and lies—and lies.
—ANITA OWEN, "Dreamy Eyes"

Drink to me only with thine eyes
And I will pledge with mine;
Or leave a kiss but in the cup
And I'll not look for wine.
—BEN JONSON, "To Celia"

It needs no dictionary of quotations to remind me that the
eyes are the windows of the soul.
—MAX BEERBOHM
*Zuleika Dobson*

Turn not Venus into a blinded motion
Eyes are the guides of love.
—EZRA POUND, "Quia Pauper Amavi"

A rolling eye, a roving heart.
—THOMAS ADAMS
*Sermons*

Choose a wife rather by your ear than your eye.

*English Proverb*


Keep the eyes wide open before marriage; and half-shut afterward.

—THOMAS FULLER

*Introductio ad Prudentian*


Love's tongue is in the eyes.

—PHINEAS FLETCHER

*Piscatory Epilogues*


The eyes are the silent tongues of love.

—MIGUEL DE CERVANTES

*Don Quixote*


Eyes that can feel like a hand, hands that can see like an eye.

—JOHANN WOLFGANG VON GOETHE

*Roman Elegies*


Where love is, there the eye wanders.

*Latin Proverb*


...the vice of her painted eyes

—JAMES JOYCE

*Ulysses*


Every eye forms its own beauty

—CHARLES G. HARPER

*The Brighton Road*

# Face

The glory of the day was in her face,
The beauty of the night was in her eyes.
—JAMES WELDON JOHNSON, "The Glory of the Day Was in Her
Face"

Her face was her chaperone.
—RUPERT HUGHES

As a white candle in a holy place,
So is the beauty of an aged face.
—JOSEPH CAMPBELL, "Old Woman"

My soul abhors the tasteless dry embrace
Of a stale virgin with a winter face.
—ALEXANDER POPE, "January and May"

A face like yours could
    sell a million floppy
discs, change hardened admen
    into optimists
You are as beautiful as low inflation,
    as tax evasion
—CAROL ANN DUFFY, "The Businessman's Love Poem"

My face
that my friends tell me is so full of character;
my face
I have hated for so many years,
my face
I have made an angry contract to live with
Though no one could love it.
— DIANE WAKOSKI, "I Have to Learn to Live with My Face"
*The Motorcycle Betrayal Poems*

Many a man in love with a dimple makes the mistake of marrying the whole girl.
— STEPHEN LEACOCK

It has been said that a pretty face is a passport. But it's not, it's a visa, and it runs out fast.
— JULIE BURCHILL, "Kiss and Sell"
*The Mail on Sunday*, 1988

# Faithfulness

I have been faithful to thee, Cynara! in my fashion.
— ERNEST DOWSON, "Non sum Qualis Eram Bonae Sub Regio Cynarae"

If I, by miracle, can be
This live-long minute true to thee,
'Tis all that heaven allows.
— JOHN WILMOT, Earl of Rochester, "Love and Life"

Those who are faithless know the pleasures of love; it is those who are faithful who know love's tragedies.
— OSCAR WILDE
*The Picture of Dorian Gray*

The seas shall run dry,
And the rocks melt into sands;
Then shall I love you still, my dear,
When all these things are done.
—ANONYMOUS, "The Young Man's Farewell to His Love"

# Faking It

To know how to live is to know how to simulate.
—ANTOINETTE DESHOULIÈRES
*Le Ruisseau*

Each sister faking orgasm . . . does it to survive.
—ROBIN MORGAN
*Sisterhood Is Powerful*

This is a fairly dumb analogy, but I think declaring to yourself you will have an orgasm is not unlike a politician declaring he will run for office. You have a better chance of getting nominated and elected if you "declare"—very few politicians get drafted.
—HELEN GURLEY BROWN

Women fake orgasm if they really care about the man because they don't want him to feel a sense of failure. I think it's really a kind thing that women do. But they're probably doing themselves an injustice, because probably, if they could get over it, if they didn't fake it, and they learned how to relax, they would probably have their orgasm. Some men aren't good enough to give it to you.
—ANNIE FLANDERS

The only time a woman has a true orgasm is when she is shopping. Every other time she's faking it. It's common courtesy.
—JOAN RIVERS

# Falling in Love

Falling in love with love is falling for make-believe.
—LORENZ HART

Falling in love is something you forget like pain.
—NINA BAWDEN
  *The Grain of Truth*

Do you love me or do you not?
You told me once, but I forgot.
—ANONYMOUS
  *Another Almanac of Words at Play* by Willard R. Espy

In shallow shoals, English soles do it,
Goldfish in the privacy of bowls, do it,
Let's do it, let's fall in love.
—COLE PORTER, "Let's Do It"

One doesn't fall in love; one grows into love, and love grows in him.
—KARL MENNINGER

Falling in love consists merely in uncorking the imagination and bottling the common-sense.
—HELEN ROWLAND
  *A Guide to Men*

# False Love

Farewell, false love, the oracle of lies,
A mortal foe and enemy to rest:
. . .
False Love; Desire; Beauty frail adieu
Dead is the root whence all these fancies grew.
—SIR WALTER RALEIGH, "A Farewell to False Love"


False in one thing, false in everything.
—LEGAL MAXIM


Love in her sunny eyes does basking play;
Love walks the pleasant mazes of her hair;
Love does on both her lips forever stray;
And sows and reaps a thousand kisses there.
In all her outward parts Love's always seen;
But, oh, he never went within.
—ABRAHAM COWLEY, "The Change"


False though she be to me and love,
I'll ne'er pursue revenge;
. . .
And though the present I regret,
I'm grateful for the past.
—WILLIAM CONGREVE


# Familiarity

Familiarity breeds contempt.
—PUBLILIUS SYRUS
*Sententiae*

Familiarity breeds content.
—ROY GOLIARD
*A Scholar's Glossary of Sex*


Familiarity breeds.
—LEONARD LEWIS LEVINSON
*Bartlett's Unfamiliar Quotations*


Familiarity doesn't breed contempt. It is contempt.
—FLORENCE KING


Though familiarity may not breed contempt, it takes the edge off admiration.
—WILLIAM HAZLITT
*Characteristics*


Sweets grown common lose their dear delight.
—WILLIAM SHAKESPEARE, "Sonnet 102"


The man who enters his wife's dressing room is either a philosopher or a fool.
—HONORÉ DE BALZAC
*The Physiology of Marriage*


I like familiarity. In me it does not breed contempt. Only more familiarity.
—GERTUDE STEIN (attributed)


Be thou familiar, but by no means vulgar.
—WILLIAM SHAKESPEARE
*Hamlet*

Familiarity breeds contempt—and children.
—MARK TWAIN
*Unpublished Diaries*


Familiar acts are beautiful through love.
—PERCY BYSSHE SHELLEY
*Prometheus Unbound*


# Fantasy

In maiden meditation, fancy free.
—WILLIAM SHAKESPEARE
*A Midsummer's Night's Dream*


Love brought by night a vision to my bed.
—MELEAGER


It is a terrible deception of love that it begins by engaging us in play not with a woman of the external world but with a doll fashioned in our brain—the only woman moreover that we have always at our disposal, the only one we shall ever possess.
—MARCEL PROUST
*Remembrance of Things Past: The Guermantes Way*


One's fantasy goes out for a walk and returns with a bride.
—BERNARD MALAMUD
*Long Work, Short Life*

We think about sex obsessively except during the act, when our minds tend to wander.
—HOWARD NEMEROV, "Reading Pornography in Old Age"

The Cosmo Girl was the guys' fantasy of the liberated woman, all legs and edible knickers, with her own job and own studio apartment, adept at giving head and getting great breakfast.
—LINDA GRANT
*Sexing the Millennium*

My thoughts are my trollops.
—DENIS DIDEROT

*See also:* DREAMS.

# Farewell

Ae fond kiss, and then we sever
Ae farewell, an then forever.
. . .
Fare-thee-well, thou first and fairest!
Fare-thee-well, thou best and dearest!
Thine be ilka joy and treasure
Peace, Enjoyment, Love and Pleasure!
—ROBERT BURNS, "Ae Fond Kiss"

Here is the door, and there is the way, and so . . . farewell.
—JOHN HEYWOOD
*A Dialogue Containing the Number in Effect of All the Proverbs in the English Tongue*

please
close the door
gently as you go.
—ALLAN TATE, "Letting Him Go"

Farewell! thou art too dear for my possessing.
—WILLIAM SHAKESPEARE, "Sonnet 37"

My hands have not touched water since your hands—
No;—nor my lips freed laughter since "farewell."
—HART CRANE, "Carrier Letter"

All farewells should be sudden, when forever.
—SARDANAPALUS

It may be for years, and it may be forever.
—JULIA CRAWFORD
*Kathleen Malourneen*

*See also:* PARTING.

# Fat

Love don't seem dainty on a fat woman.
—ENID BAGNOLD
*National Velvet*

An elegant degree of plumpness peculiar to the skin of the
softer sex.
—WILLIAM HOGARTH
*The Analysis of Beauty*

Outside every thin girl there is a fat man trying to get in.
—KATHERINE WHITEWHORN
*BBC Radio,* July 27, 1982


it's a sex object if you are pretty
and no love
or love and no sex if you are fat.
—NIKKI GIOVANNI, "Woman Poem"


Big fat momma with the meat shakin' on her bone,
Each time she wiggles, skinny woman loses her home.
*Blues Song*


I don't want my girl to be so skinny she can knife me with
her knee . . . nor do I want some big two-hundred-pound
tomato; meat, not suet, I hold dear.
—MARTIAL
*Epigrams* (translated by Rolfe Humphries)


He's so fat he hasn't seen his privates in twenty years.
—CARSON McCULLERS
*Ballad of the Sad Café*


The nearer the bone, the sweeter the meat.
*English Proverb*


To ask women to become unnaturally thin is to ask them
to relinquish their sexuality.
—NAOMI WOLF
*The Beauty Myth*

The flesh is aye fairest that's farthest from the bone.
*Scottish Proverb*


And a long, tall woman will make a preacher lay his
    Bible down
A long, tall woman will make a preacher lay his bible
    down. . . .
But a big, fat mama will make a mule kick his stall
    down.
—WILLIE JACKSON, Blues song


. . . unnecessary dieting is because everything from television to fashion ads has made it seem wicked to cast a
shadow. This wild, emaciated look appeals to some women,
though not many men, who are seldom seen pinning up a
*Vogue* illustration in a machine shop.
—PEG BRACKEN
*The I Hate to Cook Book*


# Faults

Faults are thick where love is thin.
—JOHN HOWELL
*Proverbs*


Where love fails we espy all faults.
—JOHN RAY
*English Proverbs*


Love sees no faults.
—THOMAS FULLER
*Gnomologia: Adages and Proverbs*

Immodest creature, you do not want a woman who will accept your faults, you want one who pretends that you are faultless — one that will caress the hand that strikes her and kiss the lips that lie to her.
—GEORGE SAND
*Intimate Journals*

Be to her virtues very kind
Be to her faults a little blind.
—MATHEW PRIOR, "An English Padlock"

# Fear

Faint heart never won fair lady.
—WILLIAM CAMDEN
*Remains Concerning Britain*

To fear love is to fear life, and those who fear life are already three parts dead.
—BERTRAND RUSSELL

Fear of sexuality is the new disease . . . the universe of fear in which everyone now lives.
—SUSAN SONTAG
*AIDS and Its Metaphors*

# Fetishes

How beautiful are thy feet with shoes,
O prince's daughter.
*Song of Songs*

The abnormal heel.
—CHARLOTTE PERKINS GILMAN
*Herland*


We, being modern and liberated and fully cognizant of women's sexual, intellectual, emotional, and economic oppression, can never for a moment cease our vigilance against the imperialistic male supremacist. We must never relax our guard against his chauvinistic sexual fantasies.

So don't even for an instant consider keeping the following hidden in the back of your closet: a see-through nurse's uniform . . . a cheerleader's costume . . . a little black French maid's outfit.

And if you do, don't tell anyone.
—CYNTHIA HEIMEL
*Sex Tips for Girls*


Let him be inflamed by the love of your dress.
—OVID
*Ars Amatoria*


Though you know the dress full well,
What know you of the wearer?
—SADI GULISTAN
*Apologue 5*


I for one venerate a petticoat.
—GEORGE GORDON, Lord Byron
*Don Juan*


Chains of iron or of silk—both are chains.
—FRIEDRICH von SCHILLER
*The Fiesco*

Like every young man grown up in England, he was conditioned to get a hard-on in the presence of certain fetishes, and then conditioned to feel shame about his new reflexes.
—THOMAS PYNCHON
*Gravity's Rainbow*


It would not grieve him to be hanged, if he might be strangled in her garters.
—ROBERT BURTON
*The Anatomy of Melancholy*


There is no unhappier creature on earth than a fetishist who yearns for a woman's shoe and has to embrace the whole woman.
—KARL KRAUS
*Aphorisms and More Aphorisms*


Prof. Higgins was right—men wish that woman's sexuality was like theirs, which it isn't. Male sexuality is far brisker and more automatic. Your clothes, breasts, odor, etc., aren't what he loves instead of you—simply the things he needs in order to set sex in motion to express love. Women find this hard to understand.
—ALEX COMFORT
*The Joy of Sex*


*See also:* CLOTHES; DRESS; LINGERIE.

# Fidelity

Fire heat shall lose, and frosts of flame be born;
Air, made to shine, as black as hell shall prove;
Earth, heaven, fire, air, the world transformed shall
    view,
Ere I prove false to faith, or strange to you.
—JOHN DOWLAND, "Dear If You Change"


A fickle thing and changeful is a woman always.
—VIRGIL
*Aeneid*


Lovers' vows do not reach the ears of the gods.
—CALLIMACHUS
*Epigrams*


It is absurd to say that a man can't love one woman all the
time as it is to say that a violinist needs several violins to
play the same piece of music.
—HONORÉ DE BALZAC


When a man declares, "I am sure of my wife," it means he
is sure of his wife. But when a woman declares, "I am sure
of my husband," it means that she is sure of herself.
—FRANCIS DE CROISSET
*Reader's Digest*, January 1943


We only part to meet again.
Change, as ye list, ye winds: my heart shall be
The faithful compass that still points to thee.
—JOHN GAY
*Sweet William's Farewell to Black-Eyed Susan*

Look you, Amanda, you may build Castles in the Air, and
fume, and fret, and grow thin and lean, and pale and ugly,
if you please. But I tell you, no man worth having is true
to his wife, or can be true to his wife, or ever was, or ever
will be so.
—SIR JOHN VANBRUGH
  *The Relapse, or Virtue in Danger*


I love I love whose lips I love
but conscience she has none
nor can I rest upon her breast
for faith's to her unknown.
—CONRAD AIKEN, "The Accomplices"


Who, who will be the next man to entrust his girl to a
friend?
Love interferes with fidelities.
—EZRA POUND, "Homage to Sextus Propertius"


# Fifty

They don't tell;
They don't yell
They don't swell;
And they're grateful as hell.
—AUTHOR UNKNOWN, "Ode to Women Over Fifty"


From 35 to 45 women are old, and at 45 the devil takes
over, and they're beautiful, splendid maternal, proud. The
acidities are gone and in their place reigns calm. They are
worth going out to find, and because of them some men
never grow old. When I see them my mouth waters.
—JEAN-BAPTISTE TROISGROS
  *The New York Times*, October 24, 1974

Love is lame at fifty years.
—THOMAS HARDY, "The Revisitation"


After 50 his performance is of poor quality, the intervals between are wide, and its satisfactions of no great value to either party; whereas his great-grandmother is as good as new. There is nothing the matter with her plant. Her candlestick is as firm as ever, whereas his candle is increasingly softened and weakened by the weather of age, as the years go by, until it can no longer stand, and is mournfully laid to rest in the hope of blessed resurrection which is never to come.
—MARK TWAIN


# First Love

One always returns to one's first love.
—CHARLES ÉTIENNE
*La Joconde*


Men always want to be a woman's first love. That is their clumsy vanity. We women have a more subtle instinct about things. What we like is to be a man's last romance.
—OSCAR WILDE
*A Woman of No Importance*


Those whom we first love we seldom marry.
—O.HENRY
*No Story*


The magic of first love is our ignorance that it can never end.
—BENJAMIN DISRAELI
*Henrietta Temple*

First love is only a little foolishness and a lot of curiosity.
—GEORGE BERNARD SHAW
*John Bull's Other Island*


We always believe our first love to be our last, and our last love our first.
—GEORGE JOHN WHYTE-MELVILLE
*Katerfelto*


O my first love, You are in my life forever
—HUGH MACDIARMID, "Of My First Love"


# First Sight

She lovede Right fro first sighte.
—GEOFFREY CHAUCER
*Troilus and Criseyde*


Who ever lov'd that lov'd not at first sight?
—CHRISTOPHER MARLOWE, "Hero and Leander"


I took one look at you
That's all I meant to do
And my heart stood still.
—LORENZ HART, "My Heart Stood Still"


Love not at the first look.
—JOHN CLARKE
*Paroemiologia Anglo-Latina*

Sudden love is latest cured.
—JEAN DE LA BRUYÈRE
*Les caractères*


The only true love is love at first sight; second sight dispels it.
—ISRAEL ZANGWILL


The moment my eyes fell on him, I was content.
—EDITH WHARTON


# Flattery

He who can not learn to love must flatter.
—JOHANN WOLFGANG GOETHE


If you want to lick the old woman's pot, scratch her back.
*Jamaican Proverb*


# Flirtation

She who trifles with all
Is less likely to fall
Than she who but trifles with one.
—JOHN GAY, "The Coquet Mother and the Coquet Daughter"


For whom does the blind man's wife paint herself.
*English Proverb*

Why does a man take it for granted that a girl who flirts with him wants him to kiss her—when, nine times out of ten, she only wants him to want to kiss her.

—HELEN ROWLAND

*A Guide to Men*

# Flowers

Why is it no ever sent me yet
One perfect limousine, do you suppose?
Ah no, it's always just my luck to get
One perfect rose.

—DOROTHY PARKER, "One Perfect Rose"

. . . .the genital
organs of plants.

—LENORE KANDEL, "Bus Ride"

A fox is a wolf who sends flowers.

—RUTH WESTON

*New York Post*, November 8, 1955

# Fool

If thou remember'st not the slightest folly
That ever love did make thee run into,
Thou has not lov'd.

—WILLIAM SHAKESPEARE

*As You Like It*

To be intimate with a foolish man is like going to bed with a razor.
—BENJAMIN FRANKLIN

One fool at least in every marriage.
—HENRY FIELDING
*Amelia*

I am two fools, I know,
For loving, and saying so
In whining poetry.
—JOHN DONNE, "The Triple Fool"

Take my word for it, the silliest woman can manage a clever man, but it takes a very clever woman to manage a fool.
—RUDYARD KIPLING, "Three and—an Extra"
*Plain Talk from the Hills*

Never let loving make a fool of you.
—SEXTUS AURELIUS PROPERTIUS

# Foreplay

License my roving hands, and let them go
Before, behind, between, above, below.
—JOHN DONNE, "To His Mistress Going to Bed"

Ye praise the wine before ye taste the grape.
—JOHN HEYWOOD
*A Dialogue Containing the Number in Effect of All the Proverbs in the English Tongue*

may i feel said he
(i'll squeal said she
just once said he)
it's fun said she

. . .

(let's go said he
not too far said she
what's too far said he
where you are said she)
—E.E. CUMMINGS, "may i feel said he"


I will go down to her, I and no other,
Close with her, kiss her and mix her with me.
—A.C. SWINBURNE, "The Triumph of Time"


Valerie fondles lovers
like a mousetrap fondles mice.
—ROGER McGOUGH


Half the time, if you really want to know the truth, when I
am horsing around with a girl I have a hellova lot of trouble finding what I am looking for . . . Take this girl I just
missed having sexual intercourse with, that I told you
about. It took me about an hour just to get her goddam
brassiere off. By the time I did get it off, she was about
ready to spit in my eye.
—J.D. SALINGER
    Catcher in the Rye


He who fondles you more than usual has either deceived
you or wants to do so.
French Proverb

i like, slowly stroking the, shocking fuzz
of your electric fur, and what-is-it comes
over parting flesh . . .

—E.E. CUMMINGS, "i like my body when it is with your body"


Let us together closely lie and kiss
There is no labour, nor no shame in this;
This hath pleased, doth please, and long will please; never
Can this decay, but is beginning ever.

—PETRONIUS ARBITER (translated from the Latin by John Dryden)


# Forgetting

No never forget! . . . Never forget any moment; they are too few.

—ELIZABETH BOWEN
*The House in Paris*


Love is so short, forgetting so long.

—PABLO NERUDA


My once dear love; hapless that I no more
Must call thee so; the rich affection's store
That fed our hopes, lies now exhaust and spent.
Like sums of treasure unto bankrupts lent.
We that did nothing study but the way
To love each other, with which thought the day
Rose with delight to us, and with them set,
Must learn the hateful art, how to forget.

—HENRY KING, "The Surrender"

The only thing that can cure love is the glass of forgetfulness.
—GRAFFITO


As one nail by strength drives out another,
So the rememberance of my former love
Is by the newer object quite forgotten.
—WILLIAM SHAKESPEARE
*Two Gentlemen from Verona*


# Forgiveness

We pardon to the extent that we love.
—FRANÇOIS, Duc de La Rochefoucauld
*Réflexions ou sentences et maximes morales*


Once a woman has forgiven her man, she must not reheat his sins for breakfast.
—MARLENE DIETRICH
*Marlene Dietrich's ABCs*


If you really worship women they'll forgive you anything, even if your balls are falling off.
—LAWRENCE DURRELL (attributed)


Women in love pardon great indiscretions more easily than little infidelities.
—FRANÇOIS, Duc de La Rochefoucauld
*Réflexions ou sentences et maximes morales*


Love is no pardoner.
—LOUIS SIMPSON, "The Man Who Married Magdalane"

# Fornication

Fornication is a filthy business,
The briefest form of lechery,
And the most boring, once you're satisfied,
So let's not rush blindly upon it
Like cows in a rut.
That's the way passion wilts
And the fire goes out.
—PETRONIUS ARBITER


Doing a filthy pleasure is, and short,
And done, we straight repent us of the sport.
—BEN JONSON


*See also:* LOVEMAKING; SEXUAL INTERCOURSE.


# Forty

At the age of forty she is very far from being cold and
insensible; her fire may be covered with ashes, but it is not
extinguished.
—MARY WORTLEY MONTAGU, Letter to Lady_____. January 13, 1716


A fool at forty is a fool indeed.
—EDWARD YOUNG
*Love of Fame*


Fat, fair and forty.
—SIR WALTER SCOTT
*St. Ronan's Well*

My notion of a wife of forty is that a man should be able to change her, like a bank note, for two twenties.
—DOUGLAS JERROLD (attributed)


Women are most fascinating between the age of thirty-five and forty after they have won a few races and know how to pace themselves. Since few ever pass forty, maximum fascination can continue indefinitely.
—CHRISTIAN DIOR


Pushing forty? She's clinging on it for dear life.
—IVY COMPTON-BURNETT (attributed)


I'm forty-nine but I could be twenty-five except for my face and legs.
—NADINE GORDIMER
*Not for Pubication and Other Stories*


# Four-letter Words

Oh perish the use of the four-letter words
Whose meanings are never obscure;
The Angles and Saxons, those bawdy old birds,
Were vulgar, obscene and impure.
But cherish the use of the weaseling phrase
That never says quite what you mean.
You had better be known for your hypocrite ways
Than vulgar, impure and obscene.
Let your morals be loose as an alderman's vest
If your language is always obscure.
Today not the act, but the word is the test
Of vulgar, obscene and impure.
—ANONYMOUS
*The Anatomy of Swearing* by Ashley Montagu

Immodest words admit no defense,
For want of decency is want of sense.
—WENTWORTH DILLON, Earl of Roscommon
*Essay on Translated Verse*


The language of sex is yet to be invented. The language of
the senses is yet to be explored.
—ANAÏS NIN
*Diary*


Not the lover but his language wins the lady.
*Japanese Proverb*


I was beyond simple desire, borne away rather by a near
swoon of lust. Couldn't she know what she did to me with
this concubine speech, with these foul, priceless words
which assail like sharp spears the bastion of my own Christian gentility with its aching repressions and restraints.
—WILLIAM STYRON
*Sophie's Choice*


Bad language or abuse
I never, never use,
Whatever the emergency;
Though "Bother it" I may
Occasionally say
I never never use a big, big D.
—W.S. GILBERT
*H.M.S. Pinafore*


Nudge, nudge, wink, wink. Know what I mean? Say no
more.
*Monty Python's Flying Circus*, BBC-TV

... of all the worn, smudged, dog-eared words in our vocabulary "love" is surely the grubbiest, smelliest, slimiest ...
—ALDOUS HUXLEY
*Tomorrow and Tomorrow and Tomorrow*


Sex is a three-letter word which sometimes needs some old-fashioned four-letter words to convey its full meaning; words like help, give, care, love.
—SAM LEVENSON
*Sex and the Single Child*


We knew, my generation
Those words and plenty more.
But liked the implication
They shocked us to the core
One offers no excuses
Hypocrisy is done
Forgive me if I mention
We found it rather fun.
—DOROTHY DRAIN, "Remember When Damn Was Spelled d..m?"


You don't know what love means. To you it's just another four-letter word.
—TENNESSEE WILLIAMS
*Cat on a Hot Tin Roof*


It is good to find modest words to express immodest things.
—AUTHOR UNKNOWN


*See also:* OBSCENITY.

# Freedom

Him that I love, I wish to be free —
even from me.
—ANNE MORROW LINDBERGH
*The Unicorn and Other Poems*

If you want something very very badly,
let it go free. If it comes back to you
it's yours forever. If it doesn't, it was
never yours to begin with.
—JESSE LAIR, "I Ain't Much Baby, But I'm All I Got"

# Free Love

Free love is sometimes love but never freedom.
—ELIZABETH BIBISCO
*Haven*

The big difference between sex for money and sex for free
is that sex for money costs a lot less.
—BRENDAN FRANCIS (attributed)

Free love is seldom free. Teens pay for it in worry—the
fear that they will be caught, or that their partner may tire
of them. It's hurried and furtive and not much fun.
—HELEN BOTTEL
*Family Circle*, November 1969

You pay a great deal too dear for what is given freely.
—WILLIAM SHAKESPEARE
*The Winter's Tale*

I have said it again and again: "Everyone who preached free love in the Sixties is responsible for AIDS." And we must accept moral responsibility for it. The idea that it is an accident, a historical accident, a microbe that sort of fell from the heaven—absurd. We must face what we did.
—CAMILLE PAGLIA
*Sex, Art, and American Culture*

# Friendship

Friendship often ends in love, but love in friendship—never.
—C.C. COLTON
*Lacon*

Love and friendship exclude one another.
—JEAN DE LA BRUYÈRE
*Les caractères*

Love is only chatter,
Friends are all that matter.
—GELLETT BURGESS
*Willy and the Lady*

A friend married is a friend lost.
—HENRIK IBSEN
*Love's Comedy*

No man can be friends with a woman he finds attractive. He always wants to have sex with her. Sex is always out there. Friendship is ultimately doomed and that's the end of the story.
—NORA EPHRON
*When Harry Met Sally*

When all is said and done, friendship is the only trustworthy fabric of the affections. So-called love is a delirious inhuman state of mind: when hot it substitutes indulgence for fair play; when cold it is cruel, but friendship is warmth in cold, firm ground in bog.
—MILES FRANKLIN
*My Career Goes Bung*

Love is like the wild rose-briar;
Friendship like the holly tree.
The holly is dark when the rose-briar blooms,
But which will bloom most constantly?
—EMILY BRONTË
*Love and Friendship*

Friendship is a disinterested commerce between equals; love an abject intercourse between tyrants and slaves.
—OLIVER GOLDSMITH
*The Good-Natured Man*

Friendship is constant in all other things
Except in the office and affairs of love.
—WILLIAM SHAKESPEARE
*Much Ado About Nothing*

# Frigidity

My love is like to ice, and I to fire:
How comes it then that this her cold so great
Is not dissolved through my hot desire,
But harder grows the more I entreat?
—EDMUND SPENSER, "My Love Is Like to Ice"

A "cold" passionless woman is a woman who has not yet
met the man she is bound to love.
—STENDHAL
*Ideal Marriage* by Th. Van de Velde


In the coldest flint there is hot fire.
—JOHN RAY
*English Proverbs*


Men always fall for frigid women because they put on the
best show.
—FANNY BRICE (attributed)


The girl who can't dance says the band can't play.
*Yiddish Proverb*


There are no frigid women, only clumsy men.
*Old Maxim*


There are both frigid women and clumsy men, and they
are usually married to each other.
—JOSEPH LoPICCOLO
*Handbook of Sex Therapy*


Show me a frigid woman and, nine times out of ten, I'll
show you a little man.
—JULIE BURCHILL
*Arena*


She looked like butter wouldn't melt in her mouth—or
anywhere else.
—ELSA LANCHESTER (attributed)

When a country wench cannot get her butter to come, she says the witch is in her churn.
—JOHN SELDON

# Frivolity

The ability to makelove frivolously is the chief character-istic which distinguishes human beings from beasts
—HEYWOOD BROUN
*The Algonquin Wits* by Robert E. Drennen

# Frustration

Frustration of sexual wishes is the exact reverse of seduc-tion. The sabotaging partner is highly sensitive to what the other desires and withholds this, usually with the excuse that the craved activity is too anxiety provoking, disgusting, taxing, or immoral.
—HELEN SINGER KAPLAN
*The New Sex Therapy*

The basic formula of all sin is: frustrated or neglected love.
—FRANZ WERFEL
*Between Heaven and Earth*

He who desires but acts not, breeds pestilence.
—WILLIAM BLAKE
*Proverbs of Hell*

# Gifts

Ever since Eve gave Adam the apple, there has been a misunderstanding between the sexes about gifts.
—NAN ROBERTSON

*The New York Times,* November 28, 1957


Win her with gifts, if she respect not words,
Dumb jewels often in their silent kind
More than quick words do move a woman's mind.
—WILLIAM SHAKESPEARE

*Two Gentlemen of Verona*


She that takes gifts herself she sells.
—DAVID FERGUSSON

*Scottish Proverbs*


She must refuse all presents offer'd her by men; for now-
a-days nothing is given for nothing.
—MOLIÈRE

*Ozell*


Frivolous minds are won by trifles.
—OVID

*Ars Amatoria*

Giving presents to a woman to secure her love is as vain as endeavoring to fill a sieve with water.
—EDWARD WARD
*Female Policy*


No: I don't want no gold and no diamonds. I'm a good girl I am.
—GEORGE BERNARD SHAW
*Pygmalion*


Faint heart ne'er won fur, lady.
—ANONYMOUS


Diamonds are a girl's best friend.
—LEO ROBIN
*Gentlemen Prefer Blondes*


I could never curl my lip
To a dazzlin' diamond clip
Though the clip meant "let 'er
rip," I'd not say nay.
—COLE PORTER, "Always True to You in My Fashion"


# Girl Friends

I don't know of any young man, black or white, who doesn't have a girl friend besides his wife. Some have three or four sneaking around.
—MUHAMMAD ALI
*The Observer,* November 28, 1975

It hurts me to say it, but I'd had given ten conversations with Einstein for a first meeting with a pretty chorus girl.
—ALBERT CAMUS
*The Fall*


If anyone wants to trade a couple of centrally located, well-cushioned show-girls for an eroded slope ninty min-utes from Broadway, I'll be on the corner tomorrow at eleven with my tongue hanging out.
—S.J. PERELMAN
*Acres and Pains*


# Gossip

Men have always detested women's gossip because they suspect the truth: their measurements are being taken and compared.
—ERICA JONG
*Fear of Flying*


Whoever gossips to you will gossip of you.
*Spanish Proverb*


Aspersion is the babbler's trade
To listen is to lend him aid.
—WILLIAM COWPER, "Friendship"

# Guilt

What is our innocence
What is our guilt? All are
naked, none is safe.
—MARIANNE MOORE, "What Are Years?"


There's nothing bolder than a woman caught;
Guilt gives 'em courage to maintain their fault.
—JUVENAL
Satire VI (translated by John Dryden)


When lovely lady stoops to folly,
And finds too late that men betray,
What charm can soothe her melancholy,
What art can wash her guilt away?
The only art her guilt to cover,
To hide her shame from every eye,
To give repentance to her lover,
And wring his bosom is — to die.
—OLIVER GOLDSMITH
The Vicar of Wakefield


When lovely woman stoops to folly and
Paces about her room again, alone
She smooths her hair with automatic hand,
And puts a record on the gramophone.
—T.S. ELIOT, "The Waste Land"

The most depressing thing, you know, the most depressing thing is that I used to feel a certain amount of post-coital tristesse. Well, guilt. But these day I can't bother to feel shifty when I get home. Extramarital sex is as overrated as premarital sex. And marital sex, come to think of it.

—SIMON GRAY

*Two Sundays*, BBC TV, 1975

Alas! how difficult it is not to betray guilt by our countenance.

—OVID

*Metamorphoses*

The follics which a man regrets most in his life are those which he did not commit when he had the opportunity.

—HELEN ROWLAND

Men's minds are very ingenious in palliating guilt in themselves

—LIVY

*History of Rome*

# Habit

Marriage must continually vanquish a monster that devours everything: the monster of habit.
—HONORÉ DE BALZAC
*Ideal Marriage* by Th. Van de Velde

Habit causes love . . . love depends on habit quite as much as the wild ways of passion.
—LUCRETIUS
*De Rerum Natura* (translated by Rolfe Humphries)

I've grown accustomed to the trace
of something in the air
Accustomed to her face.
—ALAN JAY LERNER
*My Fair Lady*

Habit has a kind of poetry.
—SIMONE DE BEAUVOIR
*The Coming of Age*

Habit is a great deadener.
—SAMUEL BECKETT
*Waiting for Godot*

[Habit] is the chloroform of love.
—GENEVIÈVE ANTOINE-DARIAUX, "The Men in Your Life"

# Hair

Fair tresses man's imperial race ensnare,
And beauty draws us with a single hair.
—ALEXANDER POPE, "The Rape of the Lock"

One strand of pubic hair can be stronger than the Atlantic cable.
—GENE FOWLER (attributed)

Ladies with curly hair
Have time to spare.
—PHYLLIS McGINLEY

# Hair-trigger Trouble

. . . like so many modern men, he was finished before he had begun.
—D.H. LAWRENCE
*Lady Chatterley's Lover*

Sad conquest: when it is the victor's fate
To die at the entrance of the opening gate.
—JOHN WILMOT, Earl of Rochester, "The Imperfect Enjoyment"

. . . he thought about everything except this, thought, counted, thought of nothing, so that this would not end, tried to fill his mind with seas, sands, winds, fruits, houses, fishes and sowings, so that it might not end . . .
—CARLOS FUENTES


Nothing is more vulgar than haste.
—RALPH WALDO EMERSON
*The Conduct of Life*


What is soon done, soon perishes.
*Latin Proverb*


. . . it was thirty seconds of action, and an hour of apology.
—MORDECAI RICHLER
*Joshua Then and Now*


Haste makes waste.
—JOHN HEYWOOD
*Proverbs*


Haste makes waste, and waste makes want, and want makes strife between the goodman and his wife.
—JOHN RAY
*English Proverbs*


Dr. Brothers advised the viewer to tell her husband to concentrate on his income tax in order to forestall his orgasm. The long form, presumably.
—PAUL KRASNER
*The Realist*, 1958

The action which we should have jointly done,
Each had unluckily performed alone;
. . .
Our flames are punish'd by their own excess,
We'd more pleasure had our loves been less.
She blush'd and frown'd, perceiving we had done
The sport she thought we scarce had yet begun.
. . .
Phyllis, let this comfort ease your care,
You'd been more happy had you been less fair.
—SIR GEORGE ETHEREGE, "The Imperfect Enjoyment"

# Hands

But when the wearied band
Swoons to a waltz, I take her hand,
And there we sit in peaceful calm,
Quietly sweating palm to palm.
—ALDOUS HUXLEY, "Frascati"


Our hands have met but not our hearts;
Our hands will never meet again.
—THOMAS HOOD, "To a False Friend"


I scarcely seem to be able to keep my hands off you.
—OVID
*Metamorphoses*


# Happiness

Happiness is having a scratch for every itch.
—OGDEN NASH

One seeks to make the loved one entirely happy, or, if that
cannot be, entirely wretched.
—JEAN DE LA BRUYÉRE
*Characters*


Happy is he who sees thee,
Happier he who hears thee,
A demigod he who kisses thee
A god he who possesses thee.
  *The Greek Anthology*


Happiness is having your girl friend's lipstick the same
color as your wife's.
—ANONYMOUS


# Hate and Love

The greatest hate springs from the greatest love.
—THOMAS FULLER
  *Gnomologia: Adagies and Proverbs*


I hated her now with a hatred more fatal than indifference
because it was the other side of love.
—AUGUST STRINDBERG
  *A Madman's Defense*


Underneath love there always lies in wait hatred.
—TH. VAN DE VELDE
  *Ideal Marriage*

The sex life of a spider is very interesting.
He screws her.
She bites his head off.

"Women's Liberation Poster"


I love her and she loves me, and we hate each other with a
wild hatred born of love.

—AUGUST STRINDBERG


Women have very little idea how much men hate them.

—GERMAINE GREER

*The Female Eunuch*


Love must be learned, and learned again and again. Hate
needs no instruction, but waits only to be provoked.

—KATHERINE ANNE PORTER

*The Days Before*


To love you was pleasant enough
And, oh! 'tis delicious to hate you!

—THOMAS MOORE, "To ___When I Lov'd You"

*Juvenile Poems*


My only love sprung from my only hate!

—WILLIAM SHAKESPEARE

*Romeo and Juliet*


I hate, I love—the cause thereof
Belike you ask of me;
I do not know, but feel 'tis so,
And I'm in agony.

—CATULLUS

*Carmina* (translated by Sir W. Marris)

Though me she hate, I cannot choose but to love her.
—WALTER DAVISON, "Ode"


No doubt in time I'd learn
To hate you like the rest
I once loved.
—W.D. SNODGRASS, "No Use"


Love is dialectic, man, back and forth, hate and sweet.
—NORMAN MAILER
*Why Are We in Vietnam?*


If we judge love by the majority of its results, it rather
resembles hatred than friendship.
—FRANÇOIS, Duc de La Rochefoucauld
*Réflexions ou sentences et maximes morales*


There never was a great love that was not followed by a
great hatred.
*Irish Proverb*


I am in someone
who hates me.
. . .
It burns the thing
inside it. And that thing
screams.
—IMANU AMIRI BARAKA, "An Agony, As Now"


We've practiced loving long enough
Let's come at last to hate.
—GEORGE HERWEGH, "Lied vom Hasse"

# Heart

The heart of a maiden is a dark forest.

*Russian Proverb*


I understand the ties that are between us too well to
talk about the heart —
that pump!
It lies between the brain box and the penis.
and when these masters stir that slave will jump.

—JAMES SIMMONS, "The Summing Up"


What they call "heart" is located far lower than the fourth
waistcoat button.

—GEORG CHRISTOPH LICHTENBERG (attributed)


When Adam found his rib was gone
He cursed and sighed and cried and swore
And looked with cold resentment on
The creature God had used it for.
. . .
Though shoulder, bosom, lip and knee
Are praised in every kind of art,
Here is love's true anatomy:
His rib is gone, he'll have her heart.

—JOHN HOLLANDER, "The Lady's Maid's Song"


Never give all the heart, for love
. . .
O never give the heart outright.

—WILLIAM BUTLER YEATS, "Never Give All the Heart"

When I was one and twenty
I heard a wise man say,
"Give crowns and pounds and guineas
But not your heart away";
. . .
And I am two-and-twenty
And oh, 'tis true 'tis true.
—A.E. HOUSEMAN, "When I Was One and Twenty"


From whence do glance love's piercing darts,
That make such holes into our hearts.
—GEORGE PEELE, "The Hunting of Cupid's Song"


What comes from the heart, goes to the heart.
—SAMUEL TAYLOR COLERIDGE


Never love with all your heart,
It only ends in aching.
—COUNTEE CULLEN


The heart is a lonely hunter.
—CARSON McCULLERS (title of novel)


My heart is a lonely hunter that hunts on a lonely hill.
—WILLIAM SHARP
*The Lonely Hunter*


The heart has its reasons, which reason does not know.
—PASCAL
*Pensées*

I thought no more was needed
Youth to prolong
Than dumbbell and foil
To keep the body young.
Oh, who could have foretold
That the heart grows old?
—WILLIAM BUTLER YEATS, "Song"


Flaubert says that the heart is like a palm tree—"it grows as soon as it is stripped"—I disagree. The heart is constantly gouged until in the end it is a ghost of a heart.
—EDNA O'BRIEN
*Our Private Lives* by D. Halpern


Nobody has ever measured, not even poets, how much the heart can hold.
—ZELDA FITZGERALD


There are strings in the human heart that had better not be vibrated.
—CHARLES DICKENS
*Barnaby Rudge*


Woman, though so kind she seems, will take your heart
    and tantalize it,
Were it made of Portland stone, she'd manage to
    McAdamize it.
Dairymaid or duchess,
Keep it from her clutches
If you ever wish to know a quiet moment more.
—JAMES PLANCHÉ, "Love You've Been a Villain"

# Heartbreak

Lie still, lie still, my breaking heart
My silent heart, lie still and break.
—CHRISTINA ROSSETTI, "Mirage"


Beauty more than bitterness
Makes the heart break.
—SARA TEASDALE, "Capri"


Don't waste time trying to break a man's heart; be satisfied if you can manage to chip it in a brand new place.
—HELEN ROWLAND
*A Guide to Men*


I was cryin'
Cause you broke my heart in two
. . .
So I was cryin'
On account of
You.
—LANGSTON HUGHES, "Late Last Night"


Broken hearts die slowly.
—THOMAS CAMPBELL, "Theodric"


Had we never loved sae kindly,
Had we never loved sae blindly,
Never met—or never parted,
We had ne'er been broken-hearted.
—ROBERT BURNS, "Ae Fond Kiss"

The day breaks not, it is my heart.
—JOHN DONNE, "Break of Day"


. . . a broken heart is what makes life so wonderful five years later, when you see the guy in the elevator and he is fat and smoking a cigar and saying long-time-no-see. If he had not broken your heart, you couldn't have that glorious feeling of relief!
—PHYLLIS BATTELLE, *New York Journal,* June 1, 1962

# Heaven and Hell

Hell, madame, is to love no longer.
—GEORGES BERNANOS
*The Diary of a Country Priest*


You fascinated me, but I loved you; so it was heaven. This sister of yours fascinates me; but I hate her; so it is hell.
—GEORGE BERNARD SHAW
*Heartbreak House*


Parting is all we know of heaven,
And all we need of hell.
—EMILY DICKINSON, "Life"


Heav'n has no rage like love to hatred turn'd
Nor hell a fury like a woman scorned.
—WILLIAM CONGREVE

O what a heaven is love!
O what a hell!
—THOMAS DEKKER
*The Honest Whore*

# Henpecked Husbands

They are sorry houses, where hennes crowe, and the cock
holds his peace.
—JOHN FLORIO
*Firste Frutes*


The missus is master. Petticoat government.
—JAMES JOYCE
*Ulysses*


But—Oh! ye lords of ladies intellectual
Inform us truly, have they not henpeck'd you all?
—GEORGE GORDON, Lord Byron
*Don Juan*


Cursed be the man, the poorest wretch in life,
The crouching vassal to the tyrant wife,
Who has no will but by her permission.
. . .
Who dreads a curtain lecture worse than hell.
—ROBERT BURNS, "The Henpecked Husband"

# Hesitation

She who hesitates is lost.
—ANONYMOUS


When love once pleads admission to our hearts
(In spight of all the virtue we can boast)
The woman that deliberates is lost.
—JOSEPH ADDISON
*Cato*


If love be timid, it is not true.
*Spanish Proverb*


He who begins timidly invites a refusal.
—SENECA
*Hippolytus*


While we ponder when to begin it becomes too late.
—QUINTILIAN
*De Institutione Oratoria*


He who hesitates is bossed.
—SONIA CHAPMAN (attributed)


# Hips

. . . the language of hips.
—JUAN GOYTISOLO
*Makbara*

(hips pumping pleasure into hips)
—E.E. CUMMINGS, "Sonnets—Actualities X"

# Honesty

No more masks! No more mythologies.
—MURIEL RUKEYSER
*No More Masks!*, by F. Howe and E. Bass

She tore off mask after mask—
Wonder Woman
Noble Martyr
Big Mama
Con Woman
Tough Broad
Sexy Kitten
Cold Bitch
Daddy's Girl
Frightened Child
Whiny Brat
and on and on . . .
—NANCY GREEN, "Masks and Mirrors"
*True to Life Adventure*

There was altogether too much candour in married life; it was an indelicate modern idea, and frequently led to upsets in the household, if not divorce.
—MURIEL SPARK
*Memento Mori*

Honesty is praised and starves.
—JUVENAL
*Satires*

# Honeymoon

When a couple are newly married, the first month is honeymoon, or smick smack; the second is hither and thither; the third is thwick thwack; the fourth, the devil take them that brought thee and I together.
—JOHN RAY
*English Proverbs*

Niagara falls is only the second biggest disappointment of the standard honeymoon.
—OSCAR WILDE

Of all the things that change
The one that shows most fickle and strange
And takes the most eccentric range
Is the moon, so called of honey.
—THOMAS HOOD
*Miss Kilmansegg*

The indifferent clerk he knowing what was going to
    happen
The lobby zombies they knowing what
The whistling elevator man he knowing
The winking bellboy knowing
Everybody knowing! I'd almost be inclined not to do
    anything!
—GREGORY CORSO, "Marriage"

The honeymoon wasn't such a ghastly experience really; it was afterwards that was really awful.
. . .
Honeymooning is a very overrated occupation.
—NOEL COWARD
*Private Lives*

The terrible question which confronts all brides is whether to pin up their curls and cream their faces before going to bed.

—VIRGINIA GRAHAM

*Everything's Too Something*

The honeymoon is over when he phones that he'll be late for supper—and she has already left a note that it's in the refrigerator.

BILL LAWRENCE

*Reader's Digest,* January 1955

# Husbands

He tells you when you've got on too much lipstick,
And helps you with your girdle when your hips stick.

—OGDEN NASH, "The Perfect Husband"

*Verses*

Marriage is not harmed by seducers but by cowardly husbands.

—SØREN KIERKEGAARD

*Either/Or*

Chumps make the best husbands. When you marry, Sally, grab a chump. Tap his forehead first, and if it rings solid, don't hesitate. All the unhappy marriages come from the husbands having brains. What good are brains to a man? They only unsettle him.

—P.G. WODEHOUSE

*The Adventures of Sally*

Changing husbands is only changing troubles.
—KATHLEEN NORRIS
*Handful of Living*


The men that women marry
And why they marry them, will always be
A marvel and a mystery to the world.
—HENRY WADSWORTH LONGFELLOW, "Michelangelo"


A husband is what is left of a lover after the nerve has been extracted.
—HELEN ROWLAND
*The Rubaiyat of a Bachelor*


The calmest husbands make the stormiest wives.
—THOMAS DEKKER
*The Honest Whore*


If ever two were one, then surely we,
If ever man were lov'd by wife, then thee.
. . .
Thy love is such I can no way repay,
The heavens reward thee manifold I pray.
—ANNE BRADSTREET, "To My Dear and Loving Husband"


There is so little difference between husbands you might as well keep the first.
—ADELA ROGERS ST. JOHN (attributed)


Husbands are like fires. They go out if unattended.
—ZSA ZSA GABOR
*Newsweek*, 1960

Lady, lady, should you meet
One whose ways are all discreet,
One who murmurs that his wife
Is the lodestar of his life,
One who keeps assuring you
That he was never untrue,
Never loved another one . . .
Lady, lady, better run.
—DOROTHY PARKER, "Social Note"


To a fond spouse a wife shows no mercy.
—JUVENAL
   *Satire VI* (translated by William Gifford)


There is only one real tragedy in a woman's life. The fact
that the past is always her lover, and the future invariably
her husband.
—OSCAR WILDE
   *An Ideal Husband*


There you are you see, quite simple. If you cannot have
your dear husband for a comfort and a delight, for a
breadwinner and a crosspatch, for a sofa, chair, or hot-
water bottle, one can use him as a Cross to be borne.
—STEVIE SMITH
   *Novel on Yellow Paper*


Who needs a husband. To hump and jump and dump and
pump.
—JOHN GREGORY DUNNE
   *Dutch Shea, Jr.*

The most popular labor-saving device is still a husband with money.
—JOEY ADAMS
*Cindy and I*


Why have scores of such lovely, gifted girls
Married impossible men?
Repeat, "impossible men": not merely rustic,
Foul-tempered or depraved
. . .
Impossible men: idle, illiterate
Self-pitying, dirty, sly,
. . .
Has God's supply of tolerable husbands
Fallen, in fact, so low?
—ROBERT GRAVES, "A Slice of Wedding Cake"


The son of a bitch is acting even when he takes his pajamas off.
—CAROLE LOMBARD (speaking about her husband William Powell)


. . . I grant the husband in the home
Disrupts its neat machinery.
His shaving brush, his sorry comb,
Mar tidy bathroom scenery.
. . .
What gadget's useful as a spouse?
Considering that a minute,
Confess that every proper house
Should have a husband in it.
—PHYLLIS McGINLEY, "Apology for Husbands"


The trouble with some women is they get excited about nothing—and then marry him.
—CHER (attributed)

To catch a husband is an art, to keep him a job.
—SIMONE DE BEAUVOIR (attributed)


I think everybody really will concede that on this, of all
days, I should begin my speech with the words "My husband and I."
—ELIZABETH II, on her 25th wedding anniversary
*The Observer,* April 26, 1972


Mender of toys, leader of boys,
Changer of fuses, kisser of bruises,
Bless him, dear Lord.
Mover of couches, soother of ouches,
Pounder of nails, teller of tales
Reward him, O Lord.
Hanger of screens, counselor of teens,
Fixer of bikes, chastiser of tykes,
Help him O Lord.
Raker of leaves, cleaner of eaves,
Dryer of dishes, fulfiller of wishes . . .
Bless him, O Lord.
—JO ANN HEIDBREDER


The lover in the husband may be lost.
—LORD LYTTELTON
*Secret Loves* by S. Friedman


You can bear your own faults, and why not a fault in your
wife?
—BENJAMIN FRANKLIN

# Imagination

My imaginations are as foul
As Vulcan's stithy.
—WILLIAM SHAKESPEARE
*Hamlet*

Nine-tenths of that which is attributed to sexuality is the work of our magnificent ability to imagine, which is no longer an instinct, but exactly the opposite: a creation.
—JOSÉ ORTEGA Y GASSET

A lady's imagination is very rapid; it jumps from admiration to love, from love to matrimony in a moment.
—JANE AUSTEN
*Pride and Prejudice*

Think of your mistress.
—HONORÉ DE BALZAC (advice to bored husbands)
*The Physiology of Marriage*

Does the imagination dwell most
Upon a woman won or lost.
—WILLIAM BUTLER YEATS, "The Tower"

The finest bosom in nature is not so fine as what imagination forms.
—DR. GREGORY
*A Father's Legacy to His Daughters*

# Imperfection

The lover who has not felt the hot tears rise at the sight of some slight, infinitely poignant imperfection in the body of the beloved, has never loved.
—MERVYN LEVY
*The Moons of Paradise*

Though love is blind, yet 'tis not for want of eyes.
—THOMAS FULLER
*English Proverbs*

... the tiniest blemish can twist the roots of the heart.
—MERVYN LEVY
*The Moons of Paradise*

In the eyes of a lover pockmarks are dimples.
*Japanese Proverb*

# Impotence

May your fire never go out.
*Traditional Irish Toast*

Gather ye rosebuds while ye may
Old time is still a-flying;
And the penis which is stiff today
Tomorrow will be dying.

—ANONYMOUS, "Chanson Antique"


I have seen it happen, often, to men who could not friggle
when they wanted, because they hadn't wanted when they
could.

—FRANÇOIS RABELAIS

*Gangantua and Pantagruel*


But on what envy God conspires
To snatch his power
yet leaves him the desire.

—JOHN WILMOT, Earl of Rochester

*The Disappointment*


Impotent with her, he is a standing bone with me.

—JOHN BARTH

*Letters*


Domine Do Little. An impotent old fellow.

—FRANCIS GROSE

*A Classical Dictionary of the Vulgar Tongue*


When all else fails, pray.

—TIM AND BEVERLY LA HAYE

*The Act of Marriage*


Use it or lose it.

*Popular Saying*

When a man tells you he's run out of steam in the sex department, I'll tell him, "Count your blessings; you've escaped from the clutches of a cruel tyrant. Enjoy!"
—RICHARD J. NEEDHAM

While a person does not give up on sex, sex does not give up on a person.
—GABRIEL GARCIA MÁRQUEZ (attributed)

She does her softest Joys dispense,
Off'ring her virgin Innocence
A victim to Love's Sacred Flame;
While the o'er Ravished Shepard lies
Unable to perform the Sacrifice.
—APHRA BEHN, "The Disappointment"

You've been a good ole wagon daddy, but you done broke down.
—BESSIE SMITH, "You've Been a Good Ole Wagon"

Trembling, confused, despairing, limber, dry
A wishing, weak, unmoving lump I lie.
—JOHN WILMOT, Earl of Rochester
*The Imperfect Enjoyment*

To succeed with the opposite sex, tell her you're impotent. She can't wait to disprove it.
—CARY GRANT (attributed), at age 72

There is nothing certain in man's life but this:
That he must lose it.
—OWEN MEREDITH
*Clytemnestra*

John Anderson, my jo, John
When first when ye began,
Ye had as good a tail-tree
As any ither man;
But now it's waxen wan, John
And aft requires my helping hand
—ROBERT BURNS, "John Anderson, My Jo"


This is the monstrosity in love lady—that the will is infinite and the execution confined, that the desire is boundless, and the act a slave to limit.
—WILLIAM SHAKESPEARE
*Troilus and Cressida*


The pitcher that goes too often to the well is broken and lost.
*English Proverb*


When the snows cover the mountains, there can be scant
heat in the valleys of the codpiece.
—FRANÇOIS RABELAIS
*Gargantua and Pantagruel*


It is vain to water the plant
When the root is dead.
—ROBERT GREENE
*Morando*


Women, fire in their crotch, won't burn out, begin by
fighting off pricks, end by going wild hunting for one that
still works.
—JOHN UPDIKE


*See also:* POTENCY.

# Impregnation

You cleft me with your beauty's pulse, and now
Your pulse has taken body.
—GENEVIEVE TAGGARD, "With Child"

He said it was artificial respiration, but now I find I am to
have his child.
—ANTHONY BURGESS
*Inside Mr. Enderby*

I pour the stuff to start sons and daughters fit for these
        States,
    I press slow rude muscle,
I brace myself effectually, I listen to no entreaties,
I dare not withdraw until I deposit what
has so long accumulated within me.
—WALT WHITMAN
*Leaves of Grass*

A surly and pessimistic Druid,
A defeatist, if only he knew it,
        Said, "The world's on the skids,
        And I think having kids
Is a waste of good seminal fluid."
*Anonymous Limerick*

# Incompatibility

A little incompatibility is the spice of life, particularly if he
has income and she is pattable.
—OGDEN NASH

The notion that a true and loving . . . wife inspires a man to high endevor is largely illusory. Every sane woman knows instinctively, as a matter of fact, that the highest aspirations of her husband are fundamentally inimical to her, and that the realization is apt to cost her her possession of him.

—H.L. MENCKEN

*Prejudices*


Dear wife, give in or get out
. . .
I like my loving in light; for you
the darkest night is still too bright.
Beneath your girdles and gowns you hide
yourself, while for me
naked is barely nude enough.

—MARTIAL

*Selected Epigrams of Martial* (translated and adapted by Donald C. Goertz)


What a woman wants, you are out of.

—O. HENRY

*Cupid à la Carte*


The distance is wide that sheets will not decide.

—JOHN RAY

*English Proverbs*


The two extremes appear as man and wife,
Coupled together for the sake of strife.

—CHARLES CHURCHILL, "The Rosciad"

# Inconstancy

She is constant only in her inconstancy.
—OVID
*Tristia*


Love lodged in a woman's breast
Is but a guest.
—SIR HENRY WOTTON
*A Woman's Heart*


A fickle and changeful thing is a woman ever.
—VIRGIL
*Aeneid*


# Indecency

The most virtuous woman is often indecent without knowing it.
—HONORÉ DE BALZAC
*The Physiology of Marriage*


Indecency and fun are old cronies.
—S.S. COX
*Why We Laugh*


The older one grows, the more one likes indecency.
—VIRGINIA WOOLF (attributed)

Is nakedness indecent? No, not inherently. It is your thought, your sophistication, your fear, your respectability, that is indecent . . . There come moods when these clothes of ours are not only irksome to wear, but are themselves indecent.

—WALT WHITMAN

# Individuality

I said
your words
till my throat
closed up
and I had
no voice
and I had no choice
but to do your song
I was your baby
I was you too long.

—DORY PREVIN, "I Was You"

You love me so much, you want to put me in your pocket. And I should die there smothered.

—D.H. LAWRENCE

*Sons and Lovers*

# Infidelity

Between a man and a woman a husband's infidelity is nothing. A man imposes no bastards on his wife.

—SAMUEL JOHNSON

*The Life of Samuel Johnson* by James Boswell

If Marilyn is in love with my husband, it proves she has good taste, for I am in love with him, too.
—SIMONE SIGNORET (on rumors linking her husband, Yves Montand, with actress Marilyn Monroe)
*New York Journal-American*, November 14, 1960

It's hard to love another woman's man.
You can't get him when you want him,
You got to catch him when you can.
—BESSIE SMITH, "Sorowful Blues"

Men are always sincere. They change sincerities, that's all.
—TRISTAN BERNARD
*Ce que l'on dit aux Femmes*

A man can have two, maybe three love affairs while he is married. After that, it is cheating.
—YVES MONTAND (attributed)

I don't think there are any men who are faithful to their wives.
—JACQUELINE KENNEDY ONASSIS (attributed)

Those who are faithful know only the trivial side of love; it is the faithless who know love's tragedies.
—OSCAR WILDE

Husbands are chiefly good lovers when they are betraying their wives.
—MARILYN MONROE

When Eve saw her reflection in a pool, she sought Adam
and accused him of infidelity.
—AMBROSE BIERCE
*The Devil's Dictionary*

There are women whose infidelities are the only link they
have with their husbands.
—SACHA GUITRY (attributed)

It is the fear of middle-age in the young, of old-age in the
middle-aged, which is the prime cause of infidelity, that
infallible rejuvenator.
—CYRIL CONNOLLY (attributed)

Love grows bitter with treason.
—A.C. SWINBURNE

*See also:* BETRAYAL.

# Insatiability

. . . it seems to make no difference how much the poor
bastard actually gets, for he is dreaming about tomorrow's
pussy even while pumping away at today's.
—PHILIP ROTH
*Portnoy's Complaint*

Verily, I can no more do without a woman than a blind man
without his staff; my gimlet must drill or I could not live.
—FRANÇOIS RABELAIS
*Gargantua and Pantagruel*

I cry we have sex in the head in the pants in the street waking sleeping reading writing thinking dying—and I have seen me and seen you wince and jerk with the heat of it beat of it meat of it and I swear there is no relief in sight.

—SEYMOUR KRIM

*Views of a Nearsighted Cannoneer*


You always have a ready mouth for a ripe cherry.

. . .

The sea complains for want of water.

—THOMAS FULLER

*Gnomologia: Adagies and Proverbs*


Like a lady can't go through a plate glass window and go to bed with you five seconds later. But every guy in the audience is the same—you can idolize your wife, just be crazy about her, be on the way home from work, have a head-on collision with a Greyhound bus, in a disaster area. Forty people lying dead on the highway—not even in the hospital, in the ambulance the guy makes a play for the nurse.

—LENNY BRUCE

*The Essential Lenny Bruce* by J. Cohen


# Intimacy

The eyes start love: intimacy perfects it.

—PUBLILIUS SYRUS

*Sententiae*


They're as thick as three in a bed.

*Scottish Proverb*

Intimacy is a difficult art.
—VIRGINIA WOOLF, "Geraldine and Jane"
*The Second Common Reader*


Sweet, casual intimacy, the soft-fleshed loveliness indisputably possessed.
—CARSON McCULLERS
*The Ballad of the Sad Café*


I said
your words
till my throat
closed up
and I had
no voice
and I had no choice
but to do your song
I was your baby
I was you too long.
—DORY PREVIN "I Was You"


You love me so much, you want to put me in your pocket.
And I should die there smothered.
—D.H. LAWRENCE
*Sons and Lovers*

# Jealousy and Suspicion

There's more self-love than love in jealousy.
—FRANÇOIS, Duc de La Rochefoucauld
*Réflexions ou sentences et maximes morales*

Jealousy, the great exaggerator.
—FRIEDRICH von SCHILLER (attributed)

It is the property of love to make to make us more distrustful and more credulous, to make us suspect the loved one, more readily than we should suspect anyone else, and be convinced more easily by her denials.
—MARCEL PROUST
*Rememberance of Things Past: Cities of the Plain*

At the gate which suspicion cometh in, love goeth out.
—STEFANO GUAZZO
*La civile conversation*

Love is sweetest seasoned with suspect.
—GEORGE CLIFFORD, "To Cynthia"

Jealousy is the great preservative of family life and marital faithfulness . . . Jealousy is the inseparable companion of love and its intensity is the pure gauge of love's strength.

—WILLIAM McDOUGAEL

*Encyclopedia of Sexual Behavior* by A. Ellis and A. Abarbanel

O! beware, my lord, of jealousy.
It is the green eye'd monster which doth mock
The meat it feeds on.

—WILLIAM SHAKESPEARE

*Othello*

Jealousy and love are sisters.

*Russian Proverb*

Love that survives jealousy is like a pretty face after small pox; a bit pockmarked forever.

—PAUL BOURGET

*La physiologie de l'amour moderne*

Thou tyrant, tyrant jealousy
Thou tyrant of the mind.

—JOHN DRYDEN, "Song of Jealousy, Love Triumphant"

Nor Jealousy
was understood, the injured lover's hell.

—JOHN MILTON

*Paradise Lost*

A woman's natural jealousy is not a man's loving another, but as his forsaking her.

—JAMES HINTON

*Life in Nature*

A lewd bachelor makes a jealous husband.
—H.G. BOHN
*Handbook of Proverbs*


Jealousy has always been the whetstone of love and some would say that without it love does not have its inner shiver.
—EDNA O'BRIEN
*Some Irish Loving*


Jealousy is the greatest of all sufferings, and the one that arouses the least pity in persons it causes.
—FRANÇOIS, Duc de La Rochefoucauld
*Réflexions ou sentences et maximes morales*


He who loves without jealousy does not truly love.
*The Zohar*


Inquisitiveness as seldom cures jealousy, as drinking in a fever quenches the thirst.
—WILLIAM WYCHERLEY
*Love in a Wood*


A jealous man always finds more than he is looking for.
—MADELINE DE SCUDÉRY, "De la jalousie"
*Choix de pensées*


And why should I be cold, my lad,
And why should you repine,
Because I love a dark head
That never shall be mine?
—EDNA ST. VINCENT MILLAY, "Sonnet"

Her jealousy never slept.
—MARY SHELLEY
*The Mortal Immortal*


Man is jealous because of his amour propre; woman is jealous because of her lack of it.
—GERMAINE GREER
*The Female Eunuch*


Jealousy is the most dreadfully involuntary of all sins.
—IRIS MURDOCH
*The Black Prince*


. . . it's matrimonial suicide to be jealous when you have a really good reason.
—CLARE BOOTH LUCE
*The Women*


The "Green-Eyed Monster" causes much woe, but the absence of this ugly serpent argues the presence of a corpse whose name is Eros.
—MINNA ANTRIM
*Naked Truths and Veiled Allusions*


Jealousy, that dragon which slays love under the pretense of keeping it alive.
—HAVELOCK ELLIS
*On Life and Sex*


The fundamental torment of adult jealousy is not the sense of betrayal but uncertainty. The jealous are driven by the need, above all, to know.
—A. ALVAREZ
*Life After Marriage*

# Kinds of Love

Inebriations of love, shadows of love, fantasies of love, but never yet the one true love.
—EDNA O'BRIEN
*Some Irish Loving*


There is only one kind of love, but there are a thousand different imitations of it.
—FRANÇOIS, Duc de La Rochefoucauld
*Réflexions ou sentences et maximes morales*


Perfect love means to love one through whom one becomes unhappy.
—SØREN KIRKEGAARD


True love comes quietly, without banners or flashing lights. If you hear bells, get your ears checked.
—ERICH SEGAL


Contrast with all loves that had failed or staled
Registered their own as love indeed.
—ROBERT GRAVES, "Never Such Love"

How do I love thee? Let me count the ways.
. . .
I love thee to the level of everyday's
Most quiet need, by sun and candlelight.
I love thee freely, as men strive for Right;
I love thee purely, as they turn from Praise.
I love thee with the passion put to use
In my old griefs, and with my childhood faith.
—ELIZABETH BARRETT BROWNING, "How do I Love Thee?"
*Sonnets from the Portuguese*

Immature love says: "I love you because I need you."
Mature love says: "I need you because I love you."
—ERICH FROMM

Nuptial love maketh mankind;
Friendly love perfecteth it;
But wanton love corrupteth and embaseth it.
—FRANCIS BACON
*Essay Ten: On Love*

Young love is a flame, often very hot and fierce but still only light and flickering. The love of the older and disciplined heart is as coals deep-burning, unquenchable.
—HENRY WARD BEECHER

# Kiss and Tell

'Gin a body, kiss a body, need the world ken.
—ROBERT BURNS, "Comin' Thro' the Rye

'Tis no sin love's fruits to steal,
But the sweet thefts to reveal;
To be taken, to be seen
These have crimes accounted been.
—BEN JONSON
*Volpone*


You must not kiss and tell.
—WILLIAM CONGREVE
*Love for Love*


Like all skirt-chasers, he had to report on his successes.
—ISAAC BASHEVIS SINGER
*Shosha*


Some men kiss and do not tell, some kiss and tell; but
George Moore told and did not kiss.
—SUSAN MITCHELL
*As I Was Going Down Sackville Street* by Oliver St. John Gogarty


# Kisses

Why this delay? Why waste the time in kissing?
What is the very meaning of a kiss?
Think of the best, the ultimate joy we are missing!
Hasten the moment of our mutual bliss.
. . .
So come to bed; there's time for dawdling after.
—PETRONIUS, "A Plea for Haste" (translated by Louis Untermeyer)

Kisses may not spread germs, but they certainly lower
resistance.
—LOUISE ERICKSON
*Reader's Digest,* May 1949


Give me a kiss, and to that kiss a score;
Then to that twenty, add a hundred more;
A thousand to that hundred; so kiss on,
To make that thousand up to a million;
Treble that million, and when that is done,
Let's kiss afresh, as when we first begun.
—ROBERT HERRICK, "To Anthea"


Let him kiss me with the kisses of his mouth:
For thy love is better than wine.
*The Song of Songs*


A kiss, when all is said, what is it?
An oath that's given closer than before;
A promise more precise; the sealing of
Confessions that till then were barely breathed;
A rosy dot placed on the i in loving;
A secret that is confined to a mouth
And not to ears.
—EDMOND ROSTAND
*Cyrano de Bergerac*


But you would have felt my soul in a kiss,
And known that once if I loved you well;
And I would have given my soul for this
To burn for ever in burning hell.
—A.C. SWINBURNE, "Les Noyades"

It takes a lot of practice for a girl to kiss like a beginner.
—ANONYMOUS
*Ladies Home Journal*


He kissed me and now I am somebody else.
—GABRIELLA MISTRAL, "He Kissed Me"


. . . kissing puberty-stricken boys until their groins turned
blue and ached.
—GILBERT SORRENTINO
*Mulligan's Stew*


I twist your arm,
You twist my leg.
I make you cry,
You make me beg.
I dry your eyes
You dry my nose,
And that's the way
The kissing goes.
—WILLIAM WOOD, "À Deux"


I fear thy kisses, gentle maiden,
Thou need not fear mine,
My spirit is too deeply laden
Ever to burden thine.
—PERCY BYSSHE SHELLEY, "To _____, I Fear Thy Kisses"


Never let a fool kiss you or a kiss fool you.
—JOEY ADAMS (attributed)

Strephon kissed in the spring,
Robin in the fall,
But Colin only looked at me
And never kissed at all.

Strephon's kiss was lost in jest,
Robin's lost in play,
But the kiss in Colin's eyes
Haunts me night and day.
—SARA TEASDALE, "The Look"


When a rogue kisses you, count your teeth.
*Yiddish Proverb*


. . . there is nothing like a kiss long and hot down to your
soul almost paralyzes you . . .
—JAMES JOYCE
*Ulysses*


Kissing is man's greatest invention. All animals copulate,
but only humans kiss.
—TOM ROBBINS
*Even Cowgirls Get the Blues*


To lip a wanton is to secure a couch.
—WILLIAM SHAKESPEARE
*Othello*


What is this thing called a kiss? French, tongue, soul,
chaste, motherly, fatherly, brotherly, sisterly, ass, genital,
Judas, trembling, rough, hesitant, sweet, soft, wet, dying,
fevered, good-night, farewell, burning, and chocolate.
—GILBERT SORRENTINO
*Mulligan's Stew*

A kiss can be a comma, a question mark or an exclamation mark. That's a basic spelling that every woman should know.
—MISTINGUETTE (attributed)

Reap many kisses and little love.
—ROBERT GREENE
*Orpharion*

The first kiss is stolen by the man;
The last is begged by the woman.
—H.L. MENCKEN
*A Mencken Chrestomanthy*

The kiss originated when the first male reptile licked the first female reptile, implying in a subtle, complimentary way that she was as succulent as the small reptile he had for dinner the night before.
—F. SCOTT FITZGERALD
*The Crack-Up*

Blondes have the hottest kisses. Redheads are fair to middling torrid, and brunettes are the frigidest of all. It's something to do with hormones, no doubt.
—RONALD REAGAN (attributed)

A fine romance with no kisses,
A fine romance, my friend, this is.
We should be like a couple of hot tomatoes,
But you're as cold as yesterday's mashed potatoes.
—DOROTHY FIELDS, "A Fine Romance"

Oh, what lies there are in kisses.
—HEINRICH HEINE, "In den Küssen welche Lüge"


Rose kissed me today.
Will she kiss me tomorrow?
Let it be as it may,
Rose kissed me today.
—AUSTIN DOBSON, "A Kiss"


You have to kiss an awful lot of frogs before you find a prince.
—GRAFFITO


i like kissing this and that of you. . .
—E.E. CUMMINGS


The storm, the storm of a kiss.
—THEODORE ROETHKE, "Her Words"


Wanton kisses are the keys of sin.
—NICHOLAS BRETON
*Crossing of Proverbs*


Some women blush when they are kissed; some call for the police; some swear; some bite; but the worst are those who laugh.
—ANONYMOUS

# Lack of Love

I saw that lack of love contaminates.
You know I know you know I know you know.
—THOM GUNN, "Carnal Knowledge"


Without love our life is . . . a ship without a rudder . . .
like a body without a soul.
—SHOLEM ALEICHEM


Life after life after life goes by
without poetry
without seemliness
without love . . .
—DENISE LEVERTOV, "The Mutes"
*The Sorrow Dance*


# Lasting Love

Of all my loves the last, for hereafter I shall glow with
passion for no other woman.
—HORACE
*Odes*

Eternity is passion, girl or boy
Cry on the onset of their sexual joy
"For ever and for ever"
—WILLIAM BUTLER YEATS, "Whence Had They Come?"


. . . so fareth love nowadays, soon hot soon cold: this is no stability. But the old love was not so.
—SIR THOMAS MALLORY
*Le Morte d'Arthur*


For the sword outwears its sheath,
And the soul outwears the breast.
And the heart must pause to breathe,
And love itself have rest.
—GEORGE GORDON, Lord Byron, "So, We'll Go No More A-Roving"


Great passions, my dear, don't exist: they're liars' fantasies. What do exist are little loves that may last for a short or longer while.
—ANNA MAGNANI
*The Egotists* by Oriana Fallaci


Parrots, tortoises and redwoods
Live longer than men do,
Men longer than dogs do,
Dogs a longer life than love does.
—EDNA ST. VINCENT MILLAY, "Pretty Love I Must Outlive You"


Love is free: to promise for ever to love the same woman is no less absurd than to promise to believe the same creed; such a vow in both cases excludes us from all inquiry.
—PERCY BYSSHE SHELLEY
*Prometheus Unbound*


*See also:* ETERNAL LOVE.

# Laughter

A maid that laughs is half taken.
—JOHN RAY
*English Proverbs*


Sexiness wears thin after a while and beauty fades, but to be married to a man who makes you laugh every day, ah, now that's a treat.
—JOANNE WOODWARD (attributed)


When the Sexual Revolution began, I tried to enlist. But I got a series of humiliating rejections. That was from the men. From the women came nothing but hysterical laughter.
—GROUCHO MARX
*Why a Duck?*


Some women blush when they are kissed; some call the police; some swear; some bite. But the worst are those that laugh.
—ANONYMOUS


# Lechery

Lechery and covetousness go together.
*English Proverb*


I am almost done with harridans, and shall soon become old enough to fall in love with girls of fourteen.
—JONATHAN SWIFT, letter to Alexander Pope at the age of 57

An itching, tainted intellectual pride
Goads the salt lecher till he has to know
Whether all women's eyes grow bright and wide
All wives and whores and virgins shudder so.

Hunters of women burn to show their skill,
Yet when the panting quarry has been caught
Mere force of habit drives them to the kill;
The soft flesh is less savory than their sport.

—JOHN PRESS, "Womanizers"


Reefer was a wenchman.

—JAMES JOYCE

*Finnegan's Wake*


You think it horrible that lust and rage
Should dance attendance upon my old age;
They were not such a plague when I was young,
What else have I to spur me to song?

—WILLIAM BUTLER YEATS, "The Spur"


I am rather prone to senile lechery just now—want to
touch the right person in the right place, in order to shake
off bodily loneliness.

—E.M. FORSTER, letter to J.R. Ackerley, October 16, 1961


He's had more dolly than you've had cream cakes.

—HAROLD PINTER

*The Homecoming*


Even dirty old men need love.

—GRAFFITO

# Lies

When the heart is full of lust the mouth's full of leasings.*
—JAMES KELLY
*Complete Collection of Scottish Proverbs*
*[leasings = lies]

Fool, not to know that love endures no tie
And Jove but laughs at lovers' perjury.
—JOHN DRYDEN
*Palamon and Arcite*

Everybody lies about sex.
—R.A. HEINLEIN
*The Notebooks of Lazurus Long*

I don't approve of guys using false pretences on dolls,
except, of course, when nothing else will do.
—DAMON RUNYON
*Take It Easy*

By the time you swear you're his,
Shivering and sighing,
And he vows his passion is
Infinite, undying—
Lady, make a note of this:
One of you is lying.
—DOROTHY PARKER, "Unfortunate Coincidence"

Every man should love his wife.
But a promise can't make you love.
It only makes you lie.
—J.L. WILLIAMS, "Why Marry?"

{ 221 }

When my love swears she is made of truth,
I do believe her, though I know she lies,
That she might think me some untutor'd youth,
Unlearned in the world's false subtleties.
—WILLIAM SHAKESPEARE, "Sonnet 138"

The cruelest lies are often told in silence.
—ROBERT LOUIS STEVENSON
*Virginibus Puerisque*

Actions lie louder than words.
—CAROLYN WELLS (attributed)

Telling lies is a fault in a boy, an art in a lover, an accomplishment in a bachelor, and second-nature in a married man.
—HELEN ROWLAND
*A Guide to Men*

# Life

Life is a sexually transmitted disease.
—GRAFFITO

An orange on the table,
Your dress on the rug,
And you in my bed,
Sweet present of the present,
Cool of night,
Warmth of my life.
—JACQUES PRÉVERT
*Paroles*

Oh, love is real enough. You'll find it some day, but it has one arch enemy—and that is life.
—JEAN ANOUILH
*Ardèle*


It's a bawdy planet.
—WILLIAM SHAKESPEARE
*The Winter's Tale*


# Lingerie

Brevity: the soul of lingerie.
—DOROTHY PARKER
*While Rome Burns*


A century ago women wore unmentionables; today they wear nothing to speak of.
—ANONYMOUS


. . . let eyesight see that the film of breast-sheath and panty-crotch are mere cloth of this world and not the webbing of paradise.
—SEYMOUR KRIM
*Views of a Nearsighted Cannoneer*


A lady is one who never shows her underwear unintentionally.
—LILLIAN DAY
*Kiss and Tell*

A century and half ago there were no knickers and girls read the *Bible*, now they wear impenetrable body stockings and read *Portnoy's Complaint*.
—KENNETH TYNAN

I consider it is better to be trussed up than flopping about, but I suppose it depends on the individual.
—JOHN CAVANAGH, comment on no-bra fashions

*See also:* CLOTHES; DRESS; FETISHES.

# Lips

Free of her lips, free of her hips.
*English Proverb*

Her lips suck forth my soul.
—CHRISTOPHER MARLOWE
*Dr. Faustus*

Kissable lips and flirtable eyes still foul the good and fool the wise.
—J.B. OPDYKE
*Amor Vitaque*

Sweet lips . . .
Men touch them, and change in a trice
The lilies and languors of virtue
For the roses and rapture of vice.
—A.C. SWINBURNE, "Dolores"

. . . her odalisk lips lusciously smeared with the salve of swine fat and rosewater.

—JAMES JOYCE

*Ulysses*

Her lips are lilies, flowing with liquid myrrh.

*Song Of Songs*

Red hair she had and golden skin,
Her sulky lips were shaped for sin.

—SIR JOHN BETJEMAN, "The Licorice Fields at Pontefract"

*A Few Late Chrysanthemums*

But the loveliest things of beauty God ever has showed to me,
Are her voice, and her hair, and eyes, and the dear red curve of her lips.

—JOHN MASEFIELD, "Beauty"

# Living Together

Do you think your mother and I should have liv'd comfortably so long together, if ever we had been married?

—JOHN GAY

*The Beggar's Opera*

There would be no society if living together depended upon understanding each other.

—ERIC HOFFER

*Reflections on the Human Condition*

In the old days, one married a wife; now one forms a company with a female partner, or moves in to live with a friend. Then one seduces the partner, or defiles the friend.
—AUGUST STRINDBERG
*The Father*


Come live with me and be my love.
And we will all the pleasures prove . . .
—CHRISTOPHER MARLOWE, "The Passionate Shepherd to His Love"


Come live with me and be my love
And we will all the pleasures prove
Of peace and plenty, bed and board
That chance employment may afford.
—C. DAY LEWIS, "Come Live With Me"


Come live with me and be my love
In statutory Christian sin.
And we shall all the pleasures prove
Of two-room flats and moral gin.
—SAMUEL HOFFENSTEIN, "Invocation"


Horses (thou sayest) and asses men may try,
And ring suspected vessels ere they buy;
But wives, a random choice, untried that take,
They dream in courtship, but in wedlock wake.
—GEOFFREY CHAUCER
*The Wife of Bath's Tale* (translated by A. Pope)

# Loneliness

Be good and you will be lonesome.
—MARK TWAIN
*Following the Equator*


If you are afraid of loneliness, do not marry.
—ANTON CHEKHOV


Sadly, there are whole segments of the population that believe the answer to existential loneliness is the next passing crotch.
—JUDIANNE DENSEN-GERBER
*Walk in My Shoes*


The physical union of the sexes only intensifies man's sense of solitude.
—NICHOLAS BERDYAEV


We live, as we dream—alone.
—JOSEPH CONRAD
*Heart of Darkness*


Love is made by two people, in different kinds of solitude.
—JOSÉ-PIERRE LOUIS ARAGON
*Recherches sur la sexualité*


God created man, finding him not sufficiently alone, gave him a female companion to make him feel his solitude more keenly.
—PAUL VALÉRY
*Mauvaises pensées et autres*

I have not known no loneliness like this
Locked in your arms and bent beneath your kiss.
—BABETTE DEUTSCH, "Solitude"
*Banners*


Marriage is lonelier than solitude.
—ADRIENNE RICH
*Poems*


The desert of loneliness and recrimination that men call love.
—SAMUEL BECKETT


Forever at her side, yet always alone.
—FELIX ARVERS
*Mes heures perdues*


Two fears alternate in marriage, the one of loneliness and
the other of bondage. The dread of loneliness is greater
than the fear of bondage so we get married.
—CYRIL CONNOLLY
*The Unquiet Grave*


But when he's gone
Me and them lonesome blues collide
The bed's too big
The frying pan is too wide.
—JONI MITCHELL, "My Old Man"


What makes loneliness an anguish
Is not that I have no one to share my burden
But this: I have only my own burden to bear.
—DAG HAMMARSKJÖLD
*Markings*

# Longing

Will these wild oats never be sown?
—THOMAS HEYWOOD
  *The Wise Woman of Hogsdown*


I have heard mermaids singing, each to each,
I do not think they will sing for me.
—T.S. ELIOT, "The Love Song of J. Alfred Prufrock"


Love will come again, but in circuitous paths.
—WILLIE MORRIS
  *New York Days*


Oh lovelorn heart, give o'er—
Cease thy vain dreams of beauty's warmth—forget
The face thou longest for.
—MELEAGER, "Lost Desire"


I am a lover and have not found my thing to love.
—SHERWOOD ANDERSON
  *Winesburg, Ohio*


I know I am but summer to your heart,
And not the full four seasons of the year.
—EDNA ST. VINCENT MILLAY, "I Know That I Am but Summer to Your
  Heart"


If you shall find my lover, what shall you say to him? Tell
him I am sick with love.
  *Song of Songs*

Somewhere there was a gentle man with a cock that wore
a jaunty grin and stayed long enough for you to get to
know him.
—JILL ROBINSON
*Bed/Time/Story*


Everywhere pass, with lips for me unmoved
The lovely ladies that I might have loved
That never now will love me, late or soon.
. . .
O loves forbidden, I'll go home and start
My pipe and light my fire and break my heart
And read a book on sexual morality.
—GERALD GOULD, "From Monogamy"


Why am I crying after love?
—SARA TEASDALE, "Spring Night"
*Rivers to the Sea*


When you really want to love you will find it waiting for
you.
—OSCAR WILDE
*De Profundis*


Somewhere there must one
Made for this soul, to move it;
—WILLIAM JOHNSON CORY
*Amaturus*

# Looking

Loving comes from looking.
—JOHN CLARKE
*Paroemiologia Anglo-Latina*


Wine comes in at the mouth
And love comes in at the eye;
That's all we know for truth
Before we grow old and die.
I lift my glass to my mouth
I look at you, and I sigh.
—WILLIAM BUTLER YEATS, "A Drinking Song"


He gave her a look you could have poured on a waffle.
—RING LARDNER


May not a woman look, but she must love?
—ROBERT GREENE, "Metamorphosis"


Although man has learned through evolution to walk in
an upright position, his eyes still swing from limb to limb.
—MARGARET SCHOOLEY
*Reader's Digest*, January 1956


Oh! death will find me long before I tire
Of watching you.
—RUPERT BROOKE, "Sonnet"


I looked and I loved.
—EDWARD GIBBON
*Memoirs*

if the soul
is to know itself
it must look
into a soul
—GEORGE SEFERIS, "Mythistoreme: Poem IV"

# Loss of Love

'Tis not love's going hurts my days,
But that it went in little ways.
—EDNA ST. VINCENT MILLAY, "The Spring and the Fall"

I hold it true, what e'er befall;
I feel it, when I sorrow most;
'Tis better to have loved and lost
Than never to have loved at all.
—ALFRED, Lord Tennyson
*In Memoriam*

And if I never fall in love again,
That's soon enough for me.
I'm going to lock my heart and throw away the key.
—JIMMY EATON AND TERRY SHAND, "I'm Going to Lock My
Heart"

The man is quickened so with grief,
He wanders god-like or like thief
Inside and out, below, above,
Without relief seeking lost love.
—ROBERT GRAVES, "Lost Love"

Murmur, a little sadly, how love fled.
—WILLIAM BUTLER YEATS, "When You Are Old"

The kiss of virgins, first-fruits of the bed,
Soft speech, smooth touch, the lips, the maidenhead:
These, and a thousand sweets, could never be
So near, or dear, as thou wast once to me.
—ROBERT HERRICK, "His Farewell to Sack"

# Love

Without love our life is. . . . a ship without a rudder . . .
like a body without a soul.
—SHOLEM ALEICHEM

Here is a perfect poem:
to awaken a longing,
to nourish it,
to develop it,
to increase it,
to stimulate it,
to gratify it.
—HONORÉ DE BALZAC
*Ideal Marriage* by Th. Van de Velde

Love, oh love, oh careless love.
—BLUES SONG

For words of rapture groping, they
"Never such love," swore "ever before was!"
—ROBERT GRAVES, "Never Such Love"

Anyone who is repelled by his sweetheart's farts has no business talking about love.

—GUNTHER GRASS

*The Flounder*


Love must be reinvented.

—ARTHUR RIMBAUD

*A Season in Hell*


Antipathy, dissimilarity of views, hate, contempt can accompany true love.

—AUGUST STRINDBERG

*The Son of a Servant*


Love doesn't just sit there, like a stone, it has to be made, like bread, remade all the time, made new.

—URSULA LE GUIN

*The Lathe of Heaven*


I know of only one duty, and that is to love.

—ALBERT CAMUS

*The Notebooks*


I love you no matter what you do, but do you have to do so much of it?

—JEAN ILLSLEY CLARKE

*Self-Esteem: A Family Affair*


If you be loved, be worthy of love.

—OVID

Something there is moves me to love, and I
Do know I love, but know not how or why.
—ALEXANDER BROME, "Love's Without Reason"


I loved him for himself alone.
—RICHARD BRINSLEY SHERIDAN
*The Duenna*


We love being in love, that's the truth on't.
—WILLIAM MAKEPEACE THACKERY
*The History of Henry Esmond*


Love seeketh only itself to please
To bind another to its delight;
Joy in another's loss of ease,
And builds a Hell in Heaven's despite.
—WILLIAM BLAKE, "The Clod and the Pebble"
*Songs of Experience*


Love has but one word and it never repeats itself.
—LACORDAIRE


Love is like war; easy to begin but very hard to stop.
—H.L. MENCKEN


In love, there is always one who kisses and one who offers
the cheek.
*French Proverb*


Love does not brook neglect.
—MENANDER
*Fragments*

No one has ever loved anyone the way everyone wants to be loved.

—MIGNON McLAUGHLIN

A fence between makes love more keen.

—ANONYMOUS

A supreme love, a motive that gives a sublime rhythm to a woman's life, and exalts habit into partnership with the soul's highest needs, is not to be had where and how she wills.

—GEORGE ELIOT

*Felix Holt, The Radical*

If thou must love me, let it be for nought
Except for love's sake only. Do not say,
I love her for her smile . . . her look . . . her way
Of speaking gently . . . for a trick of thought
That falls in well with mine, and, certes, brought
A sense of pleasant ease on such a day—
For these things in themselves, Beloved, may
Be changed, or change for thee—and love so
        wrought.
May be unwrought so.

—ELIZABETH BARRETT BROWNING

*Sonnets from the Portuguese*

Love, Arthur, is a poodle's chance of attaining the infinite, and personally I have my pride.

—LOUIS-FERDINAND CÉLINE

*Journey to the End of the Night*

If there's delight in love, 'tis when I see
That heart, which others bleed for, bleed for me.
—WILLIAM CONGREVE
*The Way of the World*


The fate of love is that it always seems too little or too much.
—AMELIA BARR
*The Belle of Bolling Green*


After all, my estwhile dear,
My no longer cherished,
Need we say it was not love,
Now that love is perished?
—EDNA ST. VINCENT MILLAY
*Passer Mortuus Est*


Real love is a pilgrimage. It happens when there is no strategy, but it is very rare because most people are strategists.
—ANITA BROOKNER
*Women Writers Talk*


Love is most nearly itself
When here and now cease to matter.
—T.S. ELIOT
*Four Quartets*


Love's chemistry thrives best in equal heat.
—JOHN WILMOT, Earl of Rochester, "The Imperfect Enjoyment"

People need a little loving, and God, sometimes it's sad all the shit they have to go through to find some.

—RICHARD BRAUTIGAN

*The Betrayed Kingdom*

Love can deny naught to love.

"Codex Amoris"

*Ideal Marriage* by Th. Van de Velde

If thou be loved—love!

—SENECA

*Epistolae*

If of herself she will not love.
Nothing can make her.

—SIR JOHN SUCKLING, "Song"

You can't make a person love another person. You can only pray for it.

—JOHN BARTH

*Letters*

What is precious never to forget
The essential delight of blood drawn from ageless springs
. . .
Never to deny its pleasure in the morning single light
Nor its grave evening demand for love.

—STEPHEN SPENDER, "I Think Continuously of Those Who Were Truly Great"

You can give without loving, but you cannot love without giving.

—AMI CARMICHAEL

Give all to love
Obey thy heart
Friends, kindred, days,
Estate, good fame
Plans, credit, and the muse
Nothing refuse.
—RALPH WALDO EMERSON, "Give All to Love"


Oh love will make a dog howl in tune.
—FRANCIS BEAUMONT AND JOHN FLETCHER
*The Queen of Corinth*


Love is indescribable and unconditional. I could tell you a
thousand things that it is not, but not one that it is.
—DUKE ELLINGTON
*Music Is My Mistress*


A woman of 47 who has been married 27 years and has
six children knows what love really is and once described
it for me like this: "Love is what you have been through
with somebody."
—JAMES THURBER
*Life*, March 14, 1960


To some people
Love is given
To others
Only heaven.
—LANGSTON HUGHES, "Luck"


Love consists of this, that two solitudes protect and touch
and greet each other.
—RAINER MARIA RILKE
*Letters to a Young Poet* (translated by M. D. Herter Norton)

Like love we don't know where or why
Like love can't compel or fly
Like love we often weep
Like love we seldom keep.
—W.H. AUDEN, "Law Like Love"


All women think they merit to be lov'd.
—OVID
*Ars Amatoria* (translated by John Dryden)


I'll be damned if I'll love just to love—there's got to be
more to it than that.
—JULIUS J. EPSTEIN, PHILIP G. EPSTEIN, AND HOWARD KOCH
*Casablanca*, spoken by Humphrey Bogart


No, there's nothing half so sweet in life
As love's young dream.
—THOMAS MOORE, "Love's Young Dream"
*Juvenile Poems*


Amo, amas, I love a lass,
As a cedar tall and slender,
Sweet cowslip's grace
Is her nom'native case
And she's of the feminine gender.
—JOHN O'KEEFE, "Amo, Amas"
*Agreeable Surprise*


Love has as few problems as a motorcar. The only problems are the driver, the passengers, and the road.
—FRANZ KAFKA (attributed)

Love is always revolutionary.
—ANDREI VOZNESENSKY


Ah—love—the walks over soft grass, the smiles over candlelight, the arguments over just about everything else.
—MAX HEADROOM


. . . and love is only and always about the lover and never
the beloved.
—NIKKI GIOVANNI, "They Clapped"


Love wakes men, once a lifetime each.
—COVENTRY PATMORE, "The Revelation"


# Love: Against

Love says, mine. Love says, I could eat you up. Love says
stay as you are, be my private thing, don't you dare have
ideas I don't share. Love has just got to gobble the other,
bones and all, crunch. I don't want to do that. I am sure I
don't want it done to me.
—MARGE PIERCY
*Braid and Lies*


Love is monotonous, incessant, boring; no one can stand
for anyone's repeating the most ingenious statement so
many times and yet the lover demands unending reitera-
tion that his beloved adores him. And vice versa: when
someone is not in love, love bestowed upon him oppresses
him and drives him mad by its utter plodding quality.
—JOSÉ ORTEGA Y GASSET

And all the little emptiness of love.
—RUPERT BROOKE, "Peace"
*New Numbers*


To be wise, and love,
Exceeds man's might.
—WILLIAM SHAKESPEARE
*Troilus and Cressida*


Love is a game—yes?
I think it is a drowning.
—AMY LOWELL, "What O'Clock"


Love, love, love—all the wretched cant of it, masking ego-
tism, lust, masochism, fantasy under a mythology of senti-
mental postures, a welter of self-induced miseries and
joys, blinding and masking the essential personalities in
frozen gestures of courtship, in the kissing and the dating
and the desire, the compliments and quarrels which vivify
its barrenness.
—GERMAINE GREER
*The Female Eunuch*


Love is a shadow
How can you lie and cry after it.
—SYLVIA PLATH, "Elm"


She's gone. I am abused, and my relief
Must be to loathe her.
—WILLIAM SHAKESPEARE
*Othello*

Oh love you've been a villian since the days of
    Troy and Helen,
When you caused the fall of Paris and of very
    many more.
—JAMES PLANCHÉ, "Love You've Been a Villain"


Love, oh love, oh loveless love
Has set our hearts on goalless goals
From silkless silk and milkless milk
We've growing used to soulless souls.
—BILLIE HOLLIDAY, "Loveless Love"


I love not for those eyes, nor hair
Nor cheeks, nor lips, nor teeth so rare,
Nor for thy speech, thy neck, nor breast,
Nor for thy belly, nor the rest;
Nor for thy hand nor foot so small:
But woulds't thou know, dear sweet? —for All.
—THOMAS CAREW, "Love's Compliment"


If thou must love me, let it be for nought
Except for love sake's only.
—ELIZABETH BARRETT BROWNING, "If Thou Must Love Me"


Don't send me off, now that your thirst
Is quenched and all seem so stale to you.
Keep me a short three months more,
Then I'll be sated too.
—HEINRICH HEINE

# Love and Marriage

Love is often the fruit of marriage.
—MOLIÈRE


One should always be in love. That is the reason one should not marry.
—OSCAR WILDE
*A Woman of No Importance*


Love is so much better when you are not married.
—MARIA CALLAS (attributed)


Love is an ideal thing, marriage is a real thing; a confusion of the real with the ideal never goes unpunished.
—JOHANN WOLFGANG VON GOETHE


"Love, shmove," Papa used to say, "I love blintzes; Did I marry one?"
—SAM LEVENSON
*In One Era and Out the Other*


People marry for a variety of other reasons and with varying results; but to marry for love is to invite inevitable tragedy.
—JAMES BRANCH CABELL
*The Cream of the Jest*


On the whole, I haven't found men unduly loath to say, "I love you." The real trick is to get them to say, "Will you marry me?"
—ILKA CHASE
*This Week*, February 5, 1956

# Love and Money

Kissing your hand may make you feel very, very good but
a diamond and sapphire bracelet lasts forever.
—ANITA LOOS
*Gentlemen Prefer Blondes*


Money cannot buy
the fuel of love
but is excellent kindling.
—W.H. AUDEN


Women prefer men who have something tender about
them—especially the legal kind.
—KAY INGRAM
*Reader's Digest*, May 1952


Heiresses are never jilted.
—GEORGE MEREDITH


Love lasteth as long as the money endureth.
—WILLIAM CAXTON
*The Game of Chesse*


Even a bald head
A pretty girl can hold
If he is willing
To pay his weight in gold.
*English Song*


Money can't buy love—but it certainly puts you in a wonderful bargaining position.
—HARRISON BAKER (attributed)

I don't pop my cork for every guy I see.
Hey! big spender, spend a little time with me.
—DOROTHY FIELDS, "Big Spender"


Her beauty was sold for an old man's gold—
She's a bird in a gilded cage.
—ARTHUR J. LAMB, "A Bird in a Gilded Cage"


Love can't last around poverty. Neither can a woman's looks.
—KRISTIN HUNTER
*The Landlord*


Romance without finance is no good.
—WILLIE "THE LION" SMITH
*Esquire,* 1964


Love conquers all except poverty and a toothache.
—MAE WEST (attributed)


A poor beauty finds more lovers than husbands.
—GEORGE HERBERT
*Outlandish Proverbs*


Lips, however rosy, must be fed.
—A.B. CHEALES
*Proverbial Folklore*


Money is the sinew of love as well as war.
—THOMAS FULLER
*Gnomologia: Adagies and Proverbs*

You sittin' down wonderin' what it's all about,
If you got no money, they'll put you out,
Why don't you do right like some other men do?
Get out of here, and get me some money too.
—JOE McCOY, "Why Don't You Do Right"


All matters of the heart cost money. Marriage does.
Affairs do. Divorce costs most of all.
—JONATHAN GATHORME-HARDY
*Marriage, Lover, Sex, Divorce*


Brigands demand your money or your life; women
demand both.
—SAMUEL BUTLER (attributed)


# Love and Sex

You mustn't force sex to do the work of love or love to do
the work of sex.
—MARY McCARTHY
*The Group*


Love is the self-delusion we manufacture to justify the
trouble we take to have sex.
—DAN GREENBERG


Nobody dies from the lack of sex. It's lack of love we die
from.
—MARGARET ATWOOD
*The Handmaid's Tale*

Lust is what makes you keep wanting it, even when you have no desire to be with each other. Love is what makes you keep wanting to be with each other, even when you have no desire to do it.
—JUDITH VIORST


Sex is a momentary itch
Love never lets you go.
—KINGSLEY AMIS, "An Ever-Fixed Mark"


You don't get high-quality sex without love.
—ALEX COMFORT
*The Joy of Sex*


It is not until sex has died out between a man and a woman that they can really love.
—ENID BAGNOLD
*Autobiography*


# Love Letters

Love makes me write what shame forbids me speak.
—ROBERT HERRICK, "What Shame Forbids to Speak"


I am two fools, I know
For loving, and for saying so
In whining Poetry.
—JOHN DONNE, "The Triple Fool"


At the touch of love everyone becomes a poet.
—PLATO
*Symposium*

And oft the pangs of absence to remove
By letters, soft interpreters of love.
—MATHEW PRIOR, "Henry and Emma"


But a woman's sayings to her lover,
Should be in wind and running water writ.
—CATULLUS
Carmina (translated by Sir W. Marris)


I don't know what you want or what I am! You write to
me like a love, you treat me like a casual acquaintance!
—EDITH WHARTON, letter to W. Morton Fullerton


Write to me. . . . And let not the ink serve as a mask.
—MANUEL UGARTE, letter to Delmira Agustini


They [lovers] read every word three ways; they read
between the lines and in the margins . . . They even take
punctuation into account.
—MORTIMER J. ADLER
Quote, December 26, 1961


Sir, more than kisses, letters mingle souls.
—JOHN DONNE, verse letter to Sir Henry Wotton


A woman's best love letters are always written to the man
she is betraying.
—LAURENCE DURRELL
Cleo

# Lovemaking

The act of sexual union is holy and pure.
—NAHMANIDES

We indulged in some foreplay, some during-play, and sometimes even some afterplay.
—ISAAC BASHEVIS SINGER
*Shosha*

I remember lovemaking as an exploration of a sadness so deep that people must go in pairs, one cannot go alone . . .
—JOHN UPDIKE
*Couples*

It was lovemaking, Doctor, even though it was nasty. Maybe especially because it was nasty. Love is smutty business, you know.
—TOM ROBBINS
*Even Cowgirls Get the Blues*

We no longer make love. We occasionally fuck . . .
—WALTER ABISH, "Parting Shot"

Here we will strip and cool our fire
In cream below, in milk-baths higher;
And when all wells are drawn dry,
I will drink a tear out of thine eye.
—RICHARD LOVELACE, "To Amarantha, That She Would Dishevel Her Hair"

Ladies never move.
—GEORGE NATHANIEL CURZON, to his second wife, on lovemaking

Wives have no need at all
For loose and limber motions, pelvic thrusts,
Abdominal gyrations . . .
—LUCRETIUS
*The Way Things Are* (translated by Rolfe Humphries)


. . . we lie together
after making love, quiet,
touching along the length of our bodies,
familiar touch of the long-married.
—GALWAY KINNELL, "After Making Love We Hear Footsteps"


Lovemaking is radical, while marriage is conservative.
—ERIC HOFFER


In lovemaking, as in other arts, those who do it best cannot tell how it is done.
—JAMES M. BARRIE


Making love to a woman too many times is like scratching a place that doesn't itch any more.
—ANONYMOUS


The prerequisite for making love is to like someone enormously.
—HELEN GURLEY BROWN (attributed)


It's time to make love. Douse the glim.
The fireflies twinkle and dim.
The stars lean together
Like birds of a feather
And the loin lies down with the limb.
—CONRAD AIKEN, "A Seizure of Limericks"


*See also:* SEXUAL INTERCOURSE.

# Lover

A whining lover is a sorry fool.
—ALEXANDER RATCLIFF, "A Satire Against Love"


Woman: You are the greatest lover I have ever known.
Allen: Well, I practice a lot when I am alone.
—WOODY ALLEN


You are the very one I've searched for
In many lands in every weather.
You are my sort; you understand me;
As equals we can talk together.
—HEINRICH HEINE, "Ich Liebe Solche Weissen Glieder" (translated by
Louis Untermeyer)


The sweeter the apple, the blacker the core,
Scratch a lover and find a foe.
—DOROTHY PARKER
*Ballade of a Great Weariness*


Lover, lunatic.
—PLAUTUS
*Mercater*


He's a deep-sea diver with a stroke that can't go wrong,
He's a deep-sea diver with a stroke that can't go wrong,
He can touch bottom and his wind holds out so long.
—BESSIE SMITH, "Empty Bed Blues"

Just like a snail: that man of mine
He never likes to hurry; he takes his time.
—TRIXIE SMITH, "He Likes It Slow"


He fell on me like a wave. But like a wave he washed
away, leaving no sign that he had been there.
—LOUISE ERDRICH


Lover, beware your lover, might well be an old maxim.
—MAXWELL ANDERSON
*Elizabeth the Queen*


We were no longer friend and friend
But only lover and lover.
—ELINOR WYLIE, "The Puritan's Ballad"


My lover is mine and I am his.
*Song of Songs*


Notoriously, women tolerate qualities in a lover—moodi-
ness, selfishness, unreliability, brutality—that they would
never countenance in a husband, in return for excitement,
an infusion of intense feeling.
—SUSAN SONTAG
*Village Voice*, April 16, 1982


# Lovers

Lovers are always in a hurry . . . like a racing river.
—BEN AMES WILLIAMS

A difficult achievement for true lovers
Is to lie mute, without embrace or kiss,
Without a rustle or smothered sigh
Basking each in the other's glory.
—ROBERT GRAVES, "The Starred Coverlet"


Lovers behave far more respectably than married couples.
Have you ever heard of a mistress-swapping party?
—JILLY COOPER
*Men and Super Men*


In every question and every remark tossed back and forth
between lovers who have not played out the last fugue,
there is one question and it is this: "Is there someone
new?"
—EDNA O'BRIEN
*Lantern Slides*


This maiden she lived with no other thought
Than to love and be loved by me.
—EDGAR ALLEN POE, "Annabel Lee"


I would not leave my little wooden hut for you!
I've got one lover and I don't want two.
—THOMAS MELLOR, "I Wouldn't Leave My Little Wooden Hut for You"


Love lasts or—or doesn't
. . .
Lovers must never crumple like cissies
Or breakdown or cry about their wrongs
If girls are sugar, God holds the sugar tongs.
—GAVIN EWART, "Ella Mi Fu Rapita!"

The world will always welcome lovers
As time goes by.
—HERMAN HUPFELD, "As Time Goes By"

# Lust

Love comforteth like sunshine after rain,
But Lust's effect is tempest after sun;
Love's gentle spring doth always fresh remain
Lust's winter comes ere summer half be done;
Love surfeits not, Lust like a glutton dies,
Love is all truth, Lust full of forged lies.
—WILLIAM SHAKESPEARE
*Venus and Adonis*

Lust will not keep.
Something must be done about it.
Inscription on the Entrance Gate to the Yoshiwara (the redlight district of
feudal Tokyo)

I was absolutely wild for her when she was a girl and I
was a boy, absolutely off of my head with volcanic lust. I
wanted to come, come, come.
—JOSEPH HELLER
*Something Happened*

So lust, though to a radiant angel link'd,
Will sate itself in a celestial bed
And prey on garbage.
—WILLIAM SHAKESPEARE
*Hamlet*

Thou deemest lust and love convertible.
—THOMAS HOCCLEVE
*De Regimine Principum*

The new lust gives the lecher the new thrill.
—JOHN MASEFIELD, "The Widow in Bye Street"

And concerning lust . . . it is a short pleasure, bought with long pain, a honeyed poison, a gulf of shame, a pickpurse, a breeder of diseases, a gall to the conscience, a corrosive to the heart, turning man's wit to foolish madness, the body's bane, and the soul's perdition.
—JOHN TAYLOR
*The Unnatural Father*

. . . wars, fires, plagues have not done that mischief to mankind as this burning lust, this brutish passion.
—ROBERT BURTON
*The Anatomy of Melancholy*

The most malignant of thy enemies is the lust that abides within thee.
—SADI
*Gulistan*

Lust is more abstract than logic; it seeks (hope triumphing over experience) for some purely sexual, hence purely imaginary, conjunction of an impossible maleness with an impossible femaleness.
—C.S. LEWIS
*The Allegory of Love*

Nonconformity and lust stalking hand and hand through
the country, wasting and ravaging.
—EVELYN WAUGH
*Decline and Fall*


The lust of the goat is the bounty of God.
—WILLIAM BLAKE
*The Marriage of Heaven and Hell*


Our lust is brief.
—JAMES JOYCE
*Ulysses*


Men triumph over women still,
Men trample women's rights at will,
And man's lust roves the world untamed.
—JOHN MASEFIELD, "C.L.M."


Let my lusts be my ruin, then, since all else is a fake and a
mockery.
—HART CRANE


O sick, insatiable
And constant lust.
—ROY FULLER, "Spring 1942"


The life of the universe depends upon the pudendum. As
soon as the Word was made flesh, man was unable to be
quiet, or work, or think, until he had dropped his seed.
—EDWARD DAHLBERG

But when lust
By unchaste looks, loose gestures, and foul talk,
But most by lewd and lavish act of sin,
Lets in defilement to the inward parts,
The soul grows clotted by contagion . . .
—JOHN MILTON, "Comus"


I've looked at a lot of women with lust. I've committed
adultery in my heart many times. This is something God
recognizes I will do—and I have done it—and God for-
gives me.
—JIMMY CARTER


For forty years I shunned the lust
Inherent in my clay.
Death only was so amorous
I let him have his way.
—COUNTEE CULLEN, "For A Virgin Lady"


I'd call it love if love
didn't take so many years
but lust too is a jewel
a sweet flower . . .
—ADRIENNE RICH
*Necessities of Life*


Lust is like rot in the bones.
*Babylonian Talmud*


Sexual lust ties up like a rope.
—MAHABHARATA

# Male and Female

The two sexes mutually corrupt and improve each other.
—MARY WOLLSTONECRAFT
*A Vindication of the Rights of Women*


And forget the He and She.
—JOHN DONNE, "The Undertaking"


A woman is a woman until the day she dies, but a man is only a man as long as he can.
—MOMS MABLEY (attributed)


Blessings are found only where male and female are together.
*The Kabbalah*


There never will be any rest between male and female so long as more than one of each exists upon earth or anywhere else.
—CHARLES BUKOWSKI, "Back Up"


For men at most differ as Heaven and Earth
But women, worst and best, as Heaven and Hell.
—ALFRED, Lord Tennyson
*The Idylls of the King*

What is it men in women require?
The lineaments of gratified desire.
What is it women do in men require?
The lineaments of gratified desire.
—WILLIAM BLAKE, "A Question Answered"


Men and women, women and men. It will never work.
—ERICA JONG


Why can't a woman be more like a man?
—ALAN J. LERNER
*My Fair Lady*


Nothing can vex
Like the opposite sex.
—GEORGE STARBUCK GALBRAITH
*Reader's Digest*, November 1956


It takes all sorts to make a sex.
—SAKI (attributed)


Male and female sexuality exist like "His" and "Hers"
sweaters. The measurable difference is slight but it is highly
significant . . .
—BEATRICE FAUST
*Women, Sex and Pornography*


*See also:* MEN AND WOMEN IN LOVE.

# Male Chauvinism

But machismo is about the conquest and humiliation of women.
—V.S. NAIPAUL
*The Return of Eva Peron*


They fear women, so hate them, but as most are latently homosexual they fear that more, so fifty times a day boastfully and loudly proclaim for each other's benefit that they would hump a rockpile if they thought a snake were underneath it.
—ALEXANDER THEROUX
*Darconville's Cat*


Macho does not prove mucho.
—ZSA ZSA GABOR (attributed)


The male whale's penis is over six feet long . . . Whenever there is a particularly obnoxious male chauvinist doing his thing, the thought always dashes through my head. "What would you say If I made you aware at this very moment that you are no bigger than a whale's "hard-on"?
—JUDIANNE DENSEN-GERBER
*Walk in My Shoes*


Like all rogues, he was a great calumniator of the fair sex.
—SIR WALTER SCOTT
*The Heart of Midlothian*


It's up to the 'brothers'—they'll have to make up their own minds as to whether they will divested of just cock privilege or—what the hell, why not say it—divested of cocks.
—ROBIN MORGAN
*Rat. Subterranean News* (New York)

# Marital Conflict

I'm not living with you. We occupy the same cage.
—TENNESSEE WILLIAMS
*A Cat on a Hot Tin Roof*

The best part of married life are the fights. The rest is merely so-so.
—THORNTON WILDER
*The Matchmaker*

They waste their strength in venereal strife.
—LUCRETIUS
*Concerning the Nature of Love*

The only solid and lasting peace between a man and a woman is doubtless a separation.
—LORD CHESTERFIELD

The life of a wife and husband who love each other is never at rest. Whether the mariage is true or false, the marriage portion is the same: elemental discord.
—JEAN GIRAUDOUX
*Tiger at the Gates*

Don't look back in anger, look forward in fury.
—ANONYMOUS

With women the heart argues, not the mind.
—MATTHEW ARNOLD

Almost all married people fight, although many are ashamed to admit it. Actually, a marriage in which no quarreling takes place may well be one that is dead or dying from emotional undernourishment. If you care, you probably fight.

—FLORA DAVIS

*Glamour*, March 1969

In every house of marriage there's room for an interpreter.

—STANLEY KUNITZ

*Route Six*

Your old-fashioned tirade—
loving, rapid, merciless
breaks like the Atlantic Ocean over my head.

—ROBERT LOWELL, "Man and Wife"

Marriage accustomed one to the good things, so one came to take them for granted, but it magnified the bad things, so they came to feel as painful as a grain in one's eye. An open window, a forgotten quart of milk, a TV set left blaring, socks on the bathroom floor could become occasions for incredible rage.

—MARILYN FRENCH

*The Women's Room*

All married couples should learn the art of battle as they should learn the art of making love. Good battle is objective and honest—never vicious and cruel. Good battle is healthy and constructive, and brings to the marriage the principle of equal partnership.

—ANN LANDERS

*Ann Landers Says Truth Is Stranger*

Marriage is like life in this—that it is a field of battle and not a bed of roses.
ROBERT LOUIS STEVENSON
*Virginibus Puerisque*


In saying what is obvious, never choose cunning. Yelling works better.
—CYNTHIA OZICK
*The First Ms. Reader*


I find my wife hath something in her gizzard that only waits for an opportunity of being provoked to bring up; but I will not, for my content-sake, give it.
—SAMUEL PEPYS
*Diary*


I say, when there are spats, kiss and make up before the day is done and live to fight another day.
—REV. RANDOLPH RAY
*New York World-Telegraph and The Sun*


# Marriage

If it were not for the presents, an elopement would be preferable.
—GEORGE ADE


Love is often a fruit of marriage.
—MOLIÈRE
*Sganarelle*

Strange to say what delight we married people have to see poor fools decoyed into our condition.
—SAMUEL PEPYS

*Diary*


A man has no business to marry a woman who can't make him miserable. It means she can't make him happy
—ANONYMOUS


If only the strength of the love that people feel when it is reciprocated could be as intense and obsessive as the love we feel when it is not; then marriages would truly be made in heaven.
—BEN ELTON, "Private Investigations"


One should always marry in the same way as one dies; that is, only when it impossible to do otherwise.
—LEO TOLSTOY


It takes two to make a marriage a success and only one a failure.
—HERBERT LOUIS SAMUEL

*A Book of Quotations*


> To keep your marriage brimming,
> With love in the loving cup
> Whenever you're wrong, admit it;
> Whenever you're right, shut up.
> —OGDEN NASH, "A Word to Husbands"


Marriage should war incessantly against a monster that is the ruin of everything. This is the monster of custom.
—HONORÉ DE BALZAC

*The Physiology of Marriage*

I can't fall in love. That's probably what holds my marriage together.
—JOSEPH HELLER
*Something Happened*


Nor shall I presume to judge the marriage. Not only is one chap's meat another man's poison, but what nourishes at twenty may nauseate at forty, and vice versa.
—JOHN BARTH
*Letters*


A good marriage is one that can survive the ninety-day euphoria of romantic love.
—EDWARD ABBEY
*A Curmudgeon's Garden of Love* by John Winoker


There are good marriages, but there are no delicious ones.
—FRANÇOIS, Duc de La Rochefucauld
*Réflexiones ou sentences et maximes morales*


Oh, bring me gifts, or beg me gifts,
And wed me if you will!
I'd make a man a good wife,
Sensible and still.
—EDNA ST. VINCENT MILLAY, "Sonnet"


If I were a girl, I'd despair; the supply of good women far exceeds that of the men who deserve them.
—ROBERT GRAVES


If you want to sacrifice the admiration of many men for the criticism of one, go ahead and get married.
—KATHARINE HOUGHTON HEPBURN, to her daughter Katherine
*A Remarkable Woman* by Anne Edwards

The only thing about marriage that appealed to me was sex without scandal: husbands could be counted on not to ask "How come you let me go all the way?"
—FLORENCE KING
*Confessions of a Failed Southern Lady*

Marriage is our last, best chance to grow up.
—REV. JOSEPH BARTH
*Ladies Home Journal,* April 1961

By all means marry; if you get a good wife, you'll become happy; if you get a bad one, you'll become a philosopher.
—SOCRATES

A good marriage is that in which each appoints the other guardian of his solitude.
—RAINER MARIA RILKE
*Letters* (translated by Jane Barnard Greene and M.D. Herter Norton)

Is this an age to buckle with a bride?
—JUVENAL
*Satire VI* (translated by John Dryden)

Girls, leave matrimony alone; it's the hardest way on earth to get a living.
—FANNY FERN
*Feminist Dictionary* by C. Kramarae and P.A. Treichler

The trouble with wedlock is, there's not enough wed and too much lock.
—CHRISTOPHER MORLEY
*Kitty Foyle*

Thus grief still treads upon the heels of pleasure:
Marry'd in haste, we may repent in leisure.
Some by experience find these words misplac'd:
At leisure marry'd, they repent in haste.

—WILLIAM CONGREVE, "The Old Bachelor"


I wonder what Adam and Eve
think about it by this time.

—MARIANNE MOORE, "Marriage"

*Collected Poems*


Except for poverty, incompatibility, opposition of parents,
absence of love on one side and of desire to marry on
both, nothing stands in way of our happy union.

—CYRIL CONNOLLY

*Journal and Memoir* by D. Pryce-Jones


Hail wedded love, mysterious law, true source
Of human offspring, sole propriety,
In Paradise of all things common else.

—JOHN MILTON, "Comus"


I married beneath me. All women do.

—NANCY WITCHER LANGHORNE ASTOR

*The Dictionary of National Biography*


When ye unite with another, do so with deep consciousness of the greatness of the dignity of that which you do!
Give yourself to this work of love; with your souls and
with your minds, even as with your flesh.

—OMAR HALEBY

*El Ktab*

I love being married. It's so great to find the one special person you want to annoy for the rest of your life.
—RITA RUDNER

# Marriage: Against

Where I love, I must not marry;
Where I marry, cannot love.
—THOMAS MOORE, "Love and Marriage"
*Juvenile Poems*

It doesn't much signify whom one marries, for one is sure to find out the next morning it was someone else.
—WILL ROGERS (attributed)

The music of a wedding procession always reminds me of the music of soldiers going into battle.
—HEINRICH HEINE (attributed)

Marriage is a mantrap baited with simulated accomplishments and delusive idealizations.
—GEORGE BERNARD SHAW
*Man and Superman*

Marriage is a bribe to make a housekeeper think she is a householder.
—THORNTON WILDER
*The Matchmaker*

The surest way to be alone is to get married.
—GLORIA STEINEM


Marry?

. . .

Better drain a cup of shame
Than play the wedding-game.
Better wallow in the mud
Then spill the hymeneal blood.
Never shall a wife rob me
Of my treasured liberty.
—FRANÇOIS RABELAIS
*Gargantua and Pantagruel*


Marriage may be compared to a cage:
the birds outside despair to get in;
those within despair to get out.
—MICHEL DE MONTAIGNE
*Essays*


Hanging and wiving go by destiny.
—JOHN HEYWOOD
*A Dialogue Containing the Number in Effect of All the Proverbs in the English Tongue*


Marriage always demands the greatest understanding of
the art of insincerity possible between two human beings.
—VICKI BAUM
*And Life Goes On*


Marriage is like pantyhose. It all depends on what you
put into it.
—PHYLLIS SCHLAFLY
*The Boston Globe*, July 16, 1974

Take my wife . . . Please!
—HENNY YOUNGMAN

[Love] can be intimacy and attachment, the wedding of
two solids by the heat of passion in a union that may
endure forever, if it does not crack under the hammer
blows of life or waste away under the monotonous drip of
ever-haunting trivia.
—ERIC BERNE
*Games People Play*

I have always thought that every woman should marry
and no man.
—BENJAMIN DISRAELI
*Lothair*

Of all serious things, marriage is the most ludicrous.
—PIERRE-AUGUSTIN BEAUMARCHAIS
*The Marriage of Figaro*

The only charm of marriage is that it makes a life of
deception necessary for both parties.
—OSCAR WILDE

All my friends at school grew up and settled down
Then they mortgaged up their lives
. . .
They just got married 'cos there's nothing else to do.
—MICK JAGGER AND KEITH RICHARD, "Sitting on a Fence"

Marriage is rather a silly habit.
—JOHN OSBORNE (attributed)

You study one another for three weeks, you love each other for three months, you fight for three years and you tolerate the situation for thirty.
—ANDRÉ DE MISSON


Married. It was like a dream come true for Donna. Just think, soon her little girl would have unpaid bills, unplanned babies, calls from the bank, and sub-standard housing. All the things a mother dreams for her child.
—ERMA BOMBECK


For the crown of our life as it closes
Is darkness, the fruit thereof of dust
No thorns go as deep as a rose's
And love is more cruel than lust.
Time turns the old days to derision
Our love into corpses or wives
And marriage and death and division
Make barren our lives.
—A.C. SWINBURNE, "Dolores"


What revolution can appear so strange,
As such a lecher, such a life to change?
A rank, notorious whoremaster, to choose
To thrust his neck into the marriage noose!
—JUVENAL
   *Satire VI* (translated by John Dryden)


Marriage. The beginning and end are wonderful. The middle part is hell.
—ENID BAGNOLD
   *The Chalk Garden*

Two by two in the ark of
the ache of it.
—DENISE LEVERTOV, "The Ache of Marriage"


"I don't hate him," Athenaise answered . . . "It's jus' being
married that I detes' an' despise."
—KATE CHOPIN, "Athenaise"


I'll hug. I'll kiss. I'll play.
And, cock-like, hens I'll tread,
And sport in any way
But not in the bridal bed
—ROBERT HERRICK


# Marriage: For

The peace of God came into my life when I wedded her.
—ALFRED, Lord Tennyson (attributed, about his wife)


Reverend and honorable matrimony,
Mother of lawful sweets, unashamed mornings,
Dangerous pleasures.
—THOMAS MIDDLETON
  *The Phoenix*


Some pray to marry the man they love
My prayer will somewhat vary:
I humbly pray to heaven above
That I love the man I marry.
—ROSE PASTOR STOKES, "My Prayer"

Should I get married? Should I be good?
...
Because what if I am 60 years old and not married,
all alone in a furnished room with pee stains on my
underwear
and everybody else is married.
—GREGORY CORSO, "Marriage"

His pulse beats matrimony.
—JOHN RAY
*English Proverbs*

The value of marriage is not that adults produce children
but that children produce adults.
—PETER DE VRIES
*The Tunnel of Love*

# Marriage and Sex

I was about to cross legs with legs.
—LUCILIUS
*Satires*

I am wanton and lascivious,
And cannot live without a wife.
—CHRISTOPHER MARLOWE
*Dr. Faustus*

If four bare legs in bed were the main thing, mighty few
marriages would last.
—ANONYMOUS

Sex is the foundation of marriage
—TH. VAN DE VELDE
*Ideal Marriage*


It is a weak man who marries for love.
—SAMUEL JOHNSON
*The Life of Samuel Johnson* by James Boswell


Better to sit up all night than to go to bed with a dragon.
—JEREMY TAYLOR
*Holy Living*


Mighty is love, but most in naked wedlock.
— SEXTUS AURELIUS PROPERTIUS


Here's to woman! Would that we could fall into her arms without falling into her hands.
—AMBROSE BIERCE (attributed)


# Masturbation

Sophisticated persons masturbate without compunction. They do it for reasons of health, privacy, thrift, and because of the remarkable perfection of invisible partners.
—P.J. O'ROURKE
*Modern Manners*


Masturbation: the primary sexual activity of mankind. In the nineteenth century it was a disease; in the twentieth, it's a cure.
—THOMAS SZASZ, "Sex"
*The Second Sin*

Don't knock masturbation. It is sex with someone I love.
—WOODY ALLEN AND MARSHALL BRICKMAN
*Annie Hall*

If God had intended us not to masturbate he would have made our arms shorter.
—GEORGE CARLIN

Recently, when I am alone I try to talk myself out of masturbation. I ask myself why can't I just be friends with myself.
—RICHARD LEWIS

Masturbation is the thinking man's television.
—CHRISTOPHER HAMPTON (attributed)

i learned how
to masturbate
through the new york times
—SONIA SANCHEZ, "Summary"
*Black Fire*

I write in praise of the solitary act;
of not feeling as trespassing tongue
forced into one's mouth . . . Five minutes of solitude are
enough—in the bath, or to fill
the gap between the Sunday papers and lunch.
—FLEUR ADCOCK, "Against Coupling"

And while Ulysses snored, chaste Penelope
put her delicate hand to use.
—MARTIAL
*Select Epigrams of Martial* (translated and adapted by Donald G. Goertz)

Never fail to have your wife's circlet tight about your middle finger.
—FRANÇOIS RABELAIS
*Gargantua and Pantagruel*


# Memory

Lovers remember everything.
—OVID
*Heroïdes*


Wolves lose their teeth but not their memory.
—THOMAS DRAXE
*Bibliotheca*


April is the cruelest month, breeding
Lilacs out of the dead land, mixing
Memory and desire, stirring
Dull roots with spring rain.
—T.S. ELIOT, "The Waste Land"


Old as I am, for ladies' love unfit,
The power of beauty I remember yet.
—JOHN DRYDEN, "Cymon and Iphigenia"


Remember me when I am gone
Gone far away into the silent land.
. . .
Better by far you should forget and smile
Than that you should remember and be sad.
—CHRISTINA ROSSETTI, "Remember"

Hast thou forgotten ere I forget?
—A.C. SWINBURNE, "Itylus"


What lips my lips have kissed, and where, and why,
I have forgotten . . .
. . .
I can not say what loves have come and gone;
I only know that summer sang in me
A little while, that in me sings no more.
—EDNA ST. VINCENT MILLAY, "What My Lips Have Kissed"


# Men

. . . cocksure, cocky gamecock
—LUIS RAPHAEL SANCHEZ
*Macho Camacho's Beat*


Man is the only animal that eats when he is not hungry,
drinks when he is not thristy, and makes love at all seasons
—ANONYMOUS


Man is the only animal who injures his mate.
—LUDOVICO ARIOSTO
*Orlando Furioso*


Some men break your heart in two,
Some men fawn and flatter,
Some men never look at you,
and that cleans up the matter.
—DOROTHY PARKER, "Experience"

why this baby, this boy, this baby-man
he's just a mass of contradictions
claims reason for himself
institutionalizes his hatred
gives her his seat on the bus
wages war in Indochina
and nods off in front of the TV
and dreams of mommy
and dreams of power
This baby will not grow up
he thinks he can do what he wants
he has fastened his mouth on my life.
—SONDRA SEGAL, "The Baby-Man,"
*Heresies 1981*

# Men and Women in Love

To women, love is an occupation; to men it is a preoccupation.
—LIONEL STRACHEY (attributed)


When he will, she won't; and when he won't, she will.
—TERENCE


Woman wants monogamy;
Man delights in novelty.
Love is a woman's moon and sun;
Man has other forms of fun.
Woman lives but in her lord;
Count to ten and man is bored.
With this the gist and sum of it,
What earthly good can come of it?
—DOROTHY PARKER, "General Review of the Sex Situation"
*Not So Deep at the Well*

The word love has by no means the same sense for both sexes, and this is one cause of the serious misunderstandings between them.
—SIMONE DE BEAUVOIR


Man dreams of fame while woman wakes to love.
—ALFRED, Lord Tennyson
*The Idylls of the King*


Man's love is of man's life a thing apart
'Tis a woman's whole existence.
—GEORGE GORDON, Lord Byron
*Don Juan*


Man's love is of man's life a thing apart;
Girls aren't like that.
—KINGSLEY AMIS
*A Bookshop Idyll*


Man begins by making love and ends by loving a woman; woman begins by loving a man and ends by loving love.
—REMY DE GOURMONT


For a woman loves forever, but a man loves for a day . . .
But it is the woman, ever the woman, who pays.
—W.D. COBB, "It's the Woman Who Pays"


*See also:* MALE AND FEMALE.

# Middle Age

all that we might have been,
all that we were    fire, tears,
wit, taste, martyred ambition —
stirs like the memory of refused adultery
the drained and flagging bosom of our middle years.
—ADRIENNE RICH, "Snapshots of a Daughter-in-Law"


On his bold visage middle age
Had slightly press'd its signet sage,
Yet had not quenched the open truth
And fiery vehemence of youth;
Forward and frolic glee was there
The will to do, the soul to dare.
—WALTER SCOTT
  *The Lady of the Lake*


When I was young I used to have successes with women
because I was young. Now I have successes with women
because I am old. Middle age is the hardest part.
—ARTHUR RUBINSTEIN (attributed)


Older women are best because they always think they
may be doing it for the last time.
—IAN FLEMING (attributed)


Oh, come in Middle Age, come in, come in!
Come close to me, give me your hand, let me look on
your face . . . Oh . . . Is that what you really look like?
Oh God help me . . . help me.
—DOROTHY PARKER
  *The Middle or Blue Period*

# The Mind

The mind is always the dupe of the heart.
—FRANÇOIS, Duc de La Rochefaucauld
*Réflexions ou sentences et maximes morales*


. . . sex is all in the head, i.e., dumb girls, dumb screwing.
—WILLIAM STYRON
*Sophie's Choice*


Adulterers and customers of whores
And cunning takers of virginities
Caper from bed and bed, but not because
The flesh is pricked to infidelities.

The body is content with homely fare
It is the avid, curious mind that craves
New pungent sauce and strips the larder bare,
The palate and not hunger enslaves.
—JOHN PRESS, "Womanizers"


The mind is an erogenous zone.
—DAVID FROST (attributed)


Modest woman chooses a man by the mind, not the eye.
—PUBLILIUS SYRUS
*Sententiae*


When beauty fires the blood, how love exalts the mind.
—JOHN DRYDEN, "Cymon and Iphigenia"


And love's the noblest frailty of the mind.
—JOHN DRYDEN
*The Indian Emperor*

I must have women. There is nothing unbends the mind
like them.
—JOHN GAY
*The Beggar's Opera*


Beauty's the thing that counts
In women: red lips
And black eyes are better than brains.
—MARY J. ELMENDORF
*Beauty's the Thing*


There are no chaste minds. Minds copulate wherever they
meet.
—ERIC HOFFER
*Reflections on the Human Condition*


The human mind is capable of excitement without the
application of gross and violent stimulants; and he must
have a very faint perception of its beauty and dignity who
does not know this.
—WILLIAM WORDSWORTH
*Lyrical Ballads* (Preface)


People will begin to explore all the sidestreets of sexual
experience, but they will do this intellectually . . . Sex
won't take place in the bed, necessarily—it will take place
in the head!
—J.G. BALLARD
*Penthouse,* September 1980


*See also:* BRAIN.

# Mistresses

Let's face it, I have been momentary,
A luxury. A bright red sloop in the harbor.
—ANNE SEXTON, "For My Lover: Returning to His Wife"

People often say that, by pointing out to a man the faults
of his mistress, you succeed only in strengthening his
attachment to her, because he does not believe you; yet
how much more if he does!
—MARCEL PROUST
*Remembrance of Things Past: Swann in Love*

Coquettes know how to please, not how to love, that is
why men love them so.
—PIERRE MARIVAUX
*Lettres sur les habitants de Paris*

Tell him it's all a lie,
I love him as much as my life;
He wouldn't be jealous of me—
I love him and loathe his wife.
"A Learned Mistress" (translated by Frank O'Connor)
*Some Irish Loving* by Edna O'Brien

The trouble of finding a husband for one's mistress, is that
no other man seems quite good enough.
—WILLIAM COOPER
*Scenes from Provincial Life*

What is the worst portion in this mortal life?
A pensive mistress, and a yelping wife.
—THEODORE ROETHKE, "The Marrow"

So mistresses tend to get a steady diet of whipped cream, but no meat and potatoes, and wives often get the reverse, when both would like a bit of each.
—MERLE SHAIN
*Some Men Are More Perfect Than Others*


Chaste to her husband, frank to all beside,
A teeming mistress, but a barren bride.
—ALEXANDER POPE
*Moral Essays*


Buy old masters. They fetch a better price than old mistresses.
—LORD BEAVERBROOK (attributed)


When you marry your mistress, you create a job vacancy.
—SIR JAMES GOLDSMITH (attributed)


Every man wants a woman to appeal to his better side, his nobler instincts and his higher nature, and another woman to help him forget them.
—HELEN ROWLAND


No, make me mistress to the man I love
If there be yet another name more free
More fond than mistress, make me that to thee!
—ALEXANDER POPE, "Eloisa to Abelard"


The Western custom of one wife and hardly any mistresses.
—SAKI
*Reginald in Russia*

Since mistress presupposes wife
It means a doubly costly life.
—PETER DE VRIES, "To His Impassionate Mistress"


# Moderation

A great soul prefers moderation to excess.
—SENECA
*Epistulae Morales*


It is good trying the sack before it is full.
—GEORGE HERBERT
*Jacula Prudentum*


Sheer the sheep but don't flay them.
*Dutch Proverb*


Too much spoils, too little does not satisfy.
—JOHN HOWELL
*Proverbs*


Therefore love moderately; long love doth so;
Too swift arrives as tardy as too slow.
—WILLIAM SHAKESPEARE
*Romeo and Juliet*

# Modesty

Suit the action to the word, the word to the action; with this special observance, that you o'er step not the modesty of nature.
—WILLIAM SHAKESPEARE
*Hamlet*

Modesty died when clothes were born.
—MARK TWAIN (attributed)

A woman who goes to bed with a man ought to lay aside her modesty with her skirt and put it on again with her petticoat.
—MICHEL DE MONTAIGNE
*Essays*

Modesty is hardly to be described as a virtue. It is a feeling rather than a disposition. It is a kind of fear of falling into disrepute.
—ARISTOTLE
*The Nichomachean Ethics*

Women commend a modest man, but like him not.
—THOMAS FULLER
*Gnomologia: Adagies and Proverbs*

Modesty, which is regarded as a feminine characteristic *par excellence*, but is far more a matter of convention than one would think, was, in our opinion, originally designed to hide the deficiency in her genitals.
—SIGMUND FREUD
*New Introductory Lecture on Psychanalysis*

A gaudy dress and gentle air
May slightly touch the heart,
But it's innocence and modesty
That polishes the dart.
—ROBERT BURNS, "She Walks in Beauty"

# Monogamy

Love has been in perpetual strife with monogamy.
—ELLEN KAY (attributed)

It is politically incorrect
to demand monogamous
relationships
. . .
Me i am
totally opposed to
monogamous relationships
unless
i'm
in love.
—PAT PARKER, "A Small Contradiction"

Go sow your wild oats
And reap as you will
I hoe in one furrow.
—EVE MERRIAM, "Monogomania"

We tried to smash monogamy, but it was ourselves who
crashed, to slink off to coupledom and middle age.
—LINDA GRANT
*Sexing the Millennium*

*See also:* MARRIAGE; POLYGAMY.

# Morality

The so-called new morality is the old immorality condoned.
—LORD SHAWCROSS
*The Observer,* November 17, 1963

As soon as one is unhappy one becomes moral.
—MARCEL PROUST
*Within a Budding Grove*

Morality in sexual relations, when it is free from superstition, consists essentially of respect for the other person, and unwillingness to use that person solely as a means of personal gratification, without regard to his or her desires.
—BERTRAND RUSSELL
*Marriage and Morals*

Love is moral without legal marrriage, but marriage is immoral without love.
—ELLEN KEY
*The Morality of Woman and Other*

What is beautiful is moral, that is all there is to it.
—GUSTAVE FLAUBERT, letter to Guy de Maupassant

We are told by moralists with the plainest faces that immorality will spoil our looks.
—LOGAN PEARSALL SMITH

# Music

A love song is just a caress set to music.
—SIGMUND ROMBERG (attributed)


Music is an incitement to love.
—LATIN PROVERB


The lascivious pleasing of a lute.
—WILLIAM SHAKESPEARE
*Richard III*


Music, moody food
of us that trade in love.
—WILLIAM SHAKESPEARE
*Antony and Cleopatra*


Low, raunchy music: A hard, mean fuck you! sound.
. . . cock-stroking rock 'n roll.
—ALBERT GOLDMAN
*Ladies and Gentlemen, Lenny Bruce*


My music isn't supposed to make you wanna riot! My
music is supposed to make you wanna fuck!
—JANIS JOPLIN (attributed)

# Nakedness

No woman so naked as one you can see to be naked underneath her clothes.
—MICHAEL FRAYN
  *Constructions*

I wasn't really naked. I simply didn't have any clothes on.
—JOSEPHINE BAKER

Man is the sole animal whose nudities offend his companions and the only one who, in his natural actions, withdraws and hides himself from his own kind.
—MICHEL DE MONTAIGNE
  *Essays*

As souls unbodied, bodies unclothed most be
To taste whole joys.
    . . .
To teach thee, I am naked first; why then
What need'st thou have more covering than a man.
—JOHN DONNE, "To His Mistress Going to Bed"

The body of someone we love is not altogether naked, but is clothed and framed in our feelings.

—ANATOLE BOYARD

*The New York Times*, July 4, 1979


Is nakedness indecent? No, not inherently. It is your thought, your sophistication, your fear, your respectability, that is indecent. There come moods when these clothes of ours are not only irksome to wear, but are themselves indecent.

—WALT WHITMAN

*Specimen Days*


. . . no nude, however abstract, should fail to arouse in the spectator some vestige of erotic feeling, even if it be only the faintest shadow—and if it does not do so it is bad art and false morals.

—KENNETH CLARK

*The Nude*


a pretty girl who is naked
is worth a million statues.

—E.E. CUMMINGS

*Collected Poems*


For me, the naked and nude
(By lexicographers construed
As synonyms that should express
The same deficiency of dress
Or shelter) stand as wide apart
As love from lies, as truth from art.

—ROBERT GRAVES, "The Naked and the Nude"

If God had meant people to wear clothes they would have
been born that way.
—ADVERTISEMENT
*The Village Voice*


Then she rode forth, clothed on with chastity.
—ALFRED, Lord Tennyson, "Godiva"


To be naked is to be oneself. To be nude is to be seen
naked by other, and yet not recognized for oneself . . .
Nudity is a form of dress.
—JOHN BERGER
*Ways of Seeing*


In naked beauty most adorned.
—JOHN MILTON
*Paradise Lost*


The pride of the peacock is the glory of God
The lust of the goat is the bounty of God
The wrath of the lion is the wisdom of God
The nakedness of women is the work of God.
—WILLIAM BLAKE
*Proverbs of Hell*


. . . the very sight of naked parts causes enormous,
exceeding concupiscence, and stirs up in both men and
women burning lust.
—ROBERT BURTON
*The Anatomy of Melancholy*


She shall pull off her clothing, laying bare her ripeness . . .
*The Epic Of Gilgamesh*

A woman is truly beautiful only when she is naked and she knows it.

—ANDRÉ COURRÈGES

*Metropolitan Museum of Modern Art Bulletin*


Show me thy feet, show me thy legs, thy thighs,
Show me those fleshy principalities;
Show me that hill where smiling love doth sit,
Having a living fountain under it;
Show me thy waist, then let me there withal,
By the ascension of thy lawn, see all.

—ROBERT HERRICK

*To Diareme*


Naked I came, and naked I leave the scene,
And naked was my pastime in between.

—JAMES VINCENT CUNNINGHAM, "Five Epigrams"


How idiotic civilization is! Why be given a body if you have to keep it shut up in a case like a rare, rare fiddle?

—KATHERINE MANSFIELD

*Bliss and Other Stories*


# Nature of Love

Love is begot by fancy, bred
By ignorance, by expectation fed,
Destroyed by knowledge, and at best
Lost in the moment 'tis possessed.

—GEORGE GRANVILLE, Baron Lansdowne, "Love"

It is all made of sighs and tears; —
. . .
It is all made of faith and service; —
. . .
It is all made of fantasy,
All made of passion, and all made of wishes;
All adoration, duty, and observance;
All humbleness, all patience, and impatience;
All purity, all trial, all obeisance.
  —WILLIAM SHAKESPEARE
    *As You Like It*


Soon hot, soon cold
  *English Proverb*


Love will creep where it cannot go.
  *English Proverb*


Love will find a way.
  *English Proverb*


Love begets love.
  *Latin Proverb*


In love, everything is true, everything is false; and it is the
one subject on which one cannot express an absurdity.
  —SÉB ASTION CHAMFORT
    *Maximes et pensées*


Love is an affectation of a mind that has nothing better to
engage it.
  —THEOPHRASTUS

Love is a capricious creature which desires everything
and can be contented with almost nothing.
—MADELINE DE SCUDÉRY, "De l'amour"
  *Choix de pensées*


Teenagers don't know what love is. They have mixed up
ideas. They go for a drive, and the boy runs out of gas,
and they smooch a little and the girl says she loves him.
That isn't love. Love is when you are married twenty-five
years, smooching in your living room, and he runs out of
gas and she says she still loves him. That's love.
—NORM CROSBY


A woman can be proud and stiff
When on love intent;
But Love has pitched his mansion in
The place of excrement;
For nothing can be sole or whole
That has not been rent.
—WILLIAM BUTLER YEATS, "Crazy Jane Talks With the Bishop"
  *Words for Music Perhaps*


In real love you want the other person's good. In romantic
love you want the other person.
—MARGARET ANDERSON
  *The Fiery Fountains*


# Ninety

I always felt that a woman has the right to treat the subject of her age with ambiguity until, perhaps, she passes
into the realm of over ninety. Then it is better she be candid with herself and with the world.
—HELENA RUBINSTEIN
  *My Life for Beauty*

What I wouldn't give to be seventy again!

—OLIVER WENDELL HOLMES (attributed), at age 92, upon seeing a
pretty girl struggle with her skirts in the wind

# No!

To think is to say No.

—ALAIN (ÉMILE CHARTIER)

*Le citoyen contre les pouvoirs*


It's not 'cause I shouldn't,
It's not 'cause I wouldn't,
It's not 'cause I couldn't,
It's simply because I am the laziest girl in town.

—COLE PORTER, "Laziest Girl in Town"


I must say . . . a fast word about oral contraception. I
asked a girl to go to bed with me and she said "no."

—WOODY ALLEN, at a nightclub, Washington D.C., April 1965


Say No, and you'll never be married.

—JAMES KELLY

*Complete Collection of Scottish Proverbs*


When the denial becomes fainter and fainter,
And her eyes give what her tongue does deny
Ah what a trembling I feel when I venture,
Ah what a trembling does usher my Joy!

—JOHN DRYDEN, "Love's Fancy"

Pray, don't say no, until you are asked.
—JONATHAN SWIFT
*Polite Conversations*


But fast she holds my hands, and close her thighs,
And what she longs to do, with frowns denies.
—DUKE OF BUCKINGHAM, 'The Happy Night"


Chloe blush'd and frown'd and swore,
And pushed me rudely from her;
I call'd her Faithless, Jilting Whore,
To talk to me of honour;
But when I arose and would be gone,
She cried, wither go ye?
—NICHOLAS ROWE, "Chloe Blush'd and Frown'd and Swore"


Saying no the maiden shakes her head up and down.
*Japanese Proverb*


When Venus said "Spell no for me."
"N-O," Dan Cupid wrote with glee.
And smiled at his success.
"Ah child" said Venus, laughing low.
"We women do not spell it so.
We spell it "Y-E-S."
—CAROLYN WELLS, "The Spelling Lesson"


Have you not heard it said full oft
A woman's nay doth stand for naught.
—WILLIAM SHAKESPEARE, "The Passionate Pilgrim"

Fabulla, sweet virgin, you have learned your lesson too well,
I warned you to hold off impetuous lovers,
To say "No" once, twice, even three times.
But, dear girl for whom I hunger and pine away,
I did not tell you to say "No" forever,
And to me.

—MARTIAL, "The Too Literal Pupil" (translated by Louis Untermeyer)


The swain did woo, she was nice,
Following fashion nayed him twice.

—ROBERT GREENE

*The Shepherd's Ode*


Or if thou think'st I am too quickly won,
I'll frown and be perverse and say thee nay.

—WILLIAM SHAKESPEARE

*Romeo and Juliet*


Girls are so queer you never know what they mean. They
say No when they mean Yes, and drive a man out of his
wits for the fun of it.

—LOUISE MAY ALCOTT

*Little Women*


A man assumes that a woman's refusal is just part of a
game. Or, at any rate, a lot of men assume that. When a
man says no, it's no. When a woman says no, it's yes, or at
least maybe. There's even a joke to that effect. And little
by little, women begin to believe in this view of themselves.

—ERICA JONG

*Fear of Flying*

. . . cannot go
From yes to no
For no is not love, no is no . . .
—W.H. AUDEN, "Too Dear, Too Vague"


A woman's "No" is said with one mouth only.
*Proverb*


# Novelty

Men are by nature fond of novelty.
—PLINY, The Elder
*Natural History*


The principal quality of a woman is never beauty nor
charm nor intelligence, it is novelty.
—JACQUES BAROCHE
*The Sexual Behavior of the Married Man in France*


Novelty always appears handsome.
—H.G. BOHN
*Handbook of Proverbs*


The taste of the first kiss disappointed me like a fruit
tasted for the first time. It is not in novelty, it is in habit
that we find the greatest pleasures.
—RAYMOND RADIGUET
*Le diable au corps*


By nature, men love newfangledness.
—GEOFFREY CHAUCER
*The Canterbury Tales*

# Obscenity

I have left out those words which, a little daring, might have offended eyes and ears; young girls well as ladies who are truly virtuous and wear out three lovers might have blushed and become indignant.

—HONORÉ DE BALZAC

*Contes drolatiques*

I know that the wiser sort of men will consider, and I wish the ignorant sort would learn, how it is not the baseness or homeliness, either of words or matters, that makes them foul and obscene, but their base minds, filthy conceits, or lewd intents that handle them.

—JOHN HARRINGTON

*The Metamorphosis of Ajax*

I think it is disgusting, shameful, and damaging to all things American. But if I were 22, with a great body, it would be artistic, tasteful, patriotic, and a progressive religious experience.

—SHELLEY WINTERS, comments on seeing Kenneth Tynan's nude revue

*Oh, Calcutta!*

Obscene is not the picture of a naked woman who
exposes her pubic hair but that of a fully clothed general
who exposes his medals awarded in a war of aggression.
—HERBERT MARCUSE (attributed)

# One-night Stands

'you'll have to go now
ive a lot of work to do
& i cant have a man around
here are yr pants
there's coffee on the stove
it's been very nice
but i can't see you again
you got what you came for
didn't you'
& she smiled
he wd either mumble curses bout crazy bitches
or sit dumbfounded
. . .
'i cdnt possibly wake up
with a strange man in my bed
why don't you go home'
—NTOZAKE SHANGE, "for colored girls who have considered suicide
when the rainbow is enuf"

How do you do
would you like to be friends?
No I just want a bed for the night
Someone to tell me they care.
You can fake it. That's all right
in the morning I won't be here.
—JANIS IAN, "The Come-on"

Would you care to stay till sunrise
it's completely your decision
it's just that night cut through me like a knife
would you care to stay awhile and save my life?
—DORY PREVIN, "The Lady With the Braid"


Do not exploit. Do not be exploited. Remember that sex
is not out there, but in here, in the deepest layer of your
own being. There is not only the morning after—there are
also lots of days and years afterward.
—JACOB NEUSNER


A man has missed something if he has never woken up in
an anonymous bed beside a face he'll never see again . . .
—GUSTAVE FLAUBERT (attributed)


# Open Marriage

Open marriage means an honest and open relationship
between two people based on equal freedom and identity
of both partners.
—GEORGE AND NENA O'NEILL


Open marriage is nature's way of telling you you need a
divorce.
—MARSHALL BRICKMAN


Edwina and I spent all our married lives getting into other
people's beds.
—EARL MOUNTBATTEN OF BURMA
  *Mountbatten* by P. Ziegler

I haven't known any open marriages, though quite a few have been ajar.
—ZSA ZSA GABOR (attributed)


Some people ask the secret of our long marriage. We take time to go to a restaurant two times a week. A little candlelight, dinner, music and dancing. She goes Tuesdays. I go Fridays.
—HENNY YOUNGMAN


# Optimist and Pessimist

An optimist is a girl who mistakes a bulge for a curve.
—RING LARDNER (attributed)


A pessimist is a man who thinks all women are bad. An optimist is one who hopes they are.
—CHAUNCEY M. DEPEW (attributed)


# Oral Sex

I regret to say that we of the FBI are powerless to act in cases of oral-genital intimacy, unless it has in some way obstructed interstate commerce.
—J. EDGAR HOOVER


Oral-genital sex definitely limits the amount of loving verbal communication that the husband and wife can have as they make love.
—ED AND GAYE WHEAT, "Intended for Pleasure"
*Newsweek*, February 1, 1982

He loves roast beef well who licks the spit.
—JOHN RAY
*English Proverbs*


A sip is the most that mortals are permitted from any goblet of delight.
—A.B. ALCOTT, "Habits"
*Table Talk*


. . . the business which the younger generation has graced with the unisex term "giving head". . . Wives who wanted head from their husbands and didn't get it, wives who got it and hated it, wives who didn't mind getting it if they did not have to give it, wives who loved giving head so much their clitorises indeed seemed to be, like the freckled-faced blue movie star, at the back of their throats.
—JOHN UPDIKE
*A Month of Sundays*


The only thing wrong with oral sex is the view.
—JOHN GREGORY DUNNE
*Dutch Shea, Jr.*


Graze on my lips; and if these hills be dry,
Stray lower, where the pleasant fountains lie.
—WILLIAM SHAKESPEARE
*Venus and Adonis*


His idea of oral sex is talking about himself.
—LIN FIELD
*Mrs. Murphy's Laws*

As for the topsy-turvy tangle called soixante-neuf, personally I have always felt it maddeningly confusing—like trying
to pat your head and rub your stomach at the same time.
—HELEN LAWRENSON
*Whistling Girl*


As the old saying goes, so it is today: upside down and
downside up.
—MENANDER
*The Widow*


# Orgasm

Hurry to your goal together. That is full bliss when man
and woman lie equally conquered.
—OVID


(cccome? said he
ummm said she)
you're divine! said he
(you are Mine said she).
—E.E. CUMMINGS, "may i feel said he"


On the brink of being satiated, desire still appears to be
infinite.
—JEAN ROSTAND
*Journal d'un caractère*


See my lips tremble, and my eyeballs roll
Suck my last breath, and catch my flying soul.
—ALEXANDER POPE, "Eloisa to Abelard"

. . . she used to come just from sitting on a vibrating subway
seat, never the IRT, on the IND. Took at least five stops.
—JOHN UPDIKE
*Books A Book*

[*Note: the* IRT *and* IND *are subway lines in New York City.*]


. . . the tyranny of the orgasm.
—CYRIL CONNOLLY
*Love and Will* by Rollo May


Hit the ball over the fence and you can take your time
going around the bases.
—JOHN W. RAPT, "What the World Needs"


Orgasm is like a slight case of apoplexy.
—DEMOCRITUS


He always has an orgasm and doesn't wait for me. It's unfair.
—LORENA BOBBIT, in a statement to police on questioning why she cut off
her husband's penis
*Esquire*, February 1994


It's rather like a sneeze.
—TRUMAN CAPOTE (attributed)


He said, "Maria . . . I feel as though I wanted to die when
I am loving thee."
"Oh," she said, "I die each time. Do you not die?"
"No. Almost. But did thee feel the earth move?"
"Yes. As I died. Put thy arm around me, please."
—ERNEST HEMINGWAY
*For Whom the Bell Tolls*

One orgasm in the bush is worth two in the hand.
—GRAFFITO

*Encyclopedia of Graffiti* by R. Reisner


The orgasm has replaced the Cross as the focus of longing and the image of fulfillment.
—MALCOM MUGGERIDGE, "Down With Sex"

*The Most of Malcolm Muggeridge*


I was in bed one night when my boyfriend Ernie said, "How come you never tell me when you're having an orgasm?' I said to him, "Ernie, you're never around."
—BETTE MIDLER


Instead of fulfilling the promise of orgiastic bliss, sex in America of the feminine mystique is becoming a strangely joyless national compulsion, if not a contemptuous mockery.
—BETTY FRIEDAN

*The Feminine Mystique*


I finally had an orgasm and my doctor told me it was the wrong kind.
—WOODY ALLEN

*Manhattan*


The modern erotic ideal: man and woman in loving sexual embrace experiencing simultaneous orgasm through genital intercourse. This is a psychiatric-sexual myth useful in forcing feelings of sexual inadequacy and personal inferiority. It is also a rich source of "psychiatric patients."
—THOMAS SZASZ

*The Second Sin*

And was it good for you?

. . .

Oh very. Of course, it always is.

—EVE MERRIAM, "The Love-Making: His and Hers"


Love's climax should never be rushed, I say,
But worked up slowly, lingering all the way.

—OVID

*Ars Amatoria*


O love! for love I could not speak
It left me winded, wilting, weak.

—SIR JOHN BETJEMAN, "The Licorice-Fields at Pontefract"


There is no such thing as a vaginal orgasm distinct from a clitoral orgasm. The nature of the orgasm is the same regardless of erotogenic zone stimulated to produce it.

—MARY JANE SHERFEY


All orgasms are created equal.

—DAVID REUBEN

# Pain and Torment

Only I discern
Infinite passion, and the pain
Of finite hearts that yearn.
—ROBERT BROWNING, "Two in Compagna"

Pains of love be sweeter far
Then all other pleasures are.
—JOHN DRYDEN, "Tyrannic Love"

Pains are the wages of ill pleasures
—THOMAS FULLER
*Gnomologia: Adagies and Proverbs*

And painful pleasure turns to pleasing pain.
—EDMUND SPENSER
*The Faerie Queene*

To love is to suffer, to be loved is to cause suffering.
—COMTESSE DIANE
*Maximes de la vie*

Terminate torment
of love unsatisfied
The greater torment
of love satisfied.
—T.S. ELIOT, "Ash-Wednesday"


Love is a torment of the mind
A tempest everlasting
—SAMUEL DANIEL, "Love Is a Sickness"


"Will she
Or will she not
Give me her body?"
That is the question
That teases and torments you
And sends you reeling forth
Into the night
Singing to the stars.
Or striding angrily down dusty roads,
Striking off the heads
Of helpless flowers
With your cane.
—ZELLA MURIEL WRIGHT
*The Pagan Anthology*


There can be no great love without great pain
—ANONYMOUS


There is no pain equal to that which two lovers can inflict
on one another. This should be made clear to all who
comtemplate such a union. The avoidance of this pain is
the beginning of wisdom, for it is strong enough to conta-
minate the rest of our lives.
—CYRIL CONNOLLY
*The Unquiet Grave*

# Parting

Eyes, look your last!
Arms, take your last embrace.
—WILLIAM SHAKESPEARE
*Romeo and Juliet*


Though his suit was rejected,
He sadly reflected,
That a lover forsaken
A new love may get;
But a neck that's once broken
Can never be set.
—SIR WALTER SCOTT
*Peveril of the Peak*


Come back to me in dreams, that I may give
Pulse for pulse, breath for breath:
Speak low, lean low,
As long ago, my love, how long ago.
—CHRISTINA ROSSETTI, "Echo"


Look in my face; my name is Might-Have-Been;
I am also called No-more, Too-Late, Farewell.
—DANTE GABRIEL ROSSETTI, "A Superscription"
*The House of Life*


It is our own mediocrity that makes us let go of love,
makes us renounce it. True love doesn't know the meaning of renunciation . . .
—EUGÈNE IONESCO
*The Hermit*

How can I go on living, now that we're apart?
—GEORGE BROWN (BILLY HILL), "Have You Ever Been Lonely"


We must in tears
Unwind a love knit up in many years.
In this last kiss I here surrender thee
Back to thyself, so thou again art free;
Thou in another, sad as that, resend
The truest heart that lover e'er did lend.
—HENRY KING, Bishop of Chichester, "The Surrender"


When we two parted
In silence and tears
Half broken-hearted
To sever for years.
. . .
If I should meet thee
After long years
How should I greet thee?
With silence and tears.
—GEORGE GORDON, Lord Byron, "When We Two Parted"


Only two months since you stood here!
Two short months! then tell me why
Voices are harsher than they were
And tears are longer ere they dry.
—WALTER SAVAGE LANDOR, "What News"


Oh, seek my love, your newer way;
I'll not be left in sorrow.
So long as I have yesterday
Go take your damned tomorrows.
—DOROTHY PARKER, "Godspeed"
*Enough Rope*

I will not let thee go.
Ends all our month-long love in this?
Can it be summed up so
Quit in a single kiss?
I will not let thee go.
. . .
Thou sayest farewell, and lo!
I have thee by the hand
And I will not let thee go.
—ROBERT BRIDGES, "I Will Not Let Thee Go"


Since there is no help, come let us kiss and part,
Nay, I have done; you get no more of me
And I am glad, yea glad with all my heart,
That thus so cleanly, I myself can free,
Shake hands for ever, cancel all our vows,
And when we meet at any time again,
Be it not seen in either of our brows,
That we one jot of former love retain.
—MICHAEL DRAYTON, "Sonnet"


All's over then: does truth sound bitter
As one at first believes?
—ROBERT BROWNING, "The Lost Mistress"


Abandon me to stammering, and go,
If you have tears, prepare to cry elsewhere—
I know of no emotion we can share,
Your intellectual protests are a bore.
—THOMAS GUNN, "Carnal Knowledge"


With all my will, but much against my heart,
We two now part.
—COVENTRY PATMORE, "A Farewell"

It is seldom indeed that one parts on good terms, because
if one were on good terms one would not part.
—MARCEL PROUST
*Remembrance of Things Past: The Fugitive*


To meet, to know, to love—and then to part,
Is the sad tale of many a heart.
—SAMUEL TAYLOR COLERIDGE
*Couplet Written in a Volume of Poems*


I'll see you again
When spring breaks through again.
—NOEL COWARD, "Bittersweet"


Parting is not sweet sorrow but a dry panic.
—JOHN STEINBECK (in a letter to Elaine Scott)


Get your tongue out of my mouth, I'm kissing you good-bye.
—CYNTHIA HEIMEL, (title of book)


Ah, who will shoe your feet, my love
And who will glove your hands
And who will kiss your, red, rosy lips
When I am gone to the foreign land?
—ANONYMOUS, "The Lover's Lament"


The time has come: for us to part
. . .
You're like an old shoe, I must throw away
You're just an old has-been: like a worn-out joke.
—IDA COX, "Worn-Down Daddy Blues"

# Passes

Men seldom make passes
At girls who wear glasses.
But a girl on a sofa
Is easily won ofa.
—DOROTHY PARKER, "News Item"
*Enough Rope*


Boys don't make passes at female smartasses.
—LETTY COTTIN POGREBIN
*Down With Sexist Upbringing*


Men seldom make passes at a girl who surpasses.
—FRANKLIN P. JONES (attributed)


Women don't make passes
At men who are asses.
—JANE BARTLETT
*Ms. Bartlett's Familiar Quotations*


# Passion

A man who has not passed through the inferno of his passions has not overcome them.
—CARL GUSTAV JUNG
*Memories, Dreams, Reflections*


Eternal passion!
Eternal pain!
—MATTHEW ARNOLD, "Philomela"

The duration of passion is proportionate with the original resistance of the woman.
—HONORÉ DE BALZAC (attributed)


Tenderness is the repose of passion.
—JOSEPH JOULET
*Pensées*


What is it men in women do require?
The lineaments of gratified desire.
What is it women do in men require?
The lineaments of gratified desire?
—JOHN MILTON, "The Question Answered"


Love can not grow without passion.
*Greek Proverb*


We fly to the sensation of sex in order to avoid the passion of eros.
—ROLLO MAY
*Love and Will*


Our passions are true phoenixes; as the old burn out the new straight rise up from the ashes.
. . .
Passions are vices and virtues in their highest powers.
—JOHANN WOLFGANG VON GOETHE


It is with our passions as with fire and water,
they are good servants, but bad masters.
—ROGER L'ESTRANGE
*Aesop's Fables*

One man's mate is another man's passion.
—EUGENE HEALY
*Mr. Sandman Loves His Life*


The natural man has only two primal passions, to get and beget.
—WILLIAM OSLER
*Science and Immortality*


All passions exaggerate: it is because they do that they are passions.
—NICHOLAS CHAMFORT


Wise people may say what they will but one passion is not cured by another.
—LORD CHESTERFIELD


My passions hound me like an enemy, from youth to withered old age.
—JUDAH HALEVI, "Lord, All My Longing Is Before You"


It is only with scent and silk and artifices that we raise love from an instinct to a passion.
—GEORGE MOORE


Sexual passion is the cause of war and the end of peace, the basis of what is serious, the inexhaustible source of wit, the key to all illusions . . . sexual passion is kernel of the will to live, and consequently the concentration of all desire . . .
—ARTHUR SCHOPENHAUER
*Love and Will* by Rollo May

What's called "passion," you'll learn, may be "overriding."
But not in me it doesn't: I'm that smart,
I can give everything and keep my heart.
Kisses are kisses. No need for souls to mingle.
—JONATHAN PRICE, "A Considered Reply to a Child"


If passion drives, let reason hold the reins.
—BENJAMIN FRANKLIN
*Poor Richard's Almanac*


I pray . . .
That I may seem, though I die old,
A foolish, passionate man.
—WILLIAM BUTLER YEATS


How well do I remember the aged poet,
Sophocles, when in answer to the question,
"How does love suit with age—are you
still the man you were?" replied,
"Peace, most gladly have I escaped the thing
of which you speak; I feel as if I had escaped
from a mad and furious master."
—PLATO


When passion entereth at the fore-gate, wisdom goeth out
the poster.
—THOMAS FULLER
*Gnomologia: Adagies and Proverbs*


A man in passion rides a horse that runs away with him.
—C.H. SPURGEON
*John Ploughman's Pictures*

Death is the only pure, beautiful conclusion of a great
passion.
—D.H. LAWRENCE
*Fantasia of the Unconscious*


For one heat, all know, doth drive out another,
One passion doth expel another still.
—GEORGE CHAPMAN
*Monsieur D'Olive*


Passion often turns the cleverest men into idiots
and makes the greatest blockheads clever.
—FRANÇOIS, Duc de La Rochefoucauld
*Réflexiones ou sentences et maximes morales*


It is difficult to overcome one's passion, and impossible to
satisfy them.
—MARGUERITE DE LA SABLIÈRE
*Pensées chrétiennes*


The only sin passion can commit is to be joyless.
—DOROTHY SAYERS


Ecstasy affords
the occasion and expediency determines the form.
—MARIANNE MOORE
*The Past and the Present*

# Penetration

All words,
And no performance
—PHILIP MASSINGER
*Parliament of Love*


And he came into her at once, to enter the peace on earth
of her soft, quiescent body. It was the moment of pure
peace for him, the entry into the body of a woman.
—D.H. LAWRENCE
Lady Chatterley's Lover


Why look at sexual intercourse as penetration? I have
always considered my partner enveloped. I'd rather make
a toast to all the great envelopes of the world. What say
you ladies?
—JUDIANNE DENSEN-GERBER
*Walking in My Shoes*


The moment of greatest significance in love-making is not
the moment of orgasm. It is rather the moment of
entrance, the moment of penetration . . . This is the
moment that shakes us, that has within it the great wonder, tremendous and tremulous as it may be—or disap-
pointing and despairing, which says the same thing from
the opposite point of view.
—ROLLO MAY
*Love and Will*


Bury me, bury me
Deeper, ever so deeper.
—ALFRED, Lord Tennyson, "Maud"

And when I entered you
It seemed that great happiness
Could be measured with the precision
Of sharp pain. Quick and bitter.
—YEHUDA AMICHAI, "Quick and Bitter" (translated from the Hebrew
by Assia Gutmann)


See also: SEXUAL INTERCOURSE; TECHNIQUE.


# Penis

Sensitive but resilient, equally available during the day or
night with a minimum of coaxing, it has performed pur-
posely if not skillfully for an eternity of centuries, end-
lessly searching, sensing, expanding, probing, penetrating,
throbbing, wilting and wanting more.
—GAY TALESE
*Thy Neighbor's Wife*


His penis . . . filled him with quizzical wonder, with gentle
skepticism. For the sake of those few inches of skin and
muscle, a man could ruin his reputation, his work, his life.
Absurd.
—ALAN LELCHUK
*Shrinking: The Beginning of My Ending*


I wonder why men can get serious at all. They have this
delicate long thing hanging outside their bodies, which
goes up and down by its own will . . . If I were a man I
would always be laughing at myself.
—YOKO ONO
*On Film*, 1967

It's not the size of the ship; it's the size of the waves.
—LITTLE RICHARD (attributed)


Don't let that little frankfurter ruin your life.
—BRUCE JAY FRIEDMAN
*Steam Bath*


The penis is the only muscle man has he cannot flex . . . It is the only extremity he cannot control . . . But even worse, as it affects the dignity of its owner, is its seeming obedience to that inferior thing, woman. It rises at the sight, or even the thought of a woman.
—ELIZABETH GOULD DAVIS
*Scold*


O what a peacemaker is a guide wee-willy pintle,
It is the mediator, the guarantee, the umpire,
the bond of union, the solemn league and covenant,
the plenipotentiary, the Aaron's rod, the Jacob's staff,
the prophet Elisha's pot of oil, the Ahasuerus' sceptre.
the sword of mercy, the philosopher's stone, the horn
of plenty, and the Tree of Life between Man and
     Woman.
—ROBERT BURNS
*The Merry Wives of Calcedonia*


A maiden's mouth shows the make of her chose
And a man's mentula one knows by the length of his nose.
*A Thousand and One Nights* (translated by Sir Richard Burton)


From a little spark may burst a mighty flame.
—DANTE ALIGHIERI
*Paradiso*

Men are not measured in inches.
—THOMAS FULLER
*Gnomologia: Adagies and Proverbs*


He [Homo sapiens] is proud of the fact that he has the biggest brain of all the primates, but attempts to conceal the fact that he also has the biggest penis.
—DESMOND MORRIS
*The Naked Ape*


John Thomas says good-night to Lady Jane, a little droopingly, but with a hopeful heart.
—D.H. LAWRENCE
*Lady Chatterley's Lover*


His sex beat about like the cane of a furious blind man.
—AMOS OZ (attributed)


# Perfume

So perfumed that
the winds were love-sick.
—WILLIAM SHAKESPEARE
*Antony and Cleopatra*


A woman smells best when she hath no perfume at all.
—ROBERT BURTON
*The Anatomy of Melancholy*

Oh, what perfumes, what evaporations to
coprocontaminate and scatoscandalize
the pretty little snouts of adolescent punks.
—FRANÇOIS RABELAIS
*Gargantua and Pantagruel*


It is a sad woman who buys her own perfume.
—LENA JAEGER
*The Observer*, November 25, 1955


The woman one loves always smells good.
—REMY DE GOURMONT (attributed)


Her honeyish pungent female smell monopolized the
warm bed.
—JOHN UPDIKE
*Couples*


"Where should one use perfume?" a young woman asked.
"Wherever one wants to be kissed." I said
—GABRIELLE "COCO" CHANEL (attributed)


Why are women wearing perfumes that smell like flowers? Men don't like flowers. I've been wearing a great
scent. It's called New Car Interior.
—RITA RUDNER

# Perversion

The only abnormality is the incapacity to love.
—ANAÏS NIN (attributed)


Unnatural vices
are fathered by our heroism.
—T.S. ELIOT
*Gerontion*


My own belief is that there is hardly anyone whose sexual
life, if it were broadcast, would not fill the world at large
with surprise and horror.
—W. SOMERSET MAUGHAM (attributed)


. . . every man in love is a sex pervert.
—BILLY WILDER (attributed)


Be creative, invent a sexual perversion.
—GRAFFITO


If you want to know what I think, I think you're some
kind of deviated prevert.
—PETER GEORGE, STANLEY KUBRICK, TERRY SOUTHERN
*Stanley Kubrick Directs* by A. Walker


If nature permits it, it is natural. If nature does not permit
it, it cannot be done.
—BUCKMINSTER FULLER, *Architecture as Ultra Invisible Reality*

# Platonic Love

I was that silly thing that once was wrought
To practice this thing love;
I climbed from sex to soul, from soul to thought;
But thinking there to move,
Headlong I rolled from thought to soul, and then
From soul I lighted at the sex again.
—WILLIAM CARTWRIGHT, "No Platonic Love"


Platonic affection, or more exactly Reciprocal
Platonism, is discernible only among married people.
—EDGAR SALTUS


I am convinced, and always was, that Platonic love is Pla-
tonic nonsense.
—SAMUEL RICHARDSON
*Pamela*


Platonic friendship: the short interval between introduc-
tion and seduction.
—ANONYMOUS


Of course a platonic relationship is possible—but only
between a husband and wife.
—IRVING KRISTOL (attributed)


If there is such a thing as platonic love between a man and
a woman, it is the result of some profound misunderstanding, a stifling of their true and authentic impulses.
—IVAN MESTROVIC

Platonic love is love from the neck up.
—THYRA SAMTER WINSLOW (attributed)


What I cannot love, I overlook. Is that real friendship?
—ANAÏS NIN
*The Diary of Anaïs Nin*


# Pleasure

Pleasure's a sin and sometimes sin's
a pleasure.
—GEORGE GORDON, Lord Byron
*Don Juan*


Short pleasure, long lament.
*English Proverb*


Ever let the fancy roam
Pleasure never is at home.
—JOHN KEATS, "Fancy"


Pains of love be sweeter far
Than all other pleasures are.
—JOHN DRYDEN, "Tyrannic Love"


Stolen pleasures are the sweetest.
*English Proverb*


When a man says he had pleasure with a woman, he doesn't
mean conversation.
—SAMUEL JOHNSON

The best pleasures of this world are not quite pure.
—JOHANN WOLFGANG von GOETHE
*Clavigo*


Pleasure is said by her votaries to consist of the memory
of the past, the enjoyment of the present, and the hope of
future delights.
—PHILO
*De Simniis*


The pleasure that is the safest is the least pleasure.
—OVID
*Ars Amatoria*


No pleasure is risk-free.
— JOHANN WOLFGANG von GOETHE


No pleasure lasts long enough.
—SEXTUS AURELIUS PROPERTIUS
*Elegies*


Vice poisons pleasure, passion falsifies it,
temperance sharpens it, innocence purifies it,
beneficence doubles it, friendship multiplies it.
*Chinese Proverb*


Pleasure is the object, the duty, the goal
Of all rational creatures.
—VOLTAIRE
*Epître à Madame de G.*

Most men pursue pleasure with such breathless haste that they hurry past it.
—SOREN KIERKEGAARD
*Either/Or*


There is a sting in the tail of all unlawful pleasures.
—OSWALD DYKES
*English Proverbs*


Fly the pleasure that bites tomorrow.
—GEORGE HERBERT
*Outlandish Proverbs*


My candle burns at both ends;
It will not last the night;
But, ah, my foes, and oh, my friends,
It gives a lovely light.
—EDNA ST. VINCENT MILLAY
*A Few Figs from Thistles*


# Polygamy

In pious times, e'er Priest-craft did begin,
Before Polygamy was made a sin.
—JOHN DRYDEN, "Absalom and Achitophel"


Polygamy, n.: A house of atonement, or expiatory chapel, fitted with several stools of repentance, distinguished from monogamy, which has but one.
—AMBROSE BIERCE
*The Devil's Dictionary*

Polygamy may well be held in dread,
Not only as a sin, but as a bore.
—GEORGE GORDON, Lord Byron
*Don Juan*


Marriage with more than one wife is like a man attached
to more churches than one, whereby his faith is so dis-
tracted that it becomes no faith.
—EMANUEL SWEDENBORG
*Heaven and Hell*


In every port he finds a wife.
—ISAAC BICKERSTAFFE
*Thomas and Sally*


I don't see why we can't get along with a polygamist who
doesn't polyg as we do with a lot of monogamists who
don't monog.
—THEODORE ROOSEVELT (attributed)


*See also:* MARRIAGE; MONOGAMY.


# Possession

No one worth possessing
Can be quite possessed.
—SARA TEASDALE
*Advice to a Girl*

# Post-coital Tristesse

. . . post-coital remorse surging in like the tide . . .
—JOHN BARTH
*Letters*


Every animal is sad after intercourse.
(Omne animal post coitu triste)
*Latin Proverb*


Every animal is sad after coitus except the human female
and the rooster.
(Triste est animal post coitum praeter mulierem gal-
lumque.)
—GALEN


. . . the Augustinian saying, "Omne animal post coitum
triste est", is true for me only if I fail to delight her. Otherwise, I can crow.
—ALAN WATTS
*In My Own Way: An Autobiography*


Satiety begets distaste.
—MICHEL DE MONTAIGNE
*Essays*


Minutes pass in silence. It is those few minutes that pass
after we make love that are most mysterious to me,
uncanny.
—JOYCE CAROL OATES
*The Wheel of Love and Other Stories: "Unmailed, Unwritten Letters"*

The only time human beings are sane is the ten minutes after intercourse.
—ERIC BERNE

. . . every lover will experience a marvelous disillusion after the pleasure he has at last attained . . .
—ARTHUR SCHOPENHAUER

And all this dirt for just three minutes of rapture.
—JULES LAFORGUE
*For the Book of Love*

Nothing is so good as it seemed before.
—GEORGE ELIOT
Silas Marner

What to ourselves in passion we propose,
The passion ending, doth the purpose lose.
—WILLIAM SHAKESPEARE
*Hamlet*

Come here, lie with me
And take away the pain
Then go away
I never want to see you again.
—ANONYMOUS
*Sexing the Millennium* by Linda Grant

*See also:* GUILT.

# Potency

It's not the men in my life that counts—it's the life in my men.

—MAE WEST

*I'm No Angel*


Women think of being a man as a gift. It is a duty. Even love making can be a duty. A man has always to get it up, and love isn't always enough.

—NORMAN MAILER,

*Nova Magazine*


The most distressing fact of growing older is that I find my private parts shrinking.

—CECIL BEATON (attributed)


*See also:* IMPOTENCE.


# Power

She who would long retain her power must use her lover ill.

—OVID

*Amores*


Women run the world, God dealt them all the cards between their legs.

—JAMES JONES

*From Here to Eternity*

She knows her man, and when you rant and swear,
Can draw you to her with a single hair.
—JOHN DRYDEN, "Persius"
*Satires*

One hair of a woman can draw more than a hundred pair
of oxen.
—JAMES HOWELL
*Familiar Letters*

She stoops to conquer.
—OLIVER GOLDSMITH, (title of play)

Where love rules there is no will to power; and where
power predominates, there love is lacking. The one is the
shadow of the other.
—CARL GUSTAV JUNG
*Psychological Reflections: A Jung Anthology*

In men, we various ruling passions find;
In women, two almost divide the kind;
Those, only fixed, they first or last obey,
The love of pleasure and the love of sway.
—ALEXANDER POPE
*Moral Essays*

Disguise our bondage as we will,
'Tis woman, woman, rules us still.
—THOMAS MOORE, "Sovereign Woman"
*Miscellaneous Poems*

The more developed sexual passion, in both sexes, is very largely an emotion of power, domination, or appropriation. There is no state of feeling that says "mine, mine" more fiercely.
—CHARLES HORTON COOLEY
*Human Nature and the Social Order*


The penis is mightier than the sword.
—MARK TWAIN (attributed)


Men are brought up to command, women to seduce.
—SALLY KEMPTON (attributed)


Do not put such unlimited power in the hands of husbands. Remember all men would be tyrants if they could.
—ABIGAIL ADAMS, a plea to husband John Adams
*Secret Loves* by S. Friedman


If you live with a man, you must conquer him every day. Otherwise he will go to another woman.
—BRIGITTE BARDOT


*See also:* DOMINATION.


# Pregnancy

The menace of another pregnancy hung like a sword over the head of every poor woman.
—MARGARET SANGER
*My Fight for Birth Control*

Except for women, few pregnant animals copulate.
—PLINY
*Natural History*


Once I wore my apron low
. . .
Now I wear my apron high.
—ANONYMOUS, "Love, Oh Love, Oh Careless Love"


Congratulations: we all knew you had it in you.
—DOROTHY PARKER, telegram to friend on giving birth


In the dark,
Defiant even now, it tugs and moans
To be untangled from the mother's bones.
—GENEVIEVE TAGGARD, "With Child"


Her small belly fattened, the breasts he had taught
her were beautiful
Swelled like melons, the nipples darkened. A
turmoil
Churned inside her, sharp and hard . . .
Something of her but alien.
—BETH BENTLEY, "The Birthday"


The best prescription for a discontented female is to have
a child.
—PABLO PICASSO (attributed)

No way. My womb, like my fist,
is clenched against the world.
—MARTHA SHELBY, "The Tree of Begats"


Give me children or I shall die.
—RACHEL (to Jacob)
*Genesis*


A ship under sail, a man in complete armor, and a woman
with a big belly, are the three handsomest sights in the
world.
—JAMES HOWELL
*Proverbs*


My bigness is horrible or a new form of beauty—which?
—JOHN UPDIKE
*Couples*


Love me lots
Love me little
Only leave me not
Fatter in the middle.
—LEONARD LOUIS LEVINSON
*Bartlett's Unfamiliar Quotations*


Don't litter, stop the population explosion.
—GRAFFITO

. . . lovers reading the instructions in comic books
Are turning out babies according to the instructions.
—HOWARD NEMEROV, "Make Love Not War"


The great pod of her belly swelled and grew.
—A.D. HOPE, "Imperial Adam"


# Premarital Sex

There was a young parson of Harwich,
Tried to grind his betrothed in a carriage.
   she said, "No you young goose
   just try self-abuse
And the other we'll try after marriage."
*Anonymous Limerick*


My genuine advice to a girl is to try him out in bed first
because that's where it goes or doesn't. If it goes, you've
got a chance. If it doesn't, God help you. Everything else
is propaganda.
—GEORGE M. WILLIAMS
   *The Camp*


To take meat before grace.
   *Scottish Saying*


I was born in 1896 and my parents were married in 1919.
—J.R. ACKERLEY
   *My Father and Myself*

# Pretense

I'll believe it when girls of twenty with money marry male paupers, turned sixty.
—ELBERT HUBBARD
*The Roycroft Dictionary and Book of Epigrams*

# Privacy

Sex is such a personal thing. Why do we think of sharing it with another person?
—LILY TOMLIN (attributed)

No act is so private it does not seek applause.
—JOHN UPDIKE
*Couples*

Love, in distinction from friendship, is killed, or rather extinguished, the moment it is displayed in public.
—HANNAH ARENDT

# Procreation

The act of procreation and the members employed therein are so repulsive . . .
—LEONARDO DA VINCI
*Dell' Anatomia Fogli*

The procreation of mankind is a great marvel and mystery. Had God consulted me in the matter, I should have advised him to continue the generation by fashioning them out of clay, in the way Adam was fashioned
—MARTIN LUTHER


Urge, and urge, and urge:
Always the procreant urge of the world.
—WALT WHITMAN


If you can procreate without loving . . . I find you despicable.
—MARIAMA BA
  *So Long a Letter*


Love is only the dirty trick played on us to achieve continuation of the species
—W. SOMERSET MAUGHAM
  *A Writer's Notebook*


# Promiscuity

And I shall sigh, when some will smile,
To see thy love to every one
Hath brought thee to be loved by none.
  —SIR ROBERT AYTOUN, "To His Foresaken Mistress"


A pot that belongs to many is ill-stirred and worse boiled.
—THOMAS FULLER
  *Gnomologia: Adagies and Proverbs*

I consider promiscuity immoral. Not because sex is evil, but because sex is too good and too important.
—AYN RAND
*Playboy*, 1964


. . . the simple feat of keeping her legs crossed was a structural impossibility.
—MAXWELL BODENHEIM
*Replenishing Jessica*


Elyot: It doesn't suit women to be promiscuous.
Amanda: It doesn't suit men for women to be promiscuous.
—NOEL COWARD
*Private Lives*


What is a promiscuous person? It's usually someone who is getting more sex than you are.
—VICTOR LOWNES (attributed)


She who indulges, bulges.
—GRAFFITO


You were born with your legs apart. They'll send you to the grave in a Y-shaped coffin.
—JOE ORTON
*What the Butler Saw*


Don't love everybody—specialize.
—ANONYMOUS

Votaries of the copulative cult.

—ALDOUS LEONARD HUXLEY
*Soles Occidere et Redire Possunt*


I don't screw around. If I'd done one-third of what people said I have, if I'd had half the women, I'd be a great man. But I haven't. I wish I had.

—DAN RATHER (attributed)


Promiscuous . . . That was a word I never applied to myself. Possibly no one ever does, for it is a sordid word, reducing many valuable moments to nothing more than dog-like copulation.

—MARYA MANNES
*Message from a Stranger*


So do not think of helpful whores
as aberrational blots;
I could not love you half so well
without my practice shots.

—JAMES SIMMONS, "Cavalier Lyric"


Could you endure such promiscuity?

—EZRA POUND, "Homage to Sextus Propertius"


On a sofa upholstered in panther skin
Mona did research in original sin.

—WILLIAM PLOMER, "Mews Flat Mona"

There's nothing like a good dose of another woman to make a man appreciate his wife.
—CLARE BOOTH LUCE
*The Wit of Women* by L. and M. Cowan

Your idea of fidelity is not having more than one man in bed at the same time.
*Darling* (film)

The only difference between a caprice and a lifelong passion is that the caprice lasts a little longer.
—OSCAL WILDE
*The Picture of Dorian Gray*

She could commit adultery at one end and weep for her sins at the other, and enjoy both operations at once.
—CECIL BEATON (attributed)

I'm as pure as the driven slush.
—TALLULAH BANKHEAD
*Saturday Evening Post,* 1947

# Proposals

"I'd like to marry your daughter"
"Have you seen my wife yet?"
"Yes I have. But I prefer your daughter."
—ANONYMOUS

Whoever loves, if he do not propose
The right true end of love, he's one that goes
To sea for nothing but to make him sick.
—JOHN DONNE, "Love's Progress"


You were young—but that is scarcely to your credit
Pretty—as one expects the young to be.
And you were very much in love with me.
And half I lured it on, and half I fled it,
Till honor turned its foolish face on mine
Taking for allies music and good wine—
And told me what I ought to say: I said it.
—GERALD GOULD, "Monogamy"


Will ye gang wi' me Lizzy Lindsay,
Will ye gang to the Highlands wi' me?
Will ye gang wi' me Lizzy Lindsay,
My bride and my darling to be.
—ANONYMOUS, "Lizzy Lindsay"


Man proposes; woman forecloses.
—MINNA ANTRIM
*Naked Truth and Veiled Allusions*


Let us form, as Freud has said, a group of two
You are the best thing this world can offer.
—RANDALL JARRELL, "Woman"

# Propositions

Many things are lost for want of asking.

—GEORGE HERBERT

*Jacula Prudentum*

The bashful hog eats no pears.

*Italian Proverb*

A maiden who listens is—like a besieged city that con-sents to parlay—half-way towards surrender.

—ADRIEN DE MONTLUC

*La comédie de proverbes*

I wrong you not if my thoughts reveal,
Saying how the beauty that your clothes conceal
Is like a spark that sets afire my heart.
I only ask that you then, for your part,
Will be a saddle and let me ride,
Just for this once.
. . .
Madame . . . it would prove beneficient to the common-wealth, pleasurable to your person, honorable to your progeny, and necessary to me that I cover you for the propagation of the race . . .

—FRANÇOIS RABELAIS

*Gargantua and Pantagruel*

Come live with me and be my love,
And we will some new pleasures prove.

—JOHN DONNE, "The Bait"

Come, let us go, while we are in our prime;
And take the harmless folly of the time.
—ROBERT HERRICK

*Hesperides*


Refuse or not, they'll love you more for asking.
—OVID

*Ars Amatoria*


Crave and have.
—GABRIEL HARVEY

*Marginalia*


Where is the man who has the power and skill
To stem the torrent of a woman's will
For if she will, she will, you may depend on't.
And if she won't, she won't; so there's the end on't.
—ANONYMOUS INSCRIPTION ON A PILLAR IN CANTERBURY


I never ask for what I can buy
—GEORGE BERNARD SHAW

*Major Barbara*


One boon alone I languish for: to lay
My peacock, shoveller, cockerel, popinjay
Deep in the shelter of your downy nest.
Sweet lady, once.
—FRANÇOIS RABELAIS

*Gargantua and Pantagruel*

Quit, quit for shame; this will not move;
If of herself he will not love,
Nothing will make her, the devil take her!
—SIR JOHN SUCKLING, "Song"


Take not the first refusal ill;
Tho' now she won't, anon she will.
—THOMAS D'URFEY


Make love to every woman you meet. If you get five per-
cent on your outlay, it's a good investment.
—ARNOLD BENNETT
*Reader's Digest*, June 1941


I hiss in your ear some vile suggestion,
Some delectable abomination
You smile at me indulgently: "Men, Men!"
—RANDALL JARRELL, "Woman"


Lie down, I think I love you.
—GRAFFITO

# Quality of Love

He loves but little who
Can say and count in words, how much he loves.
—DANTE ALIGHIERI
*Vita Nuova*


Yes, this was love, the ridiculous bouncing of the buttocks
and the wilting of the poor, insignificant moist little penis.
—D.H. LAWRENCE
*Lady Chatterley's Lover*


No one ever loved anyone the way everyone wants to be
loved.
—MIGNON MCLAUGHLIN (attributed)


# Quarrels

The quarrels of lovers are the renewal of love.
—HORACE
*Andria*

Love is a kind of warfare.
—OVID
*Ars Amatoria*


The anger of lovers renews their love.
—TERENCE
*The Woman from Andros*


Never go to bed mad. Stay up and fight.
—PHYLLIS DILLER (attributed)


When a woman refuses to quarrel with a man, it means she is tired of him. True lovers fight back.
—ARTHUR RICHMAN
*Reader's Digest*, October 1951


Never argue with a woman when she is tired—or rested.
—H.C. DIEFENBACH
*Reader's Digest*, November 1960


The way to fight a woman is with your hat. Grab it and run.
—JOHN BARRYMORE
*Reader's Digest*, July 1940


Love-quarrels oft in pleasing concord end.
—JOHN MILTON
*Samson Agonistes*


Thrice happy they, and more than thrice, whom an unbroken bond holds fast, and whom love, never torn asunder by foolish quarrellings, will not loose till life's last day.
—HORACE
*Odes*

# Questions That Have Yet to Be Answered

The great question that has never been answered and which I have not yet been able to answer despite my thirty years of research into the feminine soul is: what does a woman want?
—SIGMUND FREUD


How big is the normal penis?
That is the question of the century.
—DAVID REUBEN


Heaven and earth!
How is it that bodies join
but never meet?
—BEAH RICHARDS
*A Black Woman Speaks Her Mind and Other Poems*


For in what stupid age or nation
Was marriage ever out of fashion?
—SAMUEL BUTLER
*Hudibras*


Why can't a woman be more like a man?
Men are honest, so thoroughly square;
Eternally noble, historically fair;
Who, when you win, will always give your back a pat.
Why can't a woman be like that?
—ALAN JAY LERNER, "A Hymn to Him"


Why does free love cost so much?
—GRAFFITO
*Encyclopedia of Graffiti* by R. Reisner

Where's the man who could ease a heart
Like a satin gown?
—DOROTHY PARKER


Tell me, you who know, what is this thing called love?
—LORENZO DA PONTE, libretto for Mozart's *Marriage of Figaro*


Do we really know anybody? Who does not wear a face
to hide another?
—FRANCIS MARION
*Westward the Dream*


Alas! alas! who's injured by my love?
—JOHN DONNE, "The Canonization"


How can I keep my maidenhead
Among so many men?
—ROBERT BURNS, "How Can I Keep My Maidenhead"


What makes men go crazy when a woman wear her dress
so tight?
—MUDDY WATERS, blues song


How can I ever prove
What it is I love?
—EDWIN MUIR, "In Love For Long"


When marriage ends, who is left to understand?
—JOYCE CAROL OATES
*The Wheel of Love and Other Stories:* "Unmailed, unwritten letters"

If love be good, from whennes commeth my woe?
—GEOFFREY CHAUCER


Think'st thou one man is for woman meant?
—JUVENAL

*Satire* (translated by John Dryden)


Is it, in heav'n, a crime to love too well?
—ALEXANDER POPE, "Elegy to the Memory of an Unfortunate Lady"


When do I see thee most, beloved one?
—DANTE GABRIEL ROSSETTI, "Lovesight"

*The House of Life*


What shall be the maiden's fate?
Who shall be the maiden's mate?
—SIR WALTER SCOTT

*The Lay of the Last Minstrel*


Aren't women prudes if they don't and prostitutes if they do?
—KATE MILLET


The sport being such, as both alike sweet try it,
Why should one sell it and the other buy it?
—OVID

*Elegia X*


All are good lasses, but whence come bad wives?
—JAMES KELLY

*Complete Collection of Scottish Proverbs*

If I love you, what business is it of yours?
—JOHANN WOLFGANG von GOETHE


Is sex necesary?
—JAMES THURBER and E.B. WHITE (title of book)


What am I suffering from? Sexuality. Will it destroy me?
How can I rid myself of sexuality.
—THOMAS MANN,
   *Thomas Mann and His Family* by M. Reich-Raqnicki


Why are women . . . so much more interesting to men
than men are to women?
—VIRGINIA WOOLF
   *A Room of One's Own*


What else could we do, for we were in love?
—PAUL ÉLUARD, "Curfew" (translated from the French by Quentin Stevenson)


Is it too much to to ask that women be spared the daily
struggle for superhuman beauty in order to offer it to the
caresses of a subhumanly ugly man?
—GERMAINE GREER
   *The Female Eunuch*

# Reconciliation

The worst reconciliation is preferable to the best divorce.
—MIGUEL DE CERVANTES

Go, let the fatted calf be killed
My prodigal has come home at last;
With noble resolutions filled
And filled with sorrow for the past.
No more will burn with love or wine
But quite has left his women and his swine.
  —ABRAHAM COWLEY, "The Welcome"

Many promising reconciliations have broken down because,
while both parties came prepared to forgive, neither party
came prepared to be forgiven.
—CHARLES WILLIAMS

Will ye no come back again?
Better lo'ed ye canna be,
Will ye no come back again?
  —CAROLINA BARONESS NAIRNE, "Bonnie Charlie's Now Awa"
  *Life and Song*

Old porridge is sooner heated than new made.
—JOHN RAY
*English Proverbs*


I'll try, I'll try, really. I'll try again. The marriage. The baby. The house. The whole damn bore.
—ANNE STEVENSON, "From an Asylum: Kathy Chattle to Her Mother, Ruth Arbeiter"


*See also:* DIVORCE.


# Redheads

My son, I've travelled round the world
And many maids I've met
There are two kinds you should avoid
The blonde and the brunette.
—ANONYMOUS, "A Warning"


Some American delusions:
. . .
5. That Americans are highly sexed and that redheads are more highly sexed than others.
—W. SOMERSET MAUGHAM


A redheaded man will make a good stallion.
—JOHN RAY
*English Proverbs*

# Relationships

Can I ever know you
or you know me.
—SARA TEASDALE, "The Mystery"
*Flame and Shadow*

It is explained that all relationships require a little of give
and take. This is untrue. Any particular partnership
demands that we give and give and give and at the last, as
we flop into our graves exhausted, we are told that we
didn't give enough.
—QUENTIN CRISP
*How to Become a Virgin*

Almost all our relationships begin, and most of them continue as forms of mutual exploitation, a mental, or physical
barter, to be terminated when one or both run out of goods.
—W.H. AUDEN
*The Dyer's Hand*

Once the realization is accepted that even between the
closest human beings infinite distances continue to exist, a
wonderful living side by side can grow up, if they succeed
in loving the distance between them which makes it possible to see the other whole against the sky.
—RAINER MARIA RILKE
*Letters* (translated by Jane Barnard Greene and M. D. Herter Norton)

Now the whole dizzying range of sexual possibilities has
been boiled down to that one big, boring, bulimic word:
RELATIONSHIP.
—JULIE BURCHILL
*Arena*, 1988

I become through my relation to the Thou; as I become I,
I say Thou. All real living is meeting.
—MARTIN BUBER

*I-Thou*

I know loads of nice, interesting single women in their
thirties and forties who would like a relationship, not necessarily marriage. But where are the equivalent men?
They're usually married and living with Mrs. Wrong or
gay and with Mr. Right.
—AUTHOR UNKNOWN

*Sexing the Millennium* by Linda Grant

# Religion

Nothing makes religious people as nervous as sex or at
least unregulated sex. Since each religion has its own reg-
ulations, people who go to different churches get nervous
about different things.
—ERIC BERNE

*Games People Play*

Sex is the ersatz, or substitute, religion of the 20th century.
—MALCOLM MUGGERIDGE

Depending on one's sex and one's religious propensities,
love can be . . . a single gaze on God.
—EDNA O' BRIEN

*Some Irish Loving*

To fall in love is to create a religion that has a fallible god.
—JORGE LUIS BORGES

*Other Inquisitions*

Love, usually spelled s-e-x, replaced religion as the opiate of the masses.
—ANONYMOUS
*Aphra,* Fall 1969


Love is the cheapest of religons.
—CESARE PAVESE
*Burning Brand: Diaries 1935–1950*


# Remarriage

There is no fury like an ex-wife searching for a new husband.
—CYRIL CONNOLLY
*The Unquiet Grave*


Shoot the second shaft, and perhaps thou mayst find again the first.
—J. HOWELL
*Proverbs*


He swapped his hen for a hooter*
A bad mistake.
—AUTHOR UNKNOWN, [*hooter = owl]


He loves his bonds who, when the first are broke,
Submits his neck into a second yoke.
—ROBERT HERRICK
*Hesperides*

Many a man owes his success to his first wife, and his second wife to his success.
—JIM BACKUS (attributed)


Over the years I have come down, rather to my surprise, on the side of marriage, although I suspect that for a number of people, including myself, it may be necessary to marry wrong before you can marry right.
—A. ALVAREZ
*Life After Marriage: Love in the Age of Divorce*


The triumph of hope over experience.
—SAMUEL JOHNSON
*The Life of Samuel Johnson* by James Boswell


Be wary how you marry one who hath cast her rider.
*English Proverb*


I long for a way to accommodate second marriages.
—DONALD COGGAN, Archbishop of Canterbury,
*The Observer,* July 16, 1978


Find a man of forty who heaves and moans over a woman in the manner of a poet, and you will behold either a man who has ceased to develop intellectually at twenty-four or thereabout, or a fraud who has an eye on the lands, tenements, and hereditaments of the lady's first deceased husband.
—H.L. MENCKEN
*Prejudices*


There are four minds in the bed of a divorced man who marries a divorced woman.
*Babylonian Talmud*

Most used husbands come with strings attached and the
ghosts of the past are nothing to the tangles of the present.
—BETTINA ARNDT

*All About Us*

# Remembrance

I shall remember you with love, or season
My scorn with pity; let me make it plain:
I find this frenzy insufficient reason
For conversation when we meet again.
　　　—EDNA ST. VINCENT MILLAY, "Sonnet"


Remember me when I am gone away,
Gone far away into the silent land;
When you can no longer hold me by the hand
Nor half turn to go, yet turning stay.
　　　—CHRISTINA ROSSETTI, "Remember"


And if bad luck should lay my strength
Into the shallow grave
Remember all the good you can;
Don't forget my love.
　　　—JOHN CORNFORD, "Huesca"


If I should go away,
Beloved, do not say
"He has forgotten me."
For you abide,
A singing rib within my dreaming side;
You always stay.
　　　—ALUN LEWIS, "Postscript: for Gwen"

# Reputation

In love, beauty counts more than reputation.
—PUBLILIUS SYRUS
*Sententiae*


A bad reputation in a woman allures like the signs of heat in a bitch.
—ALDOUS HUXLEY
*Point Counter Point*


# Revenge

'Tis sweet to love, but when with scorn we meet,
Revenge supplies the loss with joys as great.
—GEORGE GRANVILLE, Baron Lansdowne
*The British Enchanters*


You are not permitted to kill a woman who has wronged you, but nothing forbids you to reflect that she is growing older every minute. You are avenged fourteen hundred and forty times a day.
—AMBROSE BIERCE
*Epigrams*


# Romance

Some people claim that marriage interferes with romance. There's no doubt about it. Anytime you have a romance, your wife is bound to interfere.
—GROUCHO MARX
*The Groucho Phile*

Girls and women can use romance to transform the more crudely sexual relationship offered to them by boys and men and make them more palatable for female consumption. That is, romance stresses overall sensuality and gentlenesss rather than straightforward genital sex, it demands softness rather than aggression, sensitivity rather than "screwing."
—MYRA CONNELL, et al.
*Feminism for Girls*


If there is to be any romance in marriage women must be given every chance to earn a decent living at other occupations. Otherwise no man can be sure he is loved for himself and that his wife did not come to the Registry Office because she had no luck at the Labour Exchange.
—REBECCA WEST
*Manchester Daily Dispatch*, November 26, 1912


Women have tolerated miserable sexual relationships, faked orgasms, and generally kept quiet about their needs, all in the name of Romantic Love.
—ELEANOR STEPHENS
*Spare Rib Reader* by Marsha Rowe


Romance, like the rabbit at the dog track, is the elusive, fake, and never-attained reward which for the benefit and amusement of our masters keeps us running and thinking in safe circles.
—BEVERLY JAMES
*The Florida Paper on Women's Liberation*


Nothing spoils a romance so much as a sense of humor in a woman.
—OSCAR WILDE
*A Woman of No Importance*

The concept of romantic love affords a means of emotional manipulation which the male is free to exploit, since love is the only circumstance in which the female is (ideologically) pardoned for sexual activity.
—KATE MILLET

*Sexual Politics*


When one is in love one begins by deceiving oneself, and ends by deceiving others. That is what the world calls romance.
—OSCAR WILDE

*The Picture of Dorian Gray*


For centuries romance has been the sweetner—artificial at that—of a woman's virtual serfdom within a monogamous relationship.
—CAROL CASSEL

*Swept Away: Why Women Fear Their Own Sexuality*


The worst of having a romance is that it leaves one so unromantic.
—OSCAR WILDE

*The Picture of Dorian Gray*

# Safe Sex

Books is safe sex.
—KATHY ACKER
*The Sexual Imagination from Acker to Zola* by Harriet Gilbert


If your newly found lover won't use a condom, you're in bed with a witless . . . and uncaring person.
—ALEX COMFORT
*The New Joy of Sex*


Life is still rich and sex should be abundant and sensitive. It is important that people don't feel that practicing safe sex restricts pleasure.
—JEFF KOONS
*Playboy*, March 1994


My thoughts are crowded with death
and it draws so oddly on the sexual
that I am confused
confused to be attracted
by, in effect, my own annihilation.
—THOMAS GUNN, "In the Time of the Plague"

AIDS obliges people to think of sex as having, possibly, the direst consequences: suicide. Or murder.
—SUSAN SONTAG
*AIDS and Its Metaphors*


No glove—No love.
Slogan


# Satisfaction

Venus play tricks on lovers with her game of images which never satisfy.
—LUCRETIUS
*De Rerum Natura* (translated by Rolfe Humphries)


Love that is satisfied no longer charms.
—THOMAS CORNEILLE
*Le festin de Pierre*


There is a great difference between satisfaction and satiation.
—MARY JANE SHERFEY, "A Theory on Female Sexuality"
*Journal of the American Psychoanalytical Association*, 1966


There is satiety in all things, of sleep and love, of sweet song and the goodly dance.
—HOMER
*The Iliad*

Even honey may cloy, and the gladsome flowers of
Aphrodite's garden.
—PINDAR
*Nemean Odes*


Full pigeons find cherries bitter.
—JOHN WODROEPHE
*The Spared Houres of a Souldier*


# Scolding

Husbands are in heaven whose wives scold not.
*English Proverb*


Scolding wives make the best housewives.
*English Proverb*


Every man can rule a shrew save he that hath her.
—WILLIAM C. HAZLITT
English Proverbs


If you would have a hen lay, you must bear with her cackling.
—THOMAS FULLER
*Gnomologia: Adagies and Proverbs*


If a hen does not prate, she will not lay.
—TORRIANO
*Piazza University*

# Scorn

The wages of scorned love is baneful hate.
—BEAUMONT AND FLETCHER
*The Knight of Malta*


We shall find no fiend in hell can match the fury of a disappointed woman—scorned, slighted, dismissed without a
parting pang.
—COLLEY CIBBER
*Love's Last Shift*


Scorn at first makes after-love the more.
—H.G. BOHN
*A Handbook of Proverbs*


Teach not they lips such scorn; for they were made for
kissing, not for such contempt.
—WILLIAM SHAKESPEARE
*Richard III*


To love a woman who scorns you is like licking honey
from thorn.
*Welsh Proverb*


# Search for Love

Follow love and it will flee;
Flee love and it will follow thee.
—T. HOWELL
*Devises*

Flee it and it will flee thee
Follow it and it will follow thee.
—JOHN RAY
*English Proverbs*


O, beauty, are you not enough?
Why am I crying after love?
—SARA TEASDALE, "Spring Night"
*Rivers to the Sea*


Unremembered and afar
I watched you as I watched a star,
Through darkness struggling into view
And I loved you better than you knew.
—ELIZABETH AKERS ALLEN


I'm a young woman, and I ain't done running around.
—BESSIE SMITH, "Young Woman Blues"


# Secrecy

Stolen meat is sweetest
—HEAD AND KIRKMAN
*English Rogue*


Stolen secrets are always sweeter,
Stolen kisses much completer.
—LEIGH HUNT, "Song of Fairies Robbing an Orchard"

Discreet wives have sometimes neither eyes nor ears.
—THOMAS FULLER
*Gnomologia: Adagies and Proverbs*


A man who has no secrets from his wife either has no secrets or no wife.
—AUTHOR UNKNOWN


Stolen sweets are the best.
—COLLEY CIBBER
The Rival Fools


Their best conscience
Is not to leave 't undone, but to keep 't unknown.
—WILLIAM SHAKESPEARE
*Othello*


Love ceases to be a pleasure,
When it ceases to be a secret.
—APHRA BEHN
*La Montre or The Lover's Watch, Four O'Clock*


He that kisseth his wife in the market-place shall have many teachers.
—WILLIAM CAMDEN
*Remains Concerning Britain*


The heart never keeps a secret from the head.
*Welsh Proverb*

# Seduction

All doors are open to courtesy.
—THOMAS FULLER
*Gnomologia: Adagies and Proverbs*


Don't compromise yourself. You are all you've got.
—JANIS JOPLIN
*Reader's Digest*, 1973


It's a silly goose who comes to the fox's sermon.
*English Proverb*


If a man entice a maid that is not betrothed, and lie with her, he shall surely endow her to be his wife.
*Exodus*


Feather by feather the goose is plucked.
—JOHN RAY
*English Proverbs*


Ladies pretend a great skirmish at the first, yet are boarded willingly at the last.
—JOHN LYLY
*Euphues and His England*


. . .
perplexed, confused
with love suffused
She slowly sighed her legs apart.
—GERSHON LEGMAN
*The New Limerick*

The main problem with honest women is not how to seduce them, but how to take them to a private place. Their virtue hinges on half-open doors.
—JEAN GIRAUDOUX
*Amphitryon 38*


There are no unseductable women—only inept men.
—ANONYMOUS


Nothing is more shameful than seducing an honest girl.
—WOLFGANG AMADEUS MOZART, letter, July 8, 1778


Pursuit and seduction are the essence of sexuality. It's part of the sizzle.
—CAMILLE PAGLIA
*Sex, Art, and the American Culture*


Seduction is often difficult to distinguish from rape. In seduction, the rapist often bothers to buy a bottle of wine.
—ANDREA DWORKIN
*Letters from a War-Zone*


A wise woman never yields by appointment. It should always be an unforeseen happiness.
—STENDHAL
*On Love*


You have to penetrate a woman's defenses. Getting into her head is a prerequisite to getting into her body.
—BOB GUCCIONE
*Speaking Frankly* by W. Leigh

# Self-love

He that is in love with himself has at least this advantage—he won't encounter many rivals in his love.
—GEORG CHRISTOPH LICHTENBERG
*Aphorisms*

To love oneself is the beginning of a lifelong romance.
—OSCAR WILDE
*An Ideal Husband*

We stop loving ourselves when no one loves us.
—MME. DE STAËL
*De l'Allemagne*

We had a lot in common. I loved him and he loved him.
—SHELLEY WINTERS
*Bittersweet* by Susan Steinberg

He fell in love with himself at first sight and it is a passion to which he has always remained faithful.
—ANTHONY POWELL
*Acceptance World*

The last time I saw him he was walking by himself down lovers' lane holding his own hand.
—FRED ALLEN
*Much Ado About Me*

There is no one, no one, loves you like yourself.
—BRENDAN BEHAN
*The Hostage*

# Seventy

Seventy . . . has no stamina, loves its sleep, will not stand without coaxing, draws aim more often than it fires—but it will go to't, smartly too, with the keener joy in what it can no longer take for granted.
—JOHN BARTH
*Letters*


Seventy is wormwood
Seventy is gall
But it is better to be seventy
Than not alive at all.
—PHYLLIS McGINLEY


. . . the only difference between a man of forty and one of seventy is thirty years of experience.
—MAURICE CHEVALIER (attributed)


# Sex

That pathetic shortcut suggested by Nature the supreme joker as a remedy for our loneliness, that ephemeral communion which we persuade ourselves to be of the spirit when it is in fact only of the body—durable not even in memory.
—VITA SACKVILLE-WEST
*No in the Sea*


Whatever else can be said about sex it cannot be called a dignified performance.
—HELEN LAWRENSON

Sex is sacrament. Sex is sin. Sex is aerobics for the psyche, Sex is the major cause of oppression, and the major site of resistance.
—HARRIET GILBERT
*The Sexual Imagination from Acker to Zola*


Sex alleviates tension. Love causes it.
—WOODY ALLEN


No more about sex, it's too boring. Everyone's got one. Nastiness is a real stimulant—but poor honest sex, like dying, should be a private matter.
—LAURENCE DURRELL
*Prospero's Cell*


There may be some things better than sex, and there may be some things worse. But there is nothing exactly like it.
—W.C. FIELDS (attributed)


Once sex rears its ugly 'ead it's time to steer clear.
—MARGERY ALLINGHAM
*The Fashion in Shrouds*


Sex may be a hallowing and renewing experience, but more often it will be distracting, coercive, playful, frivolous, discouraging, dutiful, or even boring.
—LESLIE H. FARBER
*The Ways of the Will*


Sex as an institution, sex as a general notion, sex as a problem, sex as a platitude—all this I find too tedious for words. Let us skip sex.
—VLADIMIR NABOKOV
*Strong Opinions*

As we live, we are transmitters of life.
And when we fail to transmit life, life fails to flow
through us.
This is part of the mystery of sex, it is a flow onwards
Sexless people transmit nothing.

—D.H. LAWRENCE, "We Are Transmitters"


There is no greater nor keener pleasure than that of bodily love—and none which is more irrational.

—PLATO

*The Republic*


Sex is a body-contact sport. It is safe to watch but more
fun to play.

—THOMAS SZASZ

*Sex by Prescription*


Sex contains all, bodies, souls,
Meanings, proofs, purities, delicacies, results, promulgations,
Songs, commands, health, pride, the maternal mystery,
the seminal milk,
All hopes, benefactions, bestowals, all the passions,
loves, beauties, delights of the earth.

—WALT WHITMAN

*Leaves of Grass*


Is sex dirty?
Only if it's done right.

—WOODY ALLEN

*Everything You've Always Wanted to Know About Sex, But Were Afraid to Ask*


Sex is wet . . . In fact it is more than wet, it is slippery.

—ERIC BERNE

*Games People Play*

Sex is one of the nine reasons for reincarnation . . . The other eight are unimportant.
—HENRY MILLER
*Big Sur and the Oranges of Hieronymous Bosch*


Sex is not something we do, it is something we are.
—MARY CALDERONE
*Human Sexual Expression*


Sex: the thing that takes up the least amount of time and causes the most amount of trouble.
—JOHN BARRYMORE (attributed)


I am against sex ed in schools, because sex is more fun when it's dirty and sinful.
—FLORENCE KING
*The Portable Curmudgeon Redux*


All I can say is that sex in Ireland is as yet in its infancy.
—EAMON DE VALERA, after visiting France


Jelly roll killed my pappy,
Drove my mamma stone blind.
*Blues Song*


An appetite placed in humans to insure breeding. It has in turn bred, as a side product, interesting and often ludicrous customs. Its suppression has led to ugly perversions and cruelty.
—JONATHAN BENTER

Sex is the great amateur sport. The professional, male or female, is frowned upon; he or she misses the whole point and spoils the show.
—DAVID CORT
*Social Astonishments*


Sex, which ought to be an incident of life, is the obsession of the well-fed world.
—REBECCA WEST
*The Clarion*, November 29, 1912


It is depressing to have to insist that sex is not an unnecessary, morally dubious self-indulgence but a basic human need, no less for women than for men.
—ELLEN WILLIS
*Beginning to See the Light*


[Sex] Can be a dreadful trap . . . There are women who become frigid, but that's not the worst thing that can happen to them. The worst thing is for women to find so much happiness in sexuality that they become more or less slaves of men and that strengthens the chain that binds them to their oppressor . . .
—SIMONE DE BEAUVOIR
*Marie-Claire* (Paris), November 1976


Sex is really something I don't understand. You never know where the hell you are. I keep making up these sex rules for myself and then I break them right away.
—J.D. SALINGER
*Catcher in the Rye*


Sex hasn't been the same since women started to enjoy it.
—LEWIS GRIZZARD (attributed)

There are only two guidelines for good sex, "Don't do anything you don't really enjoy," and "Find out your partner's needs and don't balk them if you can help it."
—ALEX COMFORT
*The Joy of Sex*

# Sex Appeal

That's it, baby. If you've got it, flaunt it.
—MEL BROOKS
*The Producers*

Odd how the erotic appeal has swung away from the legs; today a smart girl takes her legs for granted and gets herself a good sweater.
—BELLE LIVINGSTONE
*Belle Out of Order*

Think of me as a sex symbol for the men who don't give a damn.
—PHYLLIS DILLER

Being a sex symbol has to do with an attitude, not looks. Most men think it's looks, most women know otherwise.
—KATHLEEN TURNER
*The Observer,* 1986

# Sex Drive

Gored by the climacteric of his want
he stalls above me like an elephant.
—ROBERT LOWELL, "To Speak of Woe That Is in Marriage"


You put guys on a desert island and they'll do it to mud.
Mud!
—LENNY BRUCE
*The Essential Lenny Bruce*


I need a little sugar in my bowl and a little hot dog
between my roll.
—BESSIE SMITH, "Put a Little Sugar in My Bowl"


Never let us deny
The thing's necessity.
—ROBERT GRAVES, "Despite and Still"


That seems forever the spermatozoon's ambition, out.
—GUSTAV ECKSTEIN
*The Body Has a Head*


. . . if they can't get rid of the seed, they cannot stop burn-
ing.
—ROBERT BURTON
*The Anatomy of Melancholy*

# Sexual Harassment

"You worked in an office once didn't you Jill?" a feminist once asked me earnestly. "Did men ever harass you?" "Yes," I replied, 'but not nearly enough.'
—JILLY COOPER
*Women and Super Women*


Today, on an Ivy League campus, if a guy tells a girl she has great tits, she can charge him with sexual harassment. Chickenshit stuff. Is this what strong women do?
—CAMILLE PAGLIA
*Sex, Art, and American Culture*


There are women out there who equate a stranger's "Hey, baby" with rape. You don't need a weatherman to know which way the wind is blowing; you need a good lawyer and at least five witnesses.
—LYNN DARLING
*Esquire*, February 1994


Those groans men use
passing a woman on the street
or on the steps of the subway
to tell her she is a female
and their flesh knows it
. . .
Yet a woman, in spite of herself
knows it's tribute
if she were lacking all grace
they'd pass her in silence

She wants to throw the tribute away
disgusted and can't.
—DENISE LEVERTOV
The Mutes

You have kindergarden harassers. We're reaching out and identifying them at the earliest grades.
—EDWARD "TED" KENNEDY,
*Esquire*, February 1994


Sexual harassment . . . refers to the unwanted imposition of sexual requirements in the context of a relationship of unequal power. Central to the concept is the use of power derived from one social sphere to lever benefits or impose deprivations in another.
—CATHERINE A. MACKINNON
*The Sexual Harassment of Working Women*


# Sexual Intercourse

If we were to believe that sexual intercourse is repulsive, then we blaspheme God who made the genitals; hands can write a Sefer Torah [a scroll of the five books of Moses, the Pentateuch] and are then honorable and exalted. Hands can perform evil deeds, and are then ugly. Just so the genitals. Whatever use a man makes of them determines whether they are holy or unholy.
—RABBI MOSES BEN NACHMAN
*The Sexual Imagination from Acker to Zola*


Takes two to tango.
—AL HOFFMAN AND DICK MANNING, title of song


Anyone who calls it "sexual intercourse" can't possibly be interested in doing it. You might as well announce you're ready for lunch by proclaiming "I'd like to do some masticating and enzyme secreting."
—ALLAN SHERMAN

The pleasure is momentary, the position is ridiculous, and the expense damnable.
—LORD CHESTERFIELD (attributed)


I think that in the sexual act, as delightful as it can be, the very physical part of it is, yes, a hammering away. So it has a certain brutality.
—LOUISE NEVELSON
*Dawn+Dusk*


I still could not picture it all taking place on the desk. There didn't seem to be enough room for a woman so tall. I have since discovered that a thimble is room enough when they really want to, and that the whole planet itself may prove too small when they really don't.
—JOSEPH HELLER
*Something Happened*


Did you know that the male bee is nothing but a slave of the queen? And once the male bee has—how should I say it—serviced the queen, the male dies. All in all, not a bad system.
—CLORIS LEACHMAN
*The Mary Tyler Moore Show*


I am happy now that Charles calls on my bedchamber less frequently than of old. As it is, I can endure but two calls a week and when I hear his footsteps outside my door, I lie down on my bed, close my eyes, open my legs and think of England.
—ALICE, Lady Hilldingdon (attributed)

Be prepared mentally and physically for intercourse every night . . .
—MARABEL MORGAN
*The Total Woman*

# Sexuality

Sexuality throws no light on love, but only through love can we learn to understand sexuality.
—EUGEN ROSENSTOCK-HUESSY

For he [Henry Miller] captured, something in the sexuality of men as it had never been seen before, precisely that it was man's sense of awe before women, his dread of her position one step closer to eternity (for in that step were her powers) which made men detest women, revile them, humiliate them, defecate symbolically upon them, do everything to reduce them so that one might dare to enter them and take pleasure of them.
—NORMAN MAILER
*The Prisoner of Sex*

If my teacher could have influenced my sexuality, I would have turned out to be a nun.
—GEORGE CARLIN
*New York*, July 24, 1978

Sexuality is something, like nuclear energy, which may prove amenable to domestication . . . but then again may not.
—SUSAN SONTAG
*Styles of Radical Will*

# Shame and Shamelessness

Play with me and hurt me not,
Jest with me and shame me not.
—GABRIEL HARVEY
*Marginalia*


Where there is shame, there may in time be virtue.
—SAMUEL JOHNSON


The more things a man is ashamed of, the more
respectable he is.
—GEORGE BERNARD SHAW
*Man and Superman*


Without shame the man I like knows and avows the
deliciousness of his sex,
Without shame the woman I like knows and avows
hers.
—WALT WHITMAN, "A Woman Waits for Me"
*Leaves of Grass*


The secret thoughts of men run over all things, holy, pro-
fane, clean, obscene, grave and light, without shame or
blame.
—THOMAS HOBBES
*Leviathan*


I never wonder to see men wicked, but I wonder to see
them unashamed.
—JONATHAN SWIFT
*Reflections on Various Subjects*

Talk of shamelessness . . . I know a girl who lost her virginity on the night of Good Friday, at Jerusalem, just above the Church of the Holy Sepulchre.
—ALDOUS HUXLEY
*Time Must Have Stopped*


I feel that the older I get, the more shameless I feel. And in a sense, more pure.
—MARIA IRENE FORNES


# Sighs

The beginning, middle, and end of love is—a sigh.
—ARNOLD HAULTAIN, "Hints for Lovers"


You must remember this, a kiss is still a kiss,
A sigh is just a sigh;
The fundamental things apply
As time goes by.
—HERMAN HUPFELD, "As Time Goes By"


There's a sigh for yes and a sigh for no
And a sigh for I can't bear it!
O what can be done, shall we stay or run
Or cut the sweet apple and share it.
—JOHN KEATS, "Sharing Eve's Apple"


If I ever kill my self, it shall be with a sigh, not a sword.
—JOHN LYLY
*Euphues and His England*

# Sin

The world's as ugly, ay, as sin
And almost as delightful.
—FREDERICH LOCKER-LAMPSON, "The Jester's Plea"


That which we call sin in others is experiment for us.
—RALPH WALDO EMERSON


Would she could make of me a saint or I of her a sinner.
—WILLIAM CONGREVE, "Song"


The greater the sinner the greater the saint.
—E. HINCHLIFFE
Barthomley


A sin that's hidden is half forgiven.
—BOCCACCIO
*Decameron*


Should we all confess our sins to one another we would
all laugh at one another for our lack of originality.
—KAHLIL GIBRAN
*Sand and Foam*


Don't worry kid, the wages of sin is birth.
—DEREK WALCOTT, "Tales of the Islands"


Pleasure's a sin and sometimes sin's a pleasure.
—GEORGE GORDON, Lord Byron
*Don Juan*

The sins you do two by two
Ye must pay for one by one.
—RUDYARD KIPLING


This common tale, alas! few can prevent;
We first must sin, before we can repent.
—ANONYMOUS


A conscience cannot prevent sin. It only prevents you
from enjoying it.
—HARRY HERSHFIELD


Fashions in sin change.
—LILLIAN HELLMAN
  *The Watch on the Rhine*


All sin tends to be addictive, and the terminal point of
addiction is damnation.
—W.H. AUDEN, "Hell"
  *A Certain World*


# Single Life

When my bed is empty
Makes me feel awful mean and blue
My springs are getting rusty
Living single like I do.
  —BESSIE SMITH, "Empty Bed Blues"

I am anal retentive. I'm a workaholic. I have insomnia.
And I am a control freak. That's why I'm not married.
Who could stand me?
—MADONNA
*Madonna Unauthorized*


The race is run one by one and never two by two.
—RUYARD KIPLING
*Tomlinson*


. . . that man is poor
Who hath but one of many,
But crowned is he with store
That, single, may have many.
—ROBERT HERRICK


Down to Gehenna and up to the Throne
He travels the fastest who travels alone.
—RUDYARD KIPLING, "The Winners"


Who travels alone, without lover or friend,
But hurries from nothing to nought at the end.
—ELLA WHEELER WILCOX, "Reply to Kipling"


# Sixty

Man comes of age at sixty, women at fifteen.
—JAMES STEPHENS
*The Observer,* October 1, 1944

I am sixty-one today
A year beyond the barrier,
And what was once the magic flute,
Is now a water carrier.
—ANONYMOUS


When I get older losing my hair . . .
Will you still be sending me a Valentine, birthday greet-
ings, bottle of wine?
. . .
Will you still need me, will you still feed me
When I'm sixty-four?
—JOHN LENNON AND PAUL McCARTNEY, "When I'm Sixty-four?"


You can take no credit for beauty at sixteen. But if you
are beautiful at sixty, it will be your own soul's doing.
—MARIE STOPES


You must ask someone else. I am only sixty.
—PRINCESS METTERNICH, when asked when does a woman cease being
capable of sexual love


One starts to get young at sixty but then it is too late.
—PABLO PICASSO (attributed)


The pleasures that once were heaven
Look silly at sixty-seven.
—NOEL COWARD, "What's Going to Happen to the Tots?"

# Sleeping Together

And never, ever, no matter what else you do in your whole
life, never sleep with anyone whose troubles are worse
than your own.
—NELSON ALGREN,
*Conversations with Nelson Algren* by H.E.F. Donohue


I said, Baby! Baby!
Please don't snore so loud
. . .
You jest a little bit o' woman, baby
Sound like a great big crowd.
—LANGSTON HUGHES, "Morning After"


Laugh and the world laughs with you; snore and you
sleep alone.
—ANTHONY BURGESS
*Inside Mr. Enderby*

# Talk

The female and the fortress which begins to parlay is half-gain'd.
—JAMES HOWELL
*Parlay of Beasts*

Speak low, if you speak love.
—WILLIAM SHAKESPEARE
*Much Ado About Nothing*

To speak of love is to make love.
—HONORÉ DE BALZAC
*The Physiology of Marriage*

And the words which carry most knives are the blind
Phrases searching to be kind.
—STEPHEN SPENDER, "The Double Shame"

I had a feeling that Pandora's box contained the mysteries
of woman's sensuality, so different from man's, and for
which man's language was inadequate. The language of
sex is yet to be invented. The language of the senses is yet
to be explored.
—ANAÏS NIN
*Diary of Anaïs Nin*

Slow and sweet were the nights
Now as bitter and grinding as sand —
"We shall be sensible" and similar curses.
And as we stray further from love
We multiply the words,
Words and sentences long and orderly
Had we remained together
We could have become a silence.
—YEHUDA AMICHAI, "Quick and Bitter"


For God's sake hold your tongue, and let me love.
—JOHN DONNE, "The Canonization"


Aside from theology and sex there is really nothing to talk
about.
—HAROLD LASKI


He loves but little who
Can say and count in words, how much he loves.
—DANTE ALIGHIERI
"Vita Nuova"


Those that love the most speak least.
—GEORGE PETTIE
Petite Pallace: Curiatius and Horatia


Whom we love best, to them we can say the least.
—JOHN RAY
English Proverbs


I thought to undermine the heart
By whispering in the ear.
—JOHN SUCKLING, "'Tis Now, Since I Sat Down Before"

Fewer women would indulge in copulation . . .
if they could obtain in the vertical position the work of
admiration in which they need and which demand a bed.
—ANDRÉ MALRAUX
*Man's Fate*


If the art of conversation stood a little higher we would
have a lower birthrate.
—STANISLAW J. LEE


But words are words, I never yet did hear
That the bruis'd heart was pierced through the ear.
—WILLIAM SHAKESPEARE
*Othello*


You can't prevent a sexually transmitted epidemic without
talking about sex.
—SAM PUCKERT
*New York,* March 23, 1987


. . . and used all speech which might provoke and stir.
—OVID
*Amores* (translated by Christopher Marlowe)


"What are your views on love?"
"Love? I make it constantly but I never talk about it."
—MARCEL PROUST
*Remembrance of Things Past: The Guermantes Way*


With thee conversing I forget all time,
All seasons, and their change
—JOHN MILTON
*Paradise Lost*

You can stroke people with words.
—F. SCOTT FITZGERALD
*The Crack-Up*


*See also:* COMMUNICATION.


# Tears

I loved the very tears I made her shed.
—JEAN RACINE
*Britannicus*


There's nothing sooner dry than woman's tears.
—JOHN WEBSTER
*The White Devil*


She acts the jealous, And at will she cries;
For women's tears are but the sweat of eyes.
—JUVENAL
*Satire VI* (translated by John Dryden)


Beg her, with tears, thy warm desires to grant;
For tears will pierce a heart of adamant.
—OVID
*Ars Amatoria* (translated by John Dryden)


In woman's eye the unanswerable tear.
—GEORGE GORDON, Lord Byron, "The Corsair"

No more tears now; I will think upon revenge.
—MARY STUART (attributed)


It's what you do, unthinking,
That makes the quick tear start;
The tear may be forgotten —
But the hurt stays in the heart.
—ELLA HIGGENSON, "Wearing Out Love"


# Teasing

Do me the favour to deny me at once.
—BENJAMIN FRANKLIN
*Poor Richard's Almanac*


Desires are nourished by delays.
—THOMAS DRAXE
*Bibliotheca*


You . . . teasers have turned millions of brave young men,
many of who died for your precious on the battlefields of
the world, into a generation of sexual basket cases.
—WILLIAM STYRON
*Sophie's Choice*


I will kindle no more coales than I may well quenche.
—AUTHOR UNKNOWN


Refuse me, Galla—teasing keeps love strong,
But don't refuse me, Galla, for too long.
—MARTIAL
*Epigrams* (translated by Rolfe Humphries)

Another thing missing from feminist discourse . . . is that girls go after guys—that sexual sex and power and aggression are fused on both sides. Girls, in fact, are always manipulating men: It's called cockteasing.
—CAMILLE PAGLIA
*Esquire*, February 1994

Her left eye winks Yes
and her right stares No
and her smile smiles smiles.
—ALAN DUGAN, "On Rape Unattempted"

# Technique

It ain't what you do, it's the way that you do it.
—THOMAS 'FATS' WALLER

Jane Mack does it like an angel, lithely, gracefully, daintily, and above all sweetly.
—JOHN BARTH
*Letters*

Mrs. Murphy's Modified Gresham's Law: Bad screwing tends to drive out the good.
—LIN FIELD
*Mrs. Murphy's Laws*

Much smoke, little fire.
*English Proverb*

The deeper the sweeter.
—BEN JONSON


My nakedness the mask itself
covers the spirit completely
I grow large and plastic
I am the enormous doll
and you dive into me
and hold on to the limbs,
wriggling like a fish
and experience on my dry beach
and never know I am there.
—ELIZABETH FENTON, "Masks"


Ignorance and bungling with love are better than wisdom
and skill without.
—HENRY THOREAU
*A Week on the Concord and Merrimack Rivers*


The greatest strokes make not the best music.
—JOHN RAY
*English Proverbs*


Stop a little, to make an end the sooner.
—THOMAS FULLER
*Gnomologia: Adagies and Proverbs*


Fair and softly goes far in a day. He that goes softly, goes
sure and also far. He that spurs on too fast at first setting
out, tires before he comes to his journey's end.
—JOHN RAY
*English Proverbs*

Gently, gently goes far.

*Portuguese Proverb*


Now high, now low, now striking short and thick
And diving deep, pierced to the quick.

—THOMAS NASHE

*The Merrie Ballad of Nashe, His Dildo*


(tip top said he
don't stop said she
oh no said he)
go slow said she

—E.E. CUMMINGS, "may i feel said he"


I wouldn't be too ladylike in love if I were you.

—ALAN PATRICK HERBERT, "I Wouldn't Be Too Ladylike"


Never confuse movement with action.

—ERNEST HEMINGWAY

*Papa Hemingway* by A.E. Hotchner


The sickle motion from the thighs
Jackknifes upward at the knees
Then straightens out from heel to hip.

—T.S. ELIOT, "Sweeney Erect"


All too many men still seem to believe, in a rather naive
and egocentric way, that what feels good to them is auto-
matically what feels good to women.

—SHERE HITE

*The Hite Report*

# Temptation

Don't worry about avoiding temptation. As you grow older it will avoid you.
—JOEY ADAMS

I generally avoid temptation unless I can't resist it.
—MAE WEST
*My Little Chickadee*

If you can't be good, be careful.
*American Proverb*

The only way of getting rid of a temptation is to yield to it.
—OSCAR WILDE
*The Picture of Dorian Gray*

You may tempt the upper classes
With your villainous demi-tasses
But Heaven willl protect the Working Girl.
—EDGAR SMITH, "Heaven Will Protect the Working Girl"

I . . . beg you let me be quiet, for I am not over-fond of resisting temptation.
—WILLIAM BECKFORD
*Vathek*

An open door may tempt a saint.
*English Proverb*

Yield to temptation; it may not pass your way again.
—R.A. HEINLEIN
*The Notebooks of Lazurus Long*

There are several good protections against temptations, but the surest is cowardice.
—MARK TWAIN
*Pudd'nhead Wilson's Calendar*


Is this her fault or mine?
The tempter or tempted, who sins the most?
—WILLIAM SHAKESPEARE
*Measure for Measure*


Temptation discovers what we are.
—THOMAS À KEMPIS
*De Imitatione Christi*


Temptations offered I still scorn;
Denied, I cling them still;
I'll neither glut mine appetite,
Nor seek to starve my will.
—THOMAS HEYWOOD


"You oughn't to yield to temptation."
"Well, somebody must, or the thing becomes absurd."
—ANTHONY HOPE
*The Dolly Dialogues*


# Thirty Years of Age

no one touches
me anymore.
—SONIA SANCHEZ, "Poem at Thirty"

Better than old beef is the tender veal
I want no woman thirty years of age.
—GEOFFREY CHAUCER
*The Canterbury Tales*


Women over thirty are at their best, but men over thirty
are too old to recognize it.
—JEAN-PAUL BELMONDO (attributed)


# Time

Gather ye rosebuds while ye may,
Old Time is still a-flying:
And the same flower that smiles today
Tomorrow will be dying
. . .
Then be not coy, but use your time;
And while ye may, go marry;
For having lost but once your prime
You may for ever tarry.
—ROBERT HERRICK, "To Virgins, To Make Much of Time"


Time which strengthens friendships weakens love.
—JEAN DE LA BRUYÈRE
*Of Women*


Had we but world enough, and time,
This coyness, lady, were no crime.
. . .
But at my back I always hear
Time's wing'd chariot hurrying near.
And yonder all before us lie
Deserts of vast eternity.
—ANDREW MARVELL, "To His Coy Mistress"

Any time not spent on love is wasted.
—TORQUATO TASSO


Straw-in-the fire love,
It's no morality play we're in,
Nor can we trick time
Nor end where we began.
—JEAN GARRIGUE, "To Speak My Influence"


Time walks at your side ma'am, unwilling to pass.
—CHRISTOPHER FRY


Laurel is green for a season, and love is sweet for a day;
But love grows bitter with treason, the laurel outlives not
May.
—A.C. SWINBURNE, "Hymn to Proserpine"


All the while believe me, I prayed
Our night would last twice as long.
—SAPPHO, "One Night" (translated by Willis Barnstone)


If you let slip time like a languished rose
It withers on the stalk with languished head.
—JOHN MILTON
Comus


After three days men grow weary of a wench, a guest, and
rainy weather.
—BENJAMIN FRANKLIN
Poor Richard's Almanac

Never fancy Time's before you,
Youth believe me, will away;
Then, alas! who will adore you,
Or to wrinkles tribute pay?
—MATTHEW PRIOR, "Lamentation for Dorinda"
*Poems*


Time, not the mind, puts an end to love.
—PUBLILIUS SYRUS
*Sententiae*


Love makes time pass; time makes love pass.
*French Proverb*


Oh, it's a long, long while
From May to December,
But the days grow short
When you reach September.
. . .
Oh the days dwindle down
To a precious few . . .
And these few precious days
I'll spend with you.
—MAXWELL ANDERSON, "September Song"


# Togetherness

Let there be spaces in your togetherness.
—KAHLIL GIBRAN
*The Prophet*

A wall between preserves love.

—SAMUEL PALMER

*Moral Essays on Proverbs*

Constant togetherness is fine — but only for Siamese twins.

—VICTORIA BILLINGS

*The Woman's Book*

We can recognize the dawn and the decline of love by the uneasiness we feel when alone together.

—JEAN DE LA BRUYÈRE

*Caractéres*

# Tongue

For she has a tongue with a tang.

—WILLIAM SHAKESPEARE

*The Tempest*

The nimble tongue (love's lesser lightning) plaid
Within my mouth, and to my thoughts conveyed
Swift orders that I prepare to throw
The all-dissolving thunderbolt below.

—JOHN WILMOT, Earl of Rochester, "The Imperfect Enjoyment"

. . . alluring him with tongue in said George's mouth and said George's tongue in hers.

*Indictment of Anne Boleyn*

Women whose tongues won't stay in their mouths are the sexiest.
—JOHN UPDIKE
*Couples*


A liquorish tongue, a lecherous tail.
*English Proverb*


Say, buddy, what
does that whore of yours
have to say?
Not your girl friend;
I mean your tongue.
—MARTIAL
*Select Epigrams of Martial*, (translated and adapted by Donald C. Goertz)


# Truth

When my love swears that she is made of truth I do not believe her though I know she lies.
—WILLIAM SHAKESPEARE

# Ugliness

If you want to be happy for the rest of your life
Never make a pretty woman your wife.
Just from my personal point of view
Get an ugly girl to marry you.
—CALYPSO SONG

Beautiful women usually fall to the lot of ugly men.
*Italian Proverb*

Beauty is only skin deep, but ugly goes to the bone.
*English Proverb*

Now my hair is nappy and I don't wear no clothes of silk
But the cow that's black and ugly, has often got the
sweetest milk.
—SARA MARTIN, "Mean Tight Mama"

Beauty is still supposed to arouse desire. This is not the
case.
Beauty has nothing to do with the physical jerks under
the coverlet.
Ugliness is one of the most reliable stimulants.
—HENRY DE MONTHERLANT, "The Goddess Cypris"

I ain't good-lookin', but I'm somebody's angel child.
—BESSIE SMITH


No need to look at the mantelpiece when you are poking the fire.
*English Proverb*


Desire beautifies what is ugly.
—ALFRED HENDERSON
*Latin Proverbs*


All the ugly ones fuck.
—THOMAS PYNCHON
*V.*


There are no ugly women, only lazy ones.
—HELENA RUBINSTEIN
*My Life for Beauty*


# Undress

Abandoned déshabillé is one of the most sexual stimulating devices.
—MERVYN LEVY
*The Moons of Paradise*


Let me take you a button-hole lower.
—WILLIAM SHAKESPEARE
*Love's Labour Lost*

By degrees
Her rich attire creeps rustling to her knees.
—JOHN KEATS, "The Eve of St. Agnes"


Come, madam, come
. . .
Off with that girdle, like heaven's zone glittereing
But a far fairer encompasssing.world.
. . .
Unlace yourself, for that harmonious chime
Tells me from you that now it is bed-time.
. . .
Off with your hose and shoes; then softly tred
In this love's hallow'd temple, this soft bed.
—JOHN DONNE, "To His Mistress Going to Bed"


A woman undressing, how dazzling. It is like the sun
piercing the clouds . . .
—AUGUST RODIN
*Erotic Art of the West* by Robert Melville

# Vagina

By my life, this is my lady's hand! these be her C's, her U's, and her T's; and thus makes she her P's.
—WILLIAM SHAKESPEARE
*Twelfth Night*


The vagina . . . in which men drop their grief, their complaints, their guilt.
—ALEXANDER THEROUX
*Darconville's Cat*


By swift degrees advancing—where
His daring hand that Altar seized,
Where Gods of Love do sacrifice:
That awful throne, that Paradice [sic]
Where Rage is calm'd, and Anger pleas'd;
That Fountain where Delight still flows,
And gives the Universe World Repose.
—APHRA BEHN, "The Disappointment"


Convince a woman that her vagina is beautiful and you have the makeup of an equal person. This I believe with all my heart.
—NANCY FRIDAY
*My Mother, My Self*

that wonderful rare
space in you.
—RAINER MARIA RILKE
*Phallic Poems*


It is like a purple flower of crimson, full of honey and per-
fume. It is like a hydra of the sea, living and soft, open at
night. It is the humid grotto, the shelter always warm, the
Asylum where man rests on his march toward death.
—PETER LOUŸS
*Aphrodite*


Their lives center around their vaginas: what goes in and
what comes out.
—ERICA ABEEL, "Park Bench Mothers"
*New York*, May 24, 1971


The portions of a woman that appeal to a man's depravity
Are constructed with considerable care,
And what at first appears to be a simple cavity
Is in fact a most elaborate affair.
—AUTHOR UNKNOWN
*Mrs. Grundy* by Peter Fryer


On this soft anvil all mankind was made.
—JOHN WILMOT, Earl of Rochester
*Sodom*


If you have a vagina and an attitude in this town, then
that's a lethal combination.
—SHARON STONE
*Empire*, June 1992

# Variety

Age can not wither her, nor custom stale
Her infinite variety; other women cloy
The appetites they feed, but she makes hungry
Where she most satisfies.
—WILLIAM SHAKESPEARE
*Antony and Cleopatra*


Variety is the soul of pleasure.
—APHRA BEHN
*The Rover*


Every night should have its own menu.
—HONORÉ DE BALZAC


We did it in front of the mirror
And in the light. We did it in the darkness,
In water, and in the high grass.

We did it in honor of man
And in honor of beast and in honor of God.
But they didn't want to know about us,
They had already seen our sort.
—YEHUDA AMICHAI, "We Did It"


Men like new women. While women perform best with
men they know.
—JOHN UPDIKE
*Couples*


Yet still the meat's the same, the change does lie
All in the sauces' great variety.
—JOHN WILMOT, Earl of Rochester
*Sodom*

Will no other vice content you?
—JOHN DONNE, "The Indifferent"


Sour, sweet, bitter, pungent,
All must be tasted.
*Chinese Proverb*


No pleasure lasts long unless there is variety in it.
—PUBLILIUS SYRUS
*Maxims*


Variety's the very spice of life,
That gives it all its flavour.
—WILLIAM COWPER, "The Timepiece"
*The Task*


Variety's the source of joy below.
—JOHN GAY
*Epistle to Bernard Lintott*


# Vice

Vice is a monster of so frightful mien.
As to be hated needs but to be seen.
Yet so oft, familiar with her face
We first endure, then pity, then embrace.
—ALEXANDER POPE
*An Essay on Man*


Hypocrisy is a sort of homage that vice pays virtue.
—THOMAS FULLER
*Gnomologia: Adagies and Proverbs*

He hasn't a single redeeming vice.
—OSCAR WILDE


Here's a rule I recommend. Never practice two vices at once.
—TALLULAH BANKHEAD (attributed)


Vice is its own reward.
—QUENTIN CRISP (attributed)


It is the function of vice to keep virtue within bounds.
—SAMUEL BUTLER
*Notebooks*


Vice
Is nice.
But a little virtue
Won't hurt you.
—FELICIA LAMPORT, "Axioms to Grind"


# Virginity

Maidenheads are for ploughing.
—SAMUEL JOHNSON (attributed)


She has cracked her pitcher or pipkin.
—FRANCIS GROSE
*A Classical Dictionary of the Vulgar Tongue*

I'll wager you that in ten years it will be fashionable again
to be a virgin.
—BARBARA CARTLAND
*The Observer*, June 20, 1976

Do I still long
for my virginity?
—SAPPHO, "Remorse"

An isolated outbreak of virginity like
Lucinda's is a rash on the face of society.
It arouses only pity from the married, and
An embarrassment from the single.
—CHARLOTTE BINGHAM
*Lucinda*

My virginity weighed like a millstone round my neck. I
was sick of it.
—SYLVIA PLATH
*The Bell Jar*

You have kissed and nibbled and poked and prodded and
worried me there so often that my virginity was lost in the
shuffle.
—VLADIMIR NABOKOV
*Ida*

I may be dead tomorrow, uncaressed
My lips have not touched a woman's, none
Has given me a look in her soul, not one
Has ever held me swooning at her breast.
—JULES LAFORGUE
*For the Book of Love*

To All You Virgins — Thanks for Nothing.
— GRAFFITO


How can I keep my maidenhead,
My maidenhead, maidenhead,
How can I keep my maidenhead,
Among sae mony men, O.
— ROBERT BURNS, "How Can I Keep My Maidenhead"


A well preserved virginity may signify a limited capacity
to love.
— ROBERT SHIELDS
*The Observer,* June 13, 1965


Oh the innocent girl
in her maiden teens
knows perfectly well
what everything means.

If she didn't she oughter;
it's a silly shame
to pretend that your daughter
is blank at the game.
— D.H. LAWRENCE, "The Jeune Fille"
*Pansies*


Losing her virginity — losing it? She'd taken it out for a
walk in the woods and abandoned it.
— KEITH WATERHOUSE


Nature abhors a virgin — a frozen asset.
— CLARE BOOTH LUCE
*The Wit of Wisdom* by L. and M. Cowen

Ladies, just a little more virginity, if you don't mind.
—SIR HERBERT BEERBOHM TREE, to actresses auditioning for a show


What most men desire is a virgin who is a whore.
—EDWARD DAHLBERG
*Reasons of the Heart*


Maids often lose their maidenhead
Ere they set foot in nuptial bed.
—ROBERT HERRICK, "Love's Courtship"


Are there still virgins? One is tempted to answer no.
There are only girls who have not yet crossed the line,
because they want to preserve their market value . . . Call
them virgins if you will, these travelers in transit.
—FRANÇOISE GIRAUD


Virginity is now a mere preamble or waiting room to be
got out of as soon as possible . . .
—URSULA LE GUIN, "The Space Crone"
*Co-Evolution Quarterly,* Summer 1976


. . . your groin and buttocks and thighs ache like hell and
you're all wet and bloody and it wasn't like a Hollywood
movie at all but Jesus, at least you're not a virgin anymore
but is this what it is all about?
And meanwhile he's asking you, "Did you come?"
—ROBIN MORGAN
*Sisterhood Is Powerful*


I was too polite to ask.
—GORE VIDAL, when asked whether his first sexual encounter had been
hetero- or homosexual

# Virtue

Woman's virtue is man's greatest invention.
—CORNELIA OTIS SKINNER
*Paris '90*

Most plain girls are virtuous because of the scarcity of opportunity to be otherwise.
—MAYA ANGELOU
*I Know Why the Caged Bird Sings*

Or do you on your mistress' virtue dote?
Tell me, I should be very glad to know it,
What virtue dwells beneath a petticoat?
—ALEXANDER RATCLIFF, "A Satire Against Love"

The lady doth protest too much, me thinks.
—WILLIAM SHAKESPEARE
*Hamlet*

The virtues of society are the vices of the saint.
—RALPH WALDO EMERSON

Whether lust is homo- or hetero-sexual, virtue consists in dominating it.
—ANDRÉ GIDE
*Sexuality and Homosexuality*, by Arno Karlin

The virtue which requires to be ever guarded is scarcely worth the sentinel.
—OLIVER GOLDSMITH

What is virtue but the Trade Unionism of the married.
—GEORGE BERNARD SHAW
*Man and Superman*


How unhappy is the woman who is in love and virtuous at the same time.
—FRANÇOIS, Duc de La Rochefoucauld
*Maximes posthumes*


To my flaming youth let virtue be as wax.
—WILLIAM SHAKESPEARE
*Hamlet*


Virtue is its own reward.
—JOHN DRYDEN
*The Assignation*


Virtue is its own reward, alas.
—LEONARD LEWIS LEVINSON
*Bartlett's Unfamiliar Quotations*


Virtue which parlays is near surrender.
—NATHANIEL BAILEY
*An Universal Etymological English Dictionary*


Virtue is its own revenge.
—E.Y. HARBURG (attributed)

# Voice

How well a soft and libertine voice will erect your member, it is as good as fingers . . .
—JUVENAL
*Satire VI*

His voice was intimate as the rustle of sheets, and he kissed easily.
—DOROTHY PARKER
*Dusk Before Fireworks*

Always I hear the milk tones of her voice, a virgin, a whore, a woman totally aware of every dark perversion, an innocent.
—GILBERTO SORRENTINO
*Mulligan's Stew*

# Vows

The vow of love-passion they say is no vow.
—PLATO
*Symposium*

Men's vows are women's traitors.
—WILLIAM SHAKESPEARE
*Cymbeline*

Lovers' solemn oaths are much like solemn hodge-podge.
—PLAUTUS
*Cistellaria*

Vows can't change nature.
—ROBERT BROWNING, "Rabbi Ben Ezra"

Then talk not of inconstancy
False hearts and broken vows;
If I, by miracle, can be
This live-long minute true to thee,
'Tis all that heaven allows.
—JOHN WILMOT, Earl of Rochester, "Love and Love: A Song"

The lecher's vows in ashes I record.
—SOPHOCLES
*Fragments*

# Vulgarity

In every great king, in every loveliest flowery princess, in
every poet most refined, every best dressed dandy, every
holiest and spiritual teacher there lurks, waiting, waiting
for the moment to emerge, an outcaste of outcastes, a
dung carrier, a dog, lower than the lowest, bottomlessly
vulgar.
—ALDOUS HUXLEY
*Collected Essays*

Vulgarity is the garlic in the salad of taste.
—CYRIL CONNOLLY


Be thou familiar, but by no means vulgar.
—WILLIAM SHAKESPEARE
*Hamlet*


Interviewer: "You've been accused of vulgarity."
Mel Brooks: "Bullshit!"
—MEL BROOKS
*Playboy,* 1975

# Wars

In Love's wars, he who flieth is conqueror
*Proverb*

# Widows

A rich widow weeps with one eye and signals with the other.
*Portuguese Proverb*

The three merriest things in the world are a cat's kitten, a goat's kid, and a young widow.
*Irish Proverb*

A buxom widow must either be married, buried, or shut up in a convent.
*Spanish Proverb*

In my day, a college widow stood for something. She stood for plenty.
—GROUCHO MARX
*A Day at the Races*

He that would woo a maid must feign, lie, and flatter.
But he that woos a widow must down his breeches and at
her.
—NATHANIAL SMITH
*Quakers Spiritual Court*


A good season for courtship is when the widow returns
from the funeral.
—THOMAS FULLER
*Gnomologia: Adagies and Proverbs*


And yet—when asked what age of womanhood
Brings most delight, producing most good,
I turn to widowhood with tender touch,
And say: "Stop here, for widows know so much."
—ANONYMOUS, "Boyhood"
*The Point of View*


The comfortable estate of widowhood is the only hope
that keeps up a wife's spirits.
—JOHN GAY
*The Beggar's Opera*


Widow. The word consumes itself . . .
—SYLVIA PLATH, "Widow"


Be wery careful o' vidders.
—CHARLES DICKENS
*Pickwick Papers*


Rich widows are only second-hand goods that sell for
first-class prices.
—BENJAMIN FRANKLIN (attributed)

"Widow" is a harsh and hurtful word. It comes from the Sanskrit and it means "empty." I have been empty too long.
—LYNN CAINE
*Widow*


Widows are divided into two classes—the bereaved and the relieved.
—VICTOR ROBINSON
*Truth Seeker,* January 6, 1906


He first deceased: she for a little tried
To live without him, liked it not, and died.
—SIR HENRY WOTTON
*Death of Sir Albertus Moreton's Wife*


# Wives

Always seek a fellow's weak point in his wife.
—JAMES JOYCE
*Ulysses*


Gentlemen, to the lady without whom I should never have survived to eighty, nor sixty, nor yet thirty years. Her smile has been my lyric, her understanding the rhythm of the stanza. She has been the spring where from I have drawn the words. She is the poem of my life.
—OLIVER WENDELL HOLMES (attributed)


My God, who wouldn't want a wife?
—JUDY SYFERS, "I Want a Wife"

Don't expect a wife to help you or hinder you. Don't expect anything.
That is the golden rule of marriage.
—ROBERTSON DAVIES

*A Jig for the Gypsy*


A living doll, everywhere you look.
It can sew, it can cook
It can talk, talk, talk.
It works, there is nothing wrong with it.
You have a hole, it's a poultice.
You have an eye it's an image.
My boy, it's your last resort.
Will you marry it, marry it, marry it?
—SYLVIA PLATH, "The Applicant"

*Ariel*


Wife: One who knows everything except why she married you.
—ANONYMOUS


If wives were good, God would have one.

*Russian Proverb*


The trouble with my wife is that she is a whore in the kitchen and a cook in bed.
—GEOFFREY GORER (attributed)


A house-wife in bed, at table a slattern . . .
—JONATHAN SWIFT

*Portraits from Life*

One man's folly is another man's wife.
—HELEN ROWLAND
*Reflections of a Bachelor Girl*


The difference between a wife and a girl friend is the difference between routine acquiescence and enthusiastic cooperation.
—ANONYMOUS


May you live out your life
Without hate, without grief
And your hair ever blaze,
In the sun, in the sun,
When I am undone,
When I am no one.
—THEODORE ROETHKE, "Wish for a Young Wife"


She has always been there, my darling
She is, in fact, exquisite.
Fireworks in the dull middle of February
and as real as a cast-iron pot.
. . .
She is so naked and singular.
She is the sum of yourself and your dream.
Climb her like a monument, step by step.
She is solid.
—ANNE SEXTON, "For My Lover: Returning to His Wife"


Who drags the fiery artist down?
Who keeps the pioneer in town?
Who hates to let the seaman roam?
It is the wife, it is the home.
—CLARENCE DAY, JR.
*Wife and Home*

Wife: A former sweetheart.
—H.L. MENCKEN


My old flame, my wife.
—ROBERT LOWELL, "The Old Flame"


Every man gets the wife he deserves.
*Midrash: Psalms Rabbah*


Think you if Laura had been Petrarch's wife
He would have written sonnets all his life.
—GEORGE GORDON, Lord Byron
*Don Juan*


I can nail my left palm
to the left-hand cross-piece bar
I can't do everything myself
I need a hand to nail my right
A help, a love, a you, a wife.
—ALAN DUGAN


Jill-of-all-trades
Lover, mother, housewife, friend, breadwinner . . .
—GENNY LIM, "Wonder Woman"
*This Bridge Called My Back* by C. Moraga and G. Anzaldúa


Wife and servant are the same,
But only differ in the name;
And when that fatal knot is tied,
Which nothing, nothing can divide;
When she the word obey has said,
And man by law supreme was made,
Then all that's kind is laid aside,
And nothing left but state and pride.
—LADY MARY CHUDLEIGH, "To the Ladies"

. . . .wives are a dying need.
—UNA STANNARD
Mrs. Man


Honey you're awful lucky
I ever come home you're so homely
and the girls out there are so beautiful so
hell it must be love I guess.
—AL PURDY, "Engraved on a Tomb"


Meek wifehood is no part of my profession;
I am your friend, but never your possession.
—VERA BRITTAIN
Married Love


The clog of all pleasures, the luggage of life,
Is the best that can be said for a very good wife.
—JOHN WILMOT, Earl of Rochester, "On a Wife"


An ideal wife is any woman who has an ideal husband.
—BOOTH TARKINGTON
Looking Forward and Others


The people people work with best
Are often very queer
The people people own by birth
Quite shock your first idea;
The people people choose for friends
Your common sense appal
But the people people marry
Are the queerest ones of all.
—CHARLOTTE PERKINS GILMAN

He shall hold thee,
when his passion shall have spent its novel force,
Something better than his dog,
a little dearer than his horse.
—ALFRED, Lord Tennyson, "Locksley Hall"


# Women

A nymphomaniac is a woman who has just a little more
sex tension than her partner.
—WARDELL POMEROY
*Masters and Johnson Explained* by N. Lehrman


I saw pale kings, and princes too,
Pale warriors, death pale were they all;
They cried: "La belle dame sans merci
Hath thee in thrall."
—JOHN KEATS, "La Belle Dame sans Merci"


The woman one loves always smells good.
—REMY DE GOURMONT


As soon as you cannot keep anything from a woman you
love her.
—PAUL GÉRALDY


A woman should always stand by a woman.
—EURIPIDES
*Helen*


For the female of the species is deadlier than the male.
—RUDYARD KIPLING, "The Female of the Species"

She talks just like a woman, yes she does.
She makes love like a woman, yes she does.
She aches like a woman
But she breaks just like a little girl.
—BOB DYLAN, "Just Like a Woman"


There are no books like a dame
And nothin' looks like a dame.
There are no drinks like a dame
And nothin' thinks like a dame,
Nothin' acts like a dame
Or attracts like a dame.
There ain't a thing wrong with any man here
That can't be cured by putting him near
A girly, womanly, female, feminine dame!
—OSCAR HAMMERSTEIN II, "There's Nothing Like a Dame"
*South Pacific*


Oh Charles—a woman needs certain things. She needs to be loved, wanted, cherished, sought after, cossetted, pampered. She needs sympathy, affection, devotion, understanding, tenderness, infatuation, adulation, idolatry—that isn't much to ask Charles.
—BARRY TOOK AND MARTY FELDMAN
*Round the Horne*, BBC Radio, 1966


No more masks! No more mythologies.
—MURIEL RUKEYSER
*No More Masks!* by F. Howe and E. Bass

# Women's Liberation

When working toward our liberation
And basic change in civilization
"Lib" is an abbreviation
In which we hear your condemnation.
—JOANN HAUGERUD

*A Feminist Dictionary* by C. Kramarae and P.A. Treichler


A contradiction in terms.
—SUSAN SONTAG

*Partisan Review*, 1973


Whether we live with or without a man, communally or in couples or alone, are married or unmarried, live with other women, go for free love, celibacy or lesbianism, or any combination, there are only good and bad things about each bad situation. There is no 'more liberated' way; there are only bad alternatives.
—CAROL HANISCH

*Feminist Revolution*


Not only are women now openly having sex on the tube, but they are even able to admit that they do not always like it. That's liberation. We've come a long way since the days when Lucy Ricardo couldn't say "pregnant" on the war.
—*THE NEW YORK DAILY NEWS*

*Say It Again* by Dorothy Uris


I'm furious about the Women Liberationists. They keep getting up on soapboxes and proclaiming that women are brighter than men. That's true, but it should be kept very quiet or it ruins the whole racket.
—ANITA LOOS

*The Observer*, December 30, 1973

...... on some days it is hard to figure out how a species that controls 97% of the money and all the pussy can be downtrodden.
—LARRY KING (attributed)

# Wooing

Happy is the wooing that is not long a-doing.
—AUTHOR UNKNOWN

She whom I love is hard to catch and conquer,
Hard, but O the glory of winning were she won!
—GEORGE MEREDITH, "Love in the Valley"

The wooing should be a day after the wedding.
—JOHN LYLY
*Euphues and His England*

The time I have lost wooing,
In watching and pursuing
The light that lies
In woman's eyes
Has been my heart's undoing.
—THOMAS MOORE, "The Time I've Lost"
*Irish Melodies*

The sad miscarriage of their wooing.
—WILLIAM CONGREVE
*The Old Bachelor*

Men like to pursue an elusive woman, like a cake of wet
soap in a bathtub; even men who hate baths.
—GELETT BURGESS


A man is like a cat; chase him and he will run . . . Sit still
and ignore him and he'll come purring at your feet.
—HELEN ROWLAND


Why, having won her, do I woo?
Because her spirit's vestal grace
Provokes me always to pursue
But spirit-like eludes embrace.
—COVENTRY PATMORE, "The Married Lover"
*The Angel in the House*


Women are angels wooing:
Things won are done; joy's soul lies in the doing:
That she's belov'd knows nought that knows not this:
Men prize the thing ungained more than it is.
—WILLIAM SHAKESPEARE
*Troilus and Cressida*


*See also:* COURTSHIP.


# Wrinkles

Beauty is just a flower
Which wrinkles will devour.
—THOMAS NASHE, "Summer's Last Will and Testament"

Age imprints more wrinkles in the mind than it does on the face.
—MICHEL DE MONTAIGNE


Sweet dalliance keepeth away wrinkles.
—HENRY CONSTABLE, "Sonnets to Diana"


If God had to give a woman wrinkles, He might at least have put them on the soles of her feet.
—NINON DE LENCLOS


Please don't retouch my wrinkles. It took me too long to earn them.
—ANNA MAGNANI
    *Interview,* 1978 to the photographer


Women are not forgiven for aging. Robert Redford's lines of distinction are my old-age wrinkles.
—JANE FONDA

# Yes!

Some say Never
Some say Unless
It's stupid and lonely
To rush into Yes

. . .

Some go local
Some go express
Some can't wait
To answer Yes

. . .

Open your eyes
Dream but don't guess
Your biggest surprise
Comes after Yes.
  —MURIEL RUKEYSER
  *Houdini*


It is well known that we are susceptible only to those sug-
gestions with which we are already secretly in accord.
—C.G. JUNG
  *Modern Man in Search of a Soul*


You made me love you,
I didn't want to do it.
  —JOE MCCARTHY, "You Made Me Love You"

Between a woman's Yes and No, I would not venture to
stick a pin.
—MIGUEL DE CERVANTES
*Don Quixote*


My favorite word is YES.
—LENORE KANDELL


How long I pleaded I can never guess,
Nor can I recollect the things we said,
Now after months, you answer yes,
And you are in my bed.

Yet, though stretched out and naked here you lie
You close your lips, you turn away; you weep.
Finally you consent . . . And I
Worn out with coaxing, sleep.
*The Greek Anthology*


When you arouse the need in me
My heart says yes, indeed, to me
Proceed with what you are leading me to.
—CAROLYN LEIGH, "Witchcraft"


When a woman says yes to her avid lover
Should be written in wind and running water.
—CATULLUS
*Odes*


. . . she receptive but to me,
dances and sings around me
"Yes and no and maybe so
and everywhere all over.
—ALAN DUGAN, "On Rape Unattempted"

. . . and then I asked him with my eyes to ask again yes and then he asked me would I yes to say yes my mountain flower and I put my arms around him yes and drew him down to me so he could feel my breasts all perfume yes and his heart was going like mad and yes I said yes I will Yes.
—JAMES JOYCE
*Ulysses*


# Youth

When I was a school boy, I thought a fair woman a pure goddess; my mind was a soft nest in which some one of them slept, though she knew it not.
—JOHN KEATS, Letter, July 18, 1818


I am fourteen
and my skin has betrayed me
the boy I cannot live without
still sucks his thumb
in secret.
—AUDRE LORDE, "Hanging Fire"


You took my heart in your hand
With a friendly smile,
With a critical eye you scanned,
Then set it down,
And said: It is still unripe
Better wait awhile.
—CHRISTINA ROSSETTI, "Twice"


Burning youth.
—MICHEL DE MONTAIGNE
*Essays*

Unbridled youth.

−JOHN LYLY

*Euphues and His England*


How long does youth last?
So long as we are loved.

*The Golden Book of Countess Diana*


The daughters of Albion

. . .

comb their dark blonde hair in suburban bedrooms
powder their delicate nipples
wondering if tonight will be the night
their bodies pressed into dresses or sweaters

−ADRIAN HENRI, "Mrs Albion You've Got a Lovely Daughter"


Early marriage, long love.

*German Proverb*


Fifteen-year old nymphs, dawn of womanhood
Who will enter the palace of my soul?

−JULES LAFORGUE

*Les Complaintes*


But in the Lower Sixth we all got religion or Commu-
nism—it goes with acne you know. Vanishes as soon as
you have proper sexual intercourse.

−KYRIL BONFIGLIOLI

*Don't Point That Thing At Me*


They try to tell us we're too young to love
Too young to really be in love.

−SYLVIA DEE, "Too Young to Love"

Young I am, and yet unskill'd
How to make Lover yield:
How to keep and how to gain,
When to love; and when to feign.
—JOHN DRYDEN

Love Triumphant: "Song for a Girl"

From best sellers to comic books, any child who hasn't
acquired an extensive sex education by the age of 12
belongs in remedial reading.
—WILL STANTON,

*Reader's Digest*, March 1971

I was a child and she was a child,
In this kingdom by the sea;
But we loved with a love which was more than love—
I and my Annabel Lee;
With a love that the winged seraphs in heaven
Coveted her and me.
—EDGAR ALLEN POE, "Annabel Lee"

If youth knew; if age could.
—HENRI ESTIENNE

*Les Prémices*

Teenage boys, goaded by their surfing hormones . . . run in
packs. They have only a brief season of exhilarating liberty
between control by their mothers and control by their wives.
—CAMILLE PAGLIA

*Sex, Art, and American Culture*

I would there be no age between ten and three-and-
twenty, or that youth would sleep out the rest; for there is
nothing in the between but getting wenches with child,
wronging the ancientry, stealing, fighting.
—WILLIAM SHAKESPEARE

*The Winter's Tale*

# Index